WOMEN AND COMMUNITY IN
MEDIEVAL AND EARLY MODERN IBERIA

*Women and Gender in
the Early Modern World*

SERIES EDITORS

Allyson Poska
Abby Zanger

Women and Community in Medieval and Early Modern Iberia

Edited and with an introduction by
MICHELLE ARMSTRONG-PARTIDA,
ALEXANDRA GUERSON, and
DANA WESSELL LIGHTFOOT

UNIVERSITY OF NEBRASKA PRESS   LINCOLN

Portions of chapter 8 are based on the book *Entre la solitud i la llibertat. Vídues barcelonines a finals de l'Edat Mitjana* by Mireia Comas-Via.

Library of Congress Cataloging-in-Publication Data
Names: Armstrong-Partida, Michelle, 1974-editor. | Guerson, Alexandra, editor. | Lightfoot, Dana Wessell, editor.
Title: Women and community in medieval and early modern Iberia / edited and with an introduction by Michelle Armstrong-Partida, Alexandra Guerson, and Dana Wessell Lightfoot.
Description: Lincoln : University of Nebraska Press, [2020] | Series: Women and gender in the early modern world | Includes bibliographical references and index. | Summary: "Women and Community in Medieval and Early Modern Iberia draws on recent research to underscore the various ways in which women influenced and contributed to their communities, engaging with a broader academic discussion of women's agency and cultural impact in the Iberian peninsula."—Provided by publisher.
Identifiers: LCCN 2019035337 |
ISBN 9781496205117 (hardback) |
ISBN 9781496219671 (epub) |
ISBN 9781496219688 (mobi) |
ISBN 9781496219695 (pdf)
Subjects: LCSH: Women—Iberian Peninsula—History—To 1500. | Women—History—Middle Ages, 500-1500. | Communities—Iberian Peninsula—History—To 1500. | Iberian Peninsula—Social conditions.
Classification: LCC HQ1147.I23 W66 2020 | DDC 305.409366—dc23
LC record available at https://lccn.loc.gov/2019035337

Set in Arno by Laura Buis.

For Helen Nader, whose pioneering work and mentorship has inspired generations of historians of women in premodern Iberia

CONTENTS

TABLES

ACKNOWLEDGMENTS

The idea for this volume emerged in a hot summer afternoon in Girona where the three of us (Michelle, Alexandra, and Dana) were doing archival research in 2015. That spring and summer we organized sessions on women and community at the Association of Spanish and Portuguese Historical Studies in Baltimore and at the International Medieval Congress in Leeds, UK. Energized by all the recent work in the field, we felt the time was ripe for a collection reflecting the rich body of scholarship that was emerging on the topic of women and community in medieval and early modern Iberia.

Our first acknowledgment should be to our contributors, who eagerly responded to our initial call and thoughtfully engaged with our editorial suggestions to produce such excellent work for this volume. They were prompt in meeting our deadlines and made our work much easier in the process. We would also like to thank the anonymous reviewers whose commentary helped to sharpen our prose, deepen our interpretations, and make tighter connections between the various essays. Any errors remain our own.

Allyson Poska and Abby Zanger, the editors of the Women and Gender in the Early Modern World series, provided continued support and advice as this volume moved from an idea conceived in Girona to actuality. We are eternally grateful for their guidance and expertise.

The staff at the University of Nebraska Press have been extremely patient with our many queries at the final stages of the manuscript preparation.

WOMEN AND COMMUNITY IN
MEDIEVAL AND EARLY MODERN IBERIA

Introduction

Contextualizing Women, Agency, and
Communities in Premodern Iberia

MICHELLE ARMSTRONG-PARTIDA, ALEXANDRA GUERSON,
AND DANA WESSELL LIGHTFOOT

In the premodern period women and men constructed and adapted their communities to meet the needs of the group, forging relationships marked as much by commitment to each other as they were by conflict. Context matters when studying communities as multiple and intersectional factors related to socioeconomic status, religion, location, and gender impact the ways in which they were shaped and understood over time. Such historical processes are evident when we consider the medieval and early modern periods in the Iberian Peninsula. Traditional historiography has often highlighted the distinction between "the neighbourly conduct required by the ethical code of the old [i.e., medieval] village community and the increasingly individualistic form of behaviour which accompanied the economic changes of the sixteenth and seventeenth centuries."[1] Such arguments emphasize a break between the medieval and early modern worlds, linking the individualism of the early modern as a first step toward modernity while jettisoning the communal nature of the medieval to the distant past. This collection challenges such assumptions and argues that when we place women at the center of community, we can see the similarities and differences across the medieval and early modern period of women influencing, navigating, and managing their roles within their communities, including testing the bonds and limitations of the community within which they operated.

In particular, we emphasize the continuities between the medieval and early modern, arguing that women—elite, bourgeois, and peasant, Christian, Jewish, Muslim, converso, and Morisco women as well as married, widowed, and single women, in other words, women from across the socioeconomic and religious spectrum—used similar strategies to maneuver within the patriarchal structures of premodern society, using their embedded community roles as a means to do so. Such strategies saw these women taking part in the multilayered spheres of their Iberian communities, moving beyond the domestic arena into the wider spheres of influence that touched upon the social, religious, political, and economic realms that premodern people engaged with on a daily basis. Our volume highlights the diversity of women from various levels of society and underscores women's social, economic, political, and religious ties to their families and communities in both urban and rural environments. As a result, this collection further illustrates that such women belonged to, interacted with, and shifted between multiple, overlapping, and often conflicting communities, particularly as liminal agents who were able to transverse social and religious boundaries.[2] At its core, the collection of essays demonstrates the complexity of women's lives, highlighting the various roles and identities they accessed both within and beyond their kin groups. By such means, the intersectional nature of women's lives is emphasized as they exercised agency, seeking to fulfill desires and agendas that cut across different communal realms.

In the past twenty years, a number of scholars have turned to focus on the great variety of formal and informal networks and ties that bound individuals together in medieval and early modern Europe.[3] Katherine Lynch's groundbreaking work on individuals and urban communities from 1200 to 1800 has explored the complex network of communities across Europe, highlighting connections across social, political, economic, familial, and religious groups. Scholars, such as Michael J. Halvorson and Karen Spierling, in their work *Defining Community in Early Modern Europe*, have looked at these networks through the lens of religion, analyzing how membership in a particular religious confession could create and challenge communal bonds. Other studies focus on women's connections to the myriad of religious, economic, intellectual, political, and social communities in premodern Europe. *Women and Community in Medieval and Early Modern Iberia* contributes to this growing scholarship by considering women's membership in institutional, familial, and socioeconomic groups, and emphasizing how such connections demonstrate the complex nature of women's identities as individuals and community members. The absence of Iberia in previous scholarly works is striking given the growth and depth of scholarship on women's history and gender history in Iberia in the last twenty-five years, particularly for the early modern period. The economic activities of widows, women and moneylending, women and violence, religious women and their social networks, queenship, marriage, women and the law, the experiences of minority women (Muslim, Jewish, Morisco, and converso) and women's education are some of the topics that scholars of early modern, and to a lesser extent medieval, Iberia have examined.[4]

This collection draws on such research, but situates itself specifically within the framework of the intersection of women with different types of communities. Rather than focusing on particular communities, such as convents, intellectual circles, or family and social kin groups, these essays explore the multi-varied and interwoven networks that women of different religious, socioeconomic, and geographic regions were embedded within. Covering the experiences of women in Castile, Portugal, and the Crown of Aragon, the authors explore the experiences of Christian, Jewish, conversa, and Morisca women who came from families across the socioeconomic spectrum, from poor peasants to the highest nobles. Using a wide variety of source material—episcopal visitations, bishops' registers, ecclesiastical and secular court records, notarial documents, Inquisition trials, hospital registers, charters, royal letters, inventories, humanist dialogues and poems—the essays demonstrate in particular how such evidence can be used to expose these intersections of religion, socioeconomic status, and gender.

As feminist scholars, we believe it important to place gender at the center of our discussion, thinking specifically about the experiences of women and how gendered ideologies, frameworks, and expectations both worked to cement and challenge communal norms. People living in groups defined their communal norms by creating, cooperating, and regulating the relationships and codes of conduct everyone was expected to follow as a collective. Community norms, however, could be contested and conflicts within the community could play out to the point where one member became marginalized or exiled and another member supported and endorsed. Women played an integral role in promoting, monitoring, conforming to, and challenging the mores of the community and its boundaries. How premodern people in rural and urban environments established and delineated their community is important to understanding how women took part in and interwove these roles together as they functioned within their neighborhood, spheres of influence, and kinship group in their everyday lives.

The term "community" is generally employed to mean a group of people living together or is used to designate a network of friends and neighbors. However, premodern historians have worked to complicate the notion of "community" and have shown that the idea or a sense of community could be formed along the lines of religious identities (Christian, Jewish, and Muslim) or that of men and women's religious houses, geographical locations, like a neighborhood, the parish, or town, as well as social identities that stemmed from socioeconomic status and profession.[5] At their core, members of a community are likely to share the same values, concerns, and interests that create an affinity.[6] Sharon Farmer has shown how sick and impoverished migrant women living in fourteenth-century Paris formed meaningful bonds with their equally poor female neighbors when they relied on each other to survive.[7] The ties of a community, then, can be formed not only when people live in close proximity to one another but also when they are faced with a crisis, whether personal, economic, or imposed by outside forces, which causes people to work together to overcome a dire situation or to work against a common enemy in times of political conflict.[8]

A community can do more than just create a common sense of identity, however; it can also satisfy emotional needs and provide for more practical concerns like food, clothing, and shelter. Katherine Lynch has argued that "individuals and families used other associations and institutions . . . to complement or even fulfill some of the fundamental missions that families have historically provided."[9] She defines such "associations and institutions" as communities, highlighting how in urban centers in particular, individuals used a variety of familial and social kin networks as a means of support in an often-shifting society.[10] Central to the creation and maintenance of these communal ties were women who, Lynch argues, tended to develop "more and tighter connections with people residing in the same area" due to the fact that they were more spatially circumscribed than men.[11] As geographical and religious borders shifted and became blurred in the dynamic society that made up medieval and early modern Iberia, Lynch's definition of community and how gender works within it is reflected in the essays that follow. These essays examine the development of such communal ties among relatives, social kin groups, and institutional networks in both urban and rural centers, to show the extent to which women functioned in facilitating the bonds between family, institutions, and community. At the same time, the evidence presented in these essays demonstrates that women could serve as agents of conflict, competition, and even violence within the community rather than only as mediators of relationships and of mutual aid.

The twelve essays in this collection treat the theme of women and community through three lenses: economic agency, how women challenged their communities, and how institutional connections created communities among women. Although some essays could easily have been assigned to one section or another in this volume because they reasonably fit into more than one category, we assigned these works based on their ability to speak to other essays in the section.

The old adage that the two certainties of life are taxes and death is one that can be readily applied to premodern Iberia. Notarial records are rich with evidence of women of all socioeconomic and religious backgrounds engaging in business, managing property, and disposing of assets. Legal practices such as partible inheritance and the dowry system meant that women often had significant control of familial property, both moveable and immoveable. This meant that we find women participating in the credit market, making fiscal decisions, but also having their property the target of royal officials. While the works of Sarah Ifft Decker, Natalie Oeltjen, and Grace Coolidge span nearly three centuries and three different regions they all illustrate the economic agency of Jewish, conversa, and Christian women, respectively. Sarah Ifft Decker shows that Jewish women's prominent role in the credit market of Vic stemmed from a complex interplay of the needs of both the Christian majority community and the Jewish minority community. Individual Jewish women lenders relied not only on the traditions of their communities but also on their familial, social, and professional relationships with both Jews and Christians, to establish themselves as effective lenders. Natalie Oeltjen, on the other hand, shows us that political and economic crises can often affect women disproportionately. When the Jews of Mallorca were attacked in the wave of anti-Jewish violence that engulfed Castile and the Crown of Aragon in 1391, conversas (Jewish women who converted to Christianity) were affected in ways that were distinct from their male co-religionists. Oeltjen discusses how royal policies responding to the devastation of the 1391 revolts at times protected and at other times threatened the dowries of conversas that therefore impacted the family and community finances. Notarial records show women of every social status and point in the life cycle acting on their own name and representing others. Grace Coolidge's study of wills in seventeenth-century Castile uncovers the communities that were of personal and economic benefit to women. She compares the experiences of single, married, and widowed women and while the latter had the most authority, single and married women were also able to manage their own assets.

The second part of the collection develops the theme of women and community by concentrating on the diverse and imbricate religious, social, and economic roles that women were involved in at various levels of society—in their neighborhoods, villages, towns, and regions. While all the essays in this section demonstrate how women were part of an intricate web of social contacts and associations, they also highlight the conflictive role that women could play in their communities by showing how women, through their insulting speech or actions, tested the limits of neighborliness and the appropriate gender roles for women, contested the strength of marriage bonds when women refused to convert to Christianity, or pushed back against legal attempts to remove their rights as property owners and heads of households.

Michelle Armstrong-Partida and Mark Meyerson begin this section by focusing on the conflictual role of single and married women in their communities. Armstrong-Partida and Meyerson underscore how women's speech and their participation in a culture of honor made them the targets of male violence. Based on an examination of fourteenth-century Catalan episcopal visitations and court records, Armstrong-Partida shows how single women without the protection of a male family member were vulnerable to violent aggression when they verbally attacked or criticized a clergyman in their parish. Armstrong-Partida demonstrates that in spite of their marginal status these women were considered part of the village community and reveals how neighbor-women frequently came to their aid when they were incapacitated by the brutal beatings of a cleric. Conversely, men of the village could be silent or withhold from condemning the clergyman for his violent attack. Village men were more tolerant of a cleric's violent behavior against a woman when she was not under the authority of a paterfamilias, indicating that men of the community could condone the thrashing of a woman who scolded and insulted a man as a justified act that kept a woman in check for her vituperative speech. Mark Meyerson exposes a different facet of violence—one that brings to light Valencian women who incited their men-folk to enact retribution and appeared in court to either bring a claim or to refute a claim of aggression against their enemies. In these circumstances women too could be the objects of attack when an enemy violated the domestic space of an opponent to beat or slash at the face of a wife, mother, or daughter. Relying on fifteenth-century secular court cases, Meyerson argues that the home was a metaphor for the female body and that attacks on the household became a way of impugning the honor of an enemy because they publicly demonstrated that a man could not protect the women in his family. Meyerson contends that women who participated in the verbal or physical encounters, or were the victims of such attacks, were an integral part of a culture of honor where the violent contests over reputation and social standing created a sense of community in Valencia that women were very much a part of. Both Armstrong-Partida and Meyerson note the vulnerability of women to violence in their daily lives perpetrated by people who were not strangers to them.

The next two essays in this section focus on conversion and the fraught role it could play in conflicts within religious communities, but also between such communities and religious authorities, such as the medieval and early modern inquisitions in Iberia. Alexandra Guerson and Dana Wessell Lightfoot's essay on the marriage and divorce of mixed couples in Girona illustrates the changing nature of the bonds of community in Jewish and converso families after the 1391 violence forced the conversion of Jews in the Crown of Aragon. In particular, Guerson and Wessell Lightfoot place women at the center of community to flesh out the difficulties of religious identities in a mixed marriage. They demonstrate the essential function of wives in developing and preserving familial and economic connections. Their work reveals how Jewish wives could be agents of conflict when they refused to convert and, yet, at the same time, managed to maintain ties to both their Jewish and converso communities. By resisting conversion, Jewish wives tested the bonds of marriage and community in being true to their own religious conviction. Stephanie Cavanaugh considers how Morisca women in Valladolid's Barrio de Santa Maria resisted attempts to assimilate the Morisco community by dispersing it throughout the city as a whole. These women worked collectively to defend their properties and neighborhood from the Crown and Church through legal action. Economically as owners of houses and lands and as heads of households, Morisca women negotiated with the Spanish Inquisition in Valladolid to ensure the survival of their community. Cavanaugh, therefore, shows that Morisca women not only played crucial religious roles as guardians of their conversion faith but were also central as legal and economic actors. In these ways, Cavanaugh's Morisca women defended their families and faith much in the same way as Guerson and Wessell Lightfoot's Jewish and conversa women, accessing legal strategies made available to them by the Christian authorities. Altogether, the four essays in this section emphasize the complex nature of communal bonds that could simultaneously serve as sites of conflict and protection for women.

The final section of our collection explores how women often acted as important bridges between religious, intellectual, and charitable institutions and the local communities in which they lived. Miriam Shadis and Michelle Herder, in their essays on religious women, illustrate the permeable walls of the cloister by exposing that the donors, family members, clergymen, servants, and neighbors linked to women's religious houses were a part of nuns' communities. Shadis examines monastic charters to show that the royal and elite of women of Portugal were critical to the economic foundation of the thirteenth-century Cistercian house Santa Maria de Celas. She reveals that elite women invested in this convent not only as a place of refuge for donors, retirees, and the sick but also with the intended purpose of participating in the good works and prayers of the nuns themselves, thereby demonstrating that the nuns were part of a wider religious and social community in Coimbra. In contrast, by focusing on the bishop of Girona's inquiry into the circumstances of a pregnant nun in the monastery of Sant Daniel, Michelle Herder exposes the social network of neighbors, servants, and clergy that were connected to the nuns' social and economic endeavors through the routine interactions of daily life. From the testimony of witnesses, she finds that lay and clerical neighbors in proximity to the monastery viewed the nuns as part of their regional community and took particular interest in the nuns and their personal activities. Although the activities of these religious women could be a source for gossip, Herder observes that neighbors accepted the nuns' social interactions within the broader community and in large part refrained from condemning the nuns as sexually unchaste due to the sexual transgression of one nun, suggesting that people were protective of the monastery and its nuns. The role of religious women, therefore, went far beyond their immediate monastic community to encompass an array of people who had spiritual, social, and economic connections to these nuns and their pious, self-sustaining endeavors.

The essays of Mireia Comas-Via and Amanda Scott highlight the importance of the emotional and financial ties among unmarried women as a source critical to their survival and ability to serve their own community of women. Mireia Comas-Via's use of notarial documents shows that in the absence of family support destitute widows in fourteenth-century Barcelona had a preference for relying on the informal charity provided by the women in their community rather than the charitable institutions of their parish. She demonstrates that some widows migrated together to Barcelona to find economic opportunities and formed bonds of solidarity because of their difficult experiences. Poor women and women with means created networks of assistance based on class and financial need, looked after one another, and thus often lived together. Comas-Via's essay underscores how these women—out of friendship, economic need, and a sense of fellowship—helped one another to overcome illness and poverty. In sixteenth-century Basque country, Scott finds a similar spirit of cooperation among *seroras*, secular women dedicated to a religious life of devotion, often living and working alongside other women for the spiritual benefit of their parish communities. Scott shows the leadership role of women as the caretakers of the religious material objects of the parish church and its shrines, and as deeply involved participants in the daily operation of the parish's religious life and charitable duties. She underscores the affective ties these women had to other *seroras* and to their female family members. An examination of wills enables Scott to document the support *seroras* offered to their fellow sisters by way of bequests of household goods and personal possessions to sustain the *serora* community. These women also continued to support familial inheritance strategies by passing on what little wealth they possessed to their nieces and nephews. It is clear in both of these essays that women played an essential role, not only in the charitable organizations of their communities, but also in the lives of other women to aid in their day-to-day existence and devotional activities.

The final essay in this collection focuses on women within their social, religious, and familial communities in premodern Iberia who sought access to other forms of networks, such as intellectual circles, which further illustrates women's presence in every aspect of premodern life. Rachel Stapleton explores the career of one such woman, the Spanish-Portuguese humanist

Luisa Sigea of Toledo, who gained international recognition in the sixteenth century for her erudition. Stapleton examines Sigea's letters to Pope Paul III, fellow humanist Álvar Gómez de Castro, and aspiring scholar Magdalena de Padilla to consider how women were able to gain entrance to and participate in humanist networks and communities in Iberia and Europe. Sigea's letters demonstrate how deeply she was embedded within these intellectual communities, and Stapleton's essay highlights how such texts are important in the examination of humanist networks in the sixteenth century. But Stapleton also argues that Sigea's role in the household of the Infanta Maria of Portugal was crucial, demonstrating, as in the other essays of this section, the multiple and overlapping ways that women both impacted and were influenced by their various communities.

To end this volume, Allyson Poska offers an epilogue that reflects on the parallels found among medieval and early modern women's lives across five centuries in premodern Iberia. She highlights the similarities of women's experiences when acting as links between a variety of religious, social, and economic communities that went beyond family, noting that in spite of patriarchal restrictions, physical barriers, and institutional constraints, women found ways to create, defend, and challenge the communities they belonged to. Poska observes that shining a spotlight on the intricate web of women's communities allows women's self-determination to become more visible. While women's participation in communities could provide support or exclusion and offer varying degrees of agency, it could also coerce or physically punish women to follow or even transgress gendered norms. Nevertheless, it is clear that women themselves created and influenced the communities that were an integral part of their lives.

The agency of women in influencing their social, economic, religious, and cultural communities is the connecting theme between the thirteen essays in this collection. Whether using communal networks as methods of support during times of crises, such as the 1391 pogroms against the Jews and the prosecution and attempts at assimilation of Moriscos in the mid-sixteenth century, or straining community ties through physical and verbal violence, or in serving as conduits through which institutional and social networks were solidified, women of all religious backgrounds and socioeconomic statuses actively participated in shaping the public, familial, social, cultural, and religious communities of which they were a part. The emphasis on women and community allows us to more clearly see women's ability to navigate a multiplicity of identities and roles—and moves beyond the traditional approach of studying women within the confines of their families.

NOTES

1. Shepard and Withington, *Communities in Early Modern England*, 4.
2. For a larger discussion of how individuals belonged to more than one group, see Shepard and Withington, *Communities in Early Modern England*, 1–15.
3. These works include Broomhall and Tarbin, *Women, Identities, and Community*; Campbell and Larsen, *Early Modern Women*; and Watt, *Medieval Women*.
4. This historiography is extensive for the early modern period, including Poska, *Women and Authority*; Lehfeldt, *Religious Women*; Vollendorf, *The Lives of Women*; Cruz and Hernández. *Women's Literacy*; Fink de Backer, *Widowhood in Early Modern Spain*; Coolidge, *Guardianship, Gender, and the Nobility*; Perry, *The Handless Maiden*; Melammed, *Heretics or Daughters of Israel?* For the medieval period, scholarship has focused on queenship, women and the law, and marriage. See the work of Silleras-Fernández, *Power, Piety, and Patronage*; Earenfight, *The King's Other Body*; Shadis, *Berenguela of Castile (1180–1246)*; Bianchini, *The Queen's Hand*; Woodacre, *Queens Regnant of Navarre*; Kelleher, *The Measure of Woman*; Dana Wessell Lightfoot, *Women, Dowries, and Agency*.
5. See, for example, chapters 5 and 6 in Nirenberg, *Communities of Violence*; Meyerson, *The Muslims of Valencia*, 225–69; chapters 2 and 3 in Perry, *The Handless Maiden*; Robert Chazan notes in his book *Medieval Stereotypes and Modern Antisemitism* that in the High Middle Ages Christian fears of Jewish malevolence created a wider sense of a Christian community in Europe that was threatened by an internal enemy. See also French, *The People of the Parish*, 20–22; Capp, *When Gossips Meet*, 268–69; chapters 3 and 4 in Chojnacka, *Working Women*; Susan McDonough, "Being a Neighbor," 1–11.
6. Shepard and Withington, *Communities in Early Modern England*, 1–15.
7. Farmer, *Surviving Poverty in Medieval Paris*; see also Chojnacka, *Working Women*, 62–64, 91–92, 99.
8. See Coope, *The Martyrs of Cordoba*.
9. Lynch, *Individuals, Families, and Communities*, 1.
10. Lynch, *Individuals, Families, and Communities*, 2.
11. Lynch, *Individuals, Families, and Communities*, 63.

Bianchini, Janna. *The Queen's Hand: Power and Authority in the Reign of Berenguela of Castile.* Philadelphia: University of Pennsylvania Press, 2012.

Broomhall, Susan, and Stephanie Tarbin, eds. *Women, Identities, and Community in Early Modern Europe.* London: Routledge, 2008.

Campbell, Julie D., and Anne R. Larsen., eds. *Early Modern Women and Transnational Communities of Letters.* Farnham VT: Ashgate, 2009.

Capp, Bernard. *When Gossips Meet: Women, Family, and Neighborhood in Early Modern England.* Oxford: Oxford University Press, 2003.

Chazan, Robert. *Medieval Stereotypes and Modern Antisemitism.* Berkeley: University of California Press, 1997.

Chojnacka, Monica. *Working Women of Early Modern Venice.* Baltimore: Johns Hopkins University Press, 2001.

Coolidge, Grace E. *Guardianship, Gender, and the Nobility in Early Modern Spain.* London: Routledge, 2016.

Coope, Jessica A. *The Martyrs of Córdoba: Community and Family Conflict in an Age of Mass Conversion.* Lincoln: University of Nebraska Press, 1995.

Cruz, Anne J., and Rosilie Hernández., eds. *Women's Literacy in Early Modern Spain and the New World.* London: Taylor and Francis, 2016.

Earenfight, Theresa. *The King's Other Body: Maria of Castile and the Crown of Aragon.* Philadelphia: University of Pennsylvania Press, 2010.

Farmer, Sharon. *Surviving Poverty in Medieval Paris: Gender, Ideology, and the Daily Lives of the Poor.* Ithaca NY: Cornell University Press, 2002.

Fink de Backer, Stephanie. *Widowhood in Early Modern Spain: Protectors, Proprietors, and Patrons.* Leiden: Brill, 2010.

French, Katherine L. *The People of the Parish: Community Life in a Late Medieval English Diocese.* Philadelphia: University of Pennsylvania Press, 2001.

Kelleher, Marie A. *The Measure of Woman: Law and Female Identity in the Crown of Aragon.* Philadelphia: University of Pennsylvania Press, 2010.

Lehfeldt, Elizabeth A. *Religious Women in Golden Age Spain: The Permeable Cloister.* Aldershot; Burlington: Ashgate, 2005.

Lynch, Katherine. *Individuals, Families, and Communities in Europe, 1200–1800.* Cambridge University Press, 2003.

McDonough, Susan. "Being a Neighbor: Ideas and Ideals of Neighborliness in the Medieval West." *History Compass* 15, no. 9 (2017): 1–11.

Melammed, Renée Levine. *Heretics or Daughters of Israel?: The Crypto-Jewish Women of Castile.* Oxford: Oxford University Press, 1999.

Meyerson, Mark D. *The Muslims of Valencia in the Age of Fernando and Isabel: Between Coexistence and Crusade.* Berkeley: University of California Press, 1991.

Nirenberg, David. *Communities of Violence: Persecution of Minorities in the Middle Ages.* Princeton: Princeton University Press, 1996.

Perry, Mary Elizabeth. *The Handless Maiden: Moriscos and the Politics of Religion in Early Modern Spain.* Princeton: Princeton University Press, 2013.

Poska, Allyson M. *Women and Authority in Early Modern Spain: The Peasants of Galicia.* Oxford: Oxford University Press, 2010.

Shadis, Miriam. *Berenguela of Castile (1180–1246) and Political Women in the High Middle Ages.* New York: Palgrave Macmillan, 2009.

Shepard, Alexandra, and Phil Withington, eds. *Communities in Early Modern England: Networks, Place, Rhetoric.* Manchester: Manchester University Press, 2007.

Silleras-Fernández, Núria. *Power, Piety, and Patronage in Late Medieval Queenship: María de Luna.* New York: Palgrave Macmillan, 2008.

Vollendorf, Lisa. *The Lives of Women: A New History of Inquisitional Spain.* Nashville: Vanderbilt University Press, 2007.

Watt, Diane, ed. *Medieval Women and Their Communities.* Toronto: University of Toronto Press, 1997.

Wessell Lightfoot, Dana. *Women, Dowries, and Agency: Marriage in Fifteenth-Century Valencia.* Manchester: Manchester University Press, 2013.

Woodacre, Elena. *The Queens Regnant of Navarre: Succession, Politics, and Partnership, 1274–1512.* New York: Palgrave Macmillan, 2013.

Part 1

*Community Networks and
Economic Agency*

1

Credit and Connections

Jewish Women between Communities in Vic, 1250–1350

SARAH IFFT DECKER

Reina, daughter of Bonmacip, a Jew of Vic, extended her first loan on November 11, 1293.[1] Her borrowers, Agnès, widow of Pere de Puig Carbó, and her son Bernat, lived in the parish of Sant Quirze de Muntanyola, about fourteen kilometers away from Vic. They borrowed sixty sous, about enough to buy an ass or a mule, or to pay a yearly rent, and agreed to repay the loan by the end of August, in around nine months.[2] Assuming they paid on time, they would owe no interest. With this loan, Reina began her seventeen-year career as a moneylender. Through her career, she both participated in and helped to build the social and economic networks that constituted the fledgling Jewish community of Vic, and connected it to the Christian communities of Vic and its surrounding rural hinterlands.

In 1293, Vic was an episcopal city, dominated by its bishop, despite jurisdictional challenges from the count-kings of Barcelona and the Montcada viscounts.[3] Unlike neighboring Barcelona, Vic did not play a major role in Mediterranean long-distance trade, but it was an active center of artisanal production, with particularly important textile, leather, and metal industries, and home to a population of about 3,000.[4] Jews had only recently begun to settle in the city; although Jews appeared occasionally in Vic as early as 1230, only in 1240 did a Jew first describe himself as a "Jew of Vic." By the end of the thirteenth century, the community amounted to about ten families, or well under one hundred Jews.[5] Reina belonged to only the third generation of Jewish settlers; her father, Bonmacip, was the son of Bonastrug Bonissach and Reina Cabrita, the very first "Jews of Vic."[6]

Reina returned to Vic and began to work as a moneylender shortly after her first marriage ended in divorce. She had married Jucef Darahi, a Jew of Barcelona, by 1282.[7] Several contracts from 1288 refer to legal disputes between the two families, suggesting that the marriage was already on the rocks.[8] By 1293, Reina had returned to her hometown of Vic, and within a year she had remarried. Her second husband, Astrug Caravida, relocated to Vic from Girona, perhaps specifically for his marriage.[9] Over the next decade, Reina and Astrug worked to establish separate lending businesses. In the extant documentation, Reina extended forty new loans between 1293 and 1310, while Astrug extended 71. On average, Reina extended slightly larger loans than her husband; as a result, her credit transactions accounted for nearly 40 percent of the couple's total income from moneylending.[10]

Reina's career as an active moneylender and a joint breadwinner with her husband would have been impossible in most Catalan cities, but Jewish women played an extraordinarily prominent role in the credit market of Vic in the late thirteenth and early fourteenth centuries. The importance of Jewish women creditors in Vic stemmed from a complex interplay between the needs of the Christian majority community and those of the Jewish minority. Christian demand for Jewish credit, combined with the small size of Vic's Jewish population, led Jewish families in Vic to rely on women as well as men to extend credit. The memory of early women lenders influenced communal and familial choices for the next half century. Individual Jewish women lenders relied on not only the traditions of their communities, but also their familial, social, and professional relationships with both Jews and Christians, to establish themselves as effective lenders.

Katherine Lynch approaches communities as "networks of individuals" that required the conscious efforts of participants to both invent and maintain.[11] The fledgling Jewish community of Vic initially created and maintained itself as a community by developing social and economic networks that encompassed both men and women. In other times and places, men established communal networks based, at least in part, on the economic exclusion of women, as Sheilagh Ogilvie argued regarding the guilds of early modern Germany.[12] The Jews of Vic instead treated women as an important part of the economic networks that tied together a community of Jews working as moneylenders.

Jewish moneylenders, both men and women, also forged networks with the surrounding Christian community. Lynch emphasized the importance of Christian religious practice and ideology in developing the institutions that created communities in premodern Europe.[13] Hence communities were constructed in a way that excluded Jews. Economic relationships, however, crossed religious lines. Although Jews and Christians maintained distinct communities, interreligious economic networks helped to tie these communities together. The work of Jewish moneylenders like Reina helped to partially integrate the Jewish community of Vic into the Christian communities of Vic and its hinterlands.

SOURCES AND METHODOLOGY

The evidence for Jewish women's moneylending in Vic comes from a particularly well-preserved set of notarial registers. Notaries recorded a wide variety of contracts, from loans and property sales to marriage contracts and wills, for men and women from all sectors of society. Each notarial register contains hundreds of individual documents. The notariate of Vic existed by 1155, and notarial registers survive from as early as 1230.[14] The notaries provided expertise in contractual forms, but even more importantly, they imbued private transactions with public authority.[15] As records of the everyday experiences of ordinary people, notarial registers are essential sources for social history, particularly for women's history. The large number of notarial documents allows for quantitative analysis, which provides a broader picture of the options available to medieval women, and contextualizes individual women's experiences. This essay combines quantitative evidence with case studies of individual women lenders.

The notaries of Vic recorded most transactions involving Jews in dedicated registers, known as the Libri Iudeorum. Vic has one of the earliest and most complete set of thirteenth- and fourteenth-century Libri Iudeorum; twenty-eight registers cover the period between 1264 and 1354.[16] The vast majority of documents related to the Jews of Vic appear in the Libri Iudeorum series; most of these documents are loan contracts.[17] Some Jews presumably extended loans outside the bounds of the notariate, perhaps engaging in pawnbroking. However, King Jaume I mandated the notarial registration of all Jewish loans starting in 1241, and most Jewish lenders probably complied.[18] The tables below are drawn from two overlapping data sets. The first, a random sample of 2,663 Jewish loans drawn from about half of the Libri Iudeorum, places women's lending in its broader context. The second data set considers all 924 loans made by Jewish women in the extant Libri Iudeorum, in order to provide a more in-depth portrait of women's lending.

TABLE 1. Jewish women's loans in Vic, by decade, 1250–1350

Decade	Jewish loans to Christians	Loans extended by Jewish women	Loans extended by Jewish women (%)
1250–1260	107	29	27
1261–1270	129	49	38.0
1271–1280	152	35	23.0
1281–1290	230	25	10.9
1291–1300	336	30	8.9
1301–1310	113	12	10.6
1311–1320	715	96	13.4
1321–1330	337	45	13.4
1331–1340	282	14	5.0
1341–1350	262	5	1.9
	2,663	340	12.8

Jewish women played a far more prominent role in the credit market of Vic than was typical in southern European cities and towns. Jewish women's lending reached its peak in the 1260s, when women extended nearly 40 percent of Jewish loans. Women consistently extended at least 9 percent of Jewish loans until the 1330s. By way of comparison, Jewish women extended only 2 percent of Jewish loans in Barcelona and Girona, with the exception of a brief spike in women's lending in the wake of the Black Death.[19] In thirteenth-century Perpignan and Castelló d'Empúries, women lenders made about 4 percent of Jewish loans.[20] Women and groups including women together extended about 10 percent of Jewish loans in the southern French town of Manosque, but none at all in the surviving records from Montpellier.[21] Vic represents an extremely unusual case.

TABLE 2. Jewish women's loans in Vic, by marital status, 1250–1350

Decade	Widows	Wives	Unknown	Total
1250–1260	1	26	2	29
1261–1270	70	54	6	130
1271–1280	36	59	6	101
1281–1290	19	58	10	87
1291–1300	3	64	11	78
1301–1310	32	49	13	94
1311–1320	43	136	11	190
1321–1330	21	68	2	91
1331–1340	5	110	3	118
1341–1350	4	2	0	6
Total	234	626	64	924

The Jewish women of Vic differed from their counterparts elsewhere in the region not only in their higher level of activity overall, but also in their greater tendency to participate in the credit market while still married. In other Catalan cities, Jewish widows reached heights of economic independence not available to married women.[22] Although some Jewish wives extended loans, particularly in the city of Puigcerdà, regular work in the credit market was typically reserved for widows in most Catalan cities and towns.[23] A very different set of circumstances prevailed in Vic, where married women extended the majority of Jewish women's loans (67.7 percent). Even when women's involvement in credit declined in the 1330s, the most active Jewish women lenders were wives rather than widows, until the 1340s.

The unusual prominence of Jewish women lenders in general, and married Jewish women in particular, explains why Reina and women like her could establish such successful lending businesses in Vic during the late thirteenth and early fourteenth centuries. The following sections will explore how Jewish women came to play such an important role in the credit market of this Catalan city.

HISTORY, MEMORY, AND WOMEN'S MONEYLENDING

The story of Jewish women's moneylending in Vic begins with Goig, the wife of David Canviador. Goig was one of the founding members of the community, along with her sister Reina Cabrita, grandmother and namesake to Reina, the daughter of Bonmacip. Goig dominated the credit market in the 1250s and retained a substantial presence through the thirteenth century, extending ninety-four independent loans over the course of several decades.[24] Her husband, in contrast, only occasionally extended loans; given his last name, he probably worked as a money changer.[25] Money changers played an important role in local finance and trade, and Christian money changers were highly respected businessmen; in Girona, they regularly served in public office.[26] As the couple established themselves in Vic, they adopted an unusual division of labor. While David contributed to local commerce at his money changer's table or through other economic endeavors, Goig brought in additional income by extending small-scale consumption loans to local Christians.

Goig's success demonstrates the demand for Jewish credit in Vic and its hinterlands, which until the thirteenth century had lacked a substantial

Jewish presence. Given the economic vitality of the city in this period, it is hardly surprising that Vic's Christians sought new forms of credit.[27] Most of Goig's debtors (67, or 71.3 percent) came from small villages in the rural environs of Vic, while just over one-quarter (26, or 27.7 percent) lived in the city.[28] Jewish lending in Catalan cities and towns often linked urban Jews with a rural Christian clientele.[29] Goig had a more profitable lending practice than her younger contemporary Reina, with an average cash loan of about ninety-six sous, a median loan of sixty-four sous, and a maximum loan of 770 sous, as well as a larger number of total loans. Between 1252 and 1310, she loaned 7,719 sous in cash, plus an additional sum, difficult to estimate precisely, in the form of grain loans.

Goig had a broad-based clientele with varied needs. At the height of her career, in 1267, she loaned five sous to a group of three Christian borrowers—a married couple and a man of unknown relation—from the towns of Taradell and Tona, to be repaid in about six months.[30] The miniscule size of the loan, its division among multiple borrowers including a possible non-relative, and the fairly long term of repayment suggest that these borrowers were impoverished rural Christians struggling to make ends meet. Jewish credit allowed them to obtain the cash they needed without relying on the generosity of family and friends. At the other end of the scale, in 1280 Goig extended a loan of 770 sous to Berenguer d'Altarippa, his wife Elisenda, their son Ponç, and Ponç's wife, to be repaid the following month.[31] Like many well-to-do medieval families, the Altarippas probably kept their wealth in the form of precious household objects or land, rather than cash.[32] They, too, occasionally relied on Jewish creditors to provide necessary infusions of coinage, only on a much larger scale.

As the new Jewish community of Vic sought to meet the demand for Jewish credit, the small size of the community required women as well as men to share in this work. Especially given that some Jewish men, like David Canviador, chose not to work as moneylenders, the labor and capital of women was essential to meet local demand.[33] The Jewish community embraced an alternative pattern of gendered lending out of necessity. Although they may have reacted to economic exigencies posed by Christian demand, they did not follow the example of local Christians. Christian women in Vic extended only 3.2 percent of Christian loans, even less than in some larger Catalan cities.[34]

Goig did not deliberately encourage Jewish women's moneylending in Vic. She did not even promote her own daughters' economic independence in her will. She named her husband as universal heir and granted legacies ranging between 500 and 1,500 sous to her four sons.[35] She left nothing directly to her married daughter Astrugona, although she promised that Astrugona's unnamed daughter would receive a legacy of 200 sous upon her marriage. Her other daughter, Reina, received only 100 sous. The bulk of her estate, then, went to men, although she may have contributed to her daughters' dowries at the times of their marriages. Robert I. Burns, in his study on Jewish Latinate wills in thirteenth- and fourteenth-century Iberia, argued that women were more likely to recognize other women in their wills, while Kathryn Reyerson found that some elite Christian women in fourteenth-century Montpellier treated male and female descendants equally.[36] Goig demonstrated neither tendency. Rather, she resembles the Christian women Thomas Kuehn found in late medieval and early modern Florence, who repudiated their inheritances in order to concentrate property in male hands.[37] Although Goig created a Latinate will, she acted in accordance with Jewish law, prioritizing her husband as heir, followed by her sons.[38] Her daughters could make no legal claims, beyond an "appropriate" dowry, on the estate of their parents.

To the extent that Goig inspired different choices about women's economic self-determination, the beneficiaries were not her own daughters, but her daughters-in-law. Perhaps influenced by the example provided by his parents, her son Astrug shared the work of moneylending with his wife Goig, who extended twelve loans between 1285 and 1306. The example extended to yet another generation; the younger Goig's daughter-in-law Reina extended twenty-one loans between 1310 and 1317, following the death of her husband, Bonjueu Canviador. Although Goig did not encourage her daughters to follow her example, she and David inspired at least one of their sons to similarly divide household labor in a way that required his wife to engage in the public work of moneylending.

However, the memory of Goig had broader repercussions beyond her immediate family. Her most important legacy was not in her own family, but in the Jewish community of Vic as a whole. The memory of Goig as both founding member of the community and active moneylender may explain the unusual prominence of women lenders for the next several decades. The example of Goig and David, perhaps idealized by subsequent generations, might have allowed Jewish families in Vic to develop an alternative attitude toward women's work, one which encompassed management of financial resources and public labor as creditors. The value placed on women's work in credit may suggest that Jewish wives in Vic held greater authority in household decision-making more broadly, although the sources do not speak to this directly. Goig's importance may have also contributed to the creation of a community built on networks that linked men and women.

This alternative attitude lasted until about 1330, over a decade after Goig's death. In Vic, women as a group maintained a more sizable share of the credit market than in other Catalan cities, and individual women established substantial careers as lenders. Men sought out women as well as men as lending partners. Twenty women, including Goig and Reina, extended ten or more loans between 1250 and 1350. Thirteen of these twenty women extended more than twenty loans, while four extended eighty or more. Many of them, like Goig and Reina, enjoyed lengthy careers; fifteen women worked as creditors for ten years or more, while seven remained active in moneylending for at least twenty years.

The arrival of Jews in Vic, and the gradual establishment of a Jewish community there, helped stimulate a latent demand for Jewish credit in the Christian community of Vic and its hinterlands. Thanks to the small size of this community, and her own family's permissive attitude toward women's moneylending, Goig became one of a small group of Jews who filled this void. Her example, I argue, influenced other families in the community to develop alternative attitudes to the division of labor between husbands and wives, as well as to value ties to women. The following section will consider how Jewish couples in Vic negotiated the joint management of the conjugal estate.

TABLE 3. Jewish women in Vic with ten or more new loans

Name	New loans	Dates active	Maximum loan (sous)	Minimum loan (sous)	Median loan (sous)	Average loan (sous)
Tolsana, wife of Astrug Jucef	99	1310–1333	600	6	60	94.85
Goig, wife of David Canviador	94	1252–1310	770	5	65	96.9
Astruga, widow of Issach de Menorca	93	1264–1274	138.67	6.5	42	44.13
Goig, wife of Salomó Vidal	81	1317–1339	760	29	104	176.28
Astrugona, daughter of Jucef de Mallorca and widow of Astrug Bonjueu	46	1301–1316	980	4.17	61	107.31
Preciosa, wife of Jucef de Mallorca	45	1277–1320	1,000	1.5	38	82.76
Reina, daughter of Bonmacip and wife of Astrug Caravida	40	1293–1310	550	15	55.5	73
Reina, wife of Bonmacip	36	1267–1305	240	15	40	66.81
Bonadona, wife of Vidal Massana	35	1315–1328	170	14	42	54.1
Astrugona, wife/widow of Vidal Maymó	30	1318–1335	800.5	8	65	130.5
Astruga Aliofera	28	1284–1303	63	6	28.5	31
Dolça, wife/widow of Vidal Jucef	22	1309–1340	1,260	10	55	201.8

Reina, widow of Bonjueu, son of Astrug David	21	1310–1317	500	14	35.5	71.91
Reina, wife of Bonisto	16	1293–1300	215	15	37	54.97
Dolsona, wife of Ereto, son of Bonastrug de Torre	14	1273–1286	132	17	50	63.2
Astruga, wife of Vidal Durand	14	1282–1285	200	20	33.5	51.18
Reina, widow of Maymó de Menorca	13	1278–1293	120	20	50	60.5
Goig, wife of Astrug, son of David Canviador	12	1285–1306	400	23	66.5	97.08
Preciosa, wife of Jucef Llobell	11	1334–1339	780	30	130	188
Dolça, wife of Astrug Vidal	11	1335–1340	140	21	102	90.9

Although Reina and Astrug Caravida both worked as moneylenders, they did not work together publicly as business partners. They never extended a loan jointly, although Reina once, in 1299, appointed Astrug as her agent (*procurator*) to collect on a debt owed to her by a Jew of Girona.[39] Catalan Jewish women typically did not travel to conduct business; even the prolific Jewish women lenders of Vic may have hesitated to transgress that boundary.[40] By appointing her husband as agent, Reina could avoid traveling to Girona (sixty-five kilometers away). She also may have benefited from Astrug's connections in his hometown. Her willingness to rely on her husband when necessary, despite her normal independence, suggests that the couple saw themselves as economic partners, despite maintaining separate lending practices.

In an even more telling example of economic partnership, other couples worked independently when extending loans but occasionally appeared as a team to collect on debts. Tolsana, wife of Astrug Jucef, eventually surpassed even her predecessor Goig, extending ninety-nine extant loans. In 1309, before she had established her own lending career, she extended a single loan alongside her husband.[41] After 1310, she worked independently. Yet the evidence suggests that her lending business and that of her husband remained intertwined. Although she extended no loans jointly with her husband between 1315 and 1333, the couple acted together on four occasions in this period to release Christians from debts owed to the couple.[42]

As Rebecca Winer has noted, it is difficult to reconstruct commercial partnerships between Jewish husbands and wives.[43] Joint quitclaims like these hint at such partnerships. Although married couples in Vic extended only twelve loans jointly between 1250 and 1350, couples jointly accepted repayment for loans on twenty-three occasions—despite the fact that new loans vastly outnumber repayment contracts in the Libri Iudeorum evidence.[44] While couples did not typically lend jointly, they may have seen themselves as participating in a family business based on the shared capital resources of the conjugal estate. They may have made other household financial decisions jointly as well.

As I have argued elsewhere, Catalan Jewish legal practice severely limited wives' authority over conjugal property.[45] Jewish women were less likely than their Christian counterparts to participate in their husbands' transactions, and rabbinic authorities denied women the right to make claims related to their dowries while the marriage lasted.[46] Jewish families in Vic not only tasked wives as well as husbands with contributing to the household through moneylending but also granted wives greater access to the conjugal estate. Married couples' joint repayment contracts suggest that both husbands and wives relied on the shared capital of the conjugal fund, rather than on distinct sets of financial resources, to extend loans.

The distinct Jewish practices of Vic may have been adapted from their Christian neighbors, who saw marital property as subject to overlapping claims from both husband and wife and granted wives some authority over the conjugal estate. Jesús Lalinde Abadia describes the Catalan marital property regime prior to the twelfth century as a partial society of acquisitions, influenced by both Visigothic and Roman law, in which goods acquired during marriage were divided between the spouses, either equally or in accordance with their initial contributions to the marriage.[47] The twelfth century saw the advent of the dowry system in which the bride brought a sizable contribution in the form of the dowry, while her husband in return pledged half that sum from his own goods as dower and obligated his entire estate for both dowry and dower.[48] Stephen Bensch argues that by the thirteenth century, the interdependence of dowry and dower and the increased popularity of more fungible cash dowries led elite couples in Barcelona to envision their property as a jointly owned conjugal fund.[49] According to Lluís To Figueras, rural Catalans in the same period also created a conjugal community of goods based on the interchange of different forms of marital property.[50] By the fifteenth century, as Teresa Vinyoles notes, couples made deliberate choices in their marriage contracts about the structure of the family economy, with some imposing a strict separation of goods, others holding all property in common, and some combining the two systems.[51] The Jews of Vic developed a concept of a shared conjugal estate that closely resembled that of their Christian neighbors, rather than other Catalan Jews.

The existence of an alternative conception of marital property helps to explain the unusual prominence of married Jewish women lenders in Vic. Typically, Jewish wives lacked independent control over financial resources, because their wealth came in the form of dowries controlled by their husbands for the duration of the marriage.[52] Greater access to the wealth of the conjugal estate, rather than a distinct ideology surrounding daughters' inheritances, probably explains the substantial presence of married Jewish women among the moneylenders of Vic. Jewish heiresses, like Reina, daughter of Bonmacip, existed alongside women like Goig, wife of David Canviador, who all but disinherited her own daughters. Moreover, inherited wealth cannot entirely explain Reina's ability to work as a moneylender; she presumably did not have access to the bulk of her father's wealth until his death, which occurred well into her lending career.

WOMEN MONEYLENDERS AND THE CHRISTIAN COMMUNITY

Although some Catalan Jews practiced other trades, moneylending remained a quintessentially Jewish profession.[53] It is, at least, the form of Jewish economic life that produced the most documentation, due to the norms of notarial registration. Moneylending, more than many other trades, also brought Jews into regular contact with Christians, including both their Christian clientele and the Christian notaries who recorded the loans. Christians, as we have seen, sought out Jewish credit when it was available.

If Christians living in and around Vic had previously come into contact with Jewish moneylenders, they probably would have borrowed from Jewish men. However, the example of Vic suggests that the paucity of Jewish women moneylenders elsewhere in Catalonia did not stem from Christian preferences. Christian debtors in Vic willingly borrowed from Jewish women as well as Jewish men. Credit networks became gendered—specifically, male—due to systems that kept many women out of the credit market, not male reluctance to transact with women.

Scholars of Northern Europe have argued that Jewish women specialized in lending to Christian women.[54] In contrast, the few Jewish women lenders active in Mediterranean Europe mostly extended credit to individual men or to married couples.[55] Although Jewish women were far more active as moneylenders in Vic than elsewhere in the region, they maintained a clientele similar to that of their counterparts in other Catalan cities. Men borrowing independently formed a plurality of their clients (37.7 percent), followed by married couples, who received about one-quarter of Jewish women's loans. These two groups received similar proportions of Jewish loans overall; in the sample, individual men received 43.0 percent of Jewish loans, while married couples received 26.0 percent.

The Jewish women lenders of Vic demonstrated no particular tendency to lend to Christian women. Christian women debtors received 2.2 percent of Jewish loans in general, and only 1.9 percent of Jewish women's loans. They were more likely to receive loans from other Christians; in a sample of 615 loans between Christians in Vic, individual women received 3.9 percent (twenty-four loans).[56] Christian women may have preferred to avoid interacting with Jews, or Jewish moneylenders might have found them less creditworthy than men. Either way, the availability of Jewish women lenders did not particularly attract Christian women debtors; nor did Jewish women seek Christian women clients. When Jewish women moneylenders engaged with the surrounding Christian community, they did not do so along gendered lines. Rather, Jewish women and men developed a similarly gendered clientele.

TABLE 4. Gender of borrowers and lenders of Jewish loans in Vic, 1250–1350

Borrower	Jewish women lenders	All Jewish lenders
Women	18	58
Men	348	1,145
Married couples	228	692
Group (men)	122	339
Group (women)	5	7
Group (mix)	173	337
Unknown	30	85
	924	2,663

Jewish moneylenders, women as well as men, depended on their ability to forge bonds of trust with their Christian clients. Religious identity formed an important part of commercial interactions between Jews and Christians, each of whom came with their own expectations of the other.[57] Many scholars have claimed that relations between Jewish creditors and Christian debtors were normally marked by hostility.[58] Joseph Shatzmiller, in his study of the trial of a Jewish moneylender in fourteenth-century Marseille, provided a necessary, albeit exaggerated, corrective to this assumption. He argues that mutual respect and goodwill existed between some Jewish moneylenders and their clients.[59] While he may overemphasize the extent of friendship between Jewish creditors and Christian debtors, he demonstrates that successful Jewish lenders cultivated cordial business relationships with Christian clients. A Christian who had a positive experience with a Jewish moneylender would borrow from that Jew again, connect the Jewish lender to other clients, and even testify on the Jew's behalf in court. Jewish moneylenders and their Christian clients built economic networks that drew together the two religious communities.

As moneylenders, the Jewish women of Vic may have had more regular contact with the surrounding Christian community than Jewish women in other Catalan cities. The case of Reina, daughter of Bonmacip and wife of Astrug Caravida, illustrates how Jewish women developed relationships with Christian clients. Reina's first clients—Agnès, widow of Pere de Puig Carbó, and her son Bernat—apparently had a good experience, because they returned to Reina for another loan in 1301.[60] Most of her repeat clients were men from neighboring villages, like Pere de Gurri of Taradell, who received three loans from Reina between 1303 and 1307, one alone, and others alongside family and friends.[61] Neither neighborhood ties nor gender can explain Reina's relationship with Pere de Gurri; he presumably returned to her because she proved trustworthy and professional in her business practices. The networks Reina built crossed religious lines, gender lines, and the divide between the urban center and its rural hinterlands.

Reina's own family ties also helped her establish initial connections with Christian clients. Pere de Gurri and his father Bernat had previously sought a loan from her husband Astrug, in 1302.[62] Several of her other clients had also previously borrowed from her father or husband. Reina also connected her clients with male lenders in her family. Guillem Vidal of Malla and his wife Guillema, who borrowed from Reina in 1302, later received two loans from her father Bonmacip.[63]

Jewish women moneylenders only established successful businesses by cultivating ties with the community, including both Jewish colleagues and Christian clients. These were not women's networks; they were gender-neutral networks. Successful women lenders relied on their ties with male relatives within the Jewish community, rather than with other women. Jewish men in Vic cultivated relationships with both men and women within their community. By choosing to encourage women's involvement in the credit market, the Jews of Vic built communal structures and economic networks that depended on ties to women as well as men.

Because Christian men formed the majority of debtors, women creditors fostered relationships with male rather than female clients. A successful Jewish woman moneylender had to develop networks that crossed both religious and gender lines. These networks helped to integrate the Jews of Vic into the larger Christian-majority community of Vic and Osona.

THE DECLINE OF JEWISH WOMEN'S MONEYLENDING IN VIC

Jewish women's share of the credit market in Vic declined dramatically in the mid-fourteenth century (see table 1). Women extended 13.4 percent of Jewish loans in the 1320s, but only 5 percent in the 1330s, and less than 2 percent in the 1340s. Although wives still predominated among women lenders in the 1330s, they had all but disappeared by the 1340s (see table 2). Of the meager six loans extended by women in the Libri Iudeorum between 1340 and 1350, widows extended four, two-thirds of the total. Gradually, over the course of the fourteenth century, women ceased to establish substantial lending careers (see table 3). The last woman lender with over twenty extant loans began her career in 1318, and the last woman lender with at least ten extant loans began her career in 1335. Out of the twenty women with ten or more new loans, sixteen had begun their careers by 1315.

The Jewish community had grown significantly by 1330 from a handful of families to an established community with a synagogue, a cemetery, and other communal institutions.[64] With the growth of the community, the Jews of Vic no longer depended on women to meet local demand for Jewish credit. During the 1250s and 1260s, about a dozen Jews in Vic worked at least occasionally as lenders. By the mid-fourteenth century, the market was shared between over forty Jews.[65] Women became less central to the community's economic success, and networks including women became less essential.

This continued growth stemmed largely from the immigration of Jews from elsewhere in Catalonia and southern France.[66] The new arrivals did not necessarily adopt the unusual attitudes toward women's work and the conjugal fund that had prevailed among the Jewish community of Vic. Jewish families who came from outside the city may have remained reluctant to entrust the work of lending to wives. As these new arrivals became integrated into the Jewish community of Vic, they primarily sought to develop social and economic ties with other men.

Although Vic eventually came to resemble other Catalan cities and towns, the unusual case of Vic in the late thirteenth and early fourteenth centuries reveals that communities could make different choices about the role women played in the networks that tied the community together. Jewish and Christian women in Catalonia typically played a marginal role in most economic sectors and hence remained excluded from the economic networks that helped create both communities and connected them to one another. Jewish women in Vic had very different experiences from their counterparts in other Catalan communities; as active creditors, they enjoyed a central economic role in both the Jewish and Christian communities. Through their public labor in the credit market, they formed an essential part of the networks that shaped the Jewish community and helped to build the networks that linked that community to the Christian one. The Jewish women of Vic challenge and expand our understanding of what was possible for women in the premodern world.

This article expands upon a paper given at the 22nd International Medieval Congress in Leeds, in 2015, as well as material presented in the author's doctoral thesis, "Gender, Religious Difference, and the Notarial Economy in Medieval Catalonia, 1250–1350."

1. ACF 4591, fol. 3r.

2. For price equivalencies, see Emery, *Jews of Perpignan*, 130.

3. Junyent, *Ciutat de Vic*, 69–78, 95–96; Freedman, *Diocese of Vic*, 141–42.

4. Junyent, *Ciutat de Vic*, 81–82.

5. Junyent, *Ciutat de Vic*, 88–89; Llop i Jordana, "L'aljama de jueus de Vic," 54–56.

6. Ifft Decker, "Gender, Religious Difference, and the Notarial Economy in Medieval Catalonia," 150.

7. Jucef referred to Bonmacip as his father-in-law when he ceded houses in Barcelona to him in 1282 (ACF 20, fol. 69v).

8. ACF 4589, fol. 19v, 22r. See also Ifft Decker, "Gender, Religious Difference, and the Notarial Economy," 151–52.

9. Astrug first appeared in Vic in September of 1294, when he referred to himself as a "Jew of Girona, now an inhabitant of Vic"; in October, Bonmacip referred to him as his son-in-law. By January of 1259, Astrug had begun to refer to himself as a "Jew of Vic." See ACF 4591, fol. 15r, 17r, 19r–v.

10. The total volume of Reina's cash loans was 2,937 sous; the total volume of Astrug's was 4605.2 sous. Reina extended an average loan of seventy-three sous and a median loan of 55.5 sous; her smallest loan was for fifteen sous, while her largest was for 550 sous. Astrug extended an average loan of sixty-five sous and a median loan of forty sous; his loans ranged between seven sous and 1,100 sous.

11. Lynch, *Individuals, Families, and Communities*, 14–15.

12. Ogilvie, "Guilds, Efficiency, and Social Capital," 307–8, 322–29.

13. Lynch, *Individuals, Families, and Communities*, 68–69.

14. Carreras i Candi, "Desenrotllament de la institució notarial," 754; Baiges i Jardí, "Notariat català," 142; Garcia i Sanz, "Precedents, origen, i evolució," 169; Ginebra i Molins, "Escrivanies eclesiàstiques a Catalunya," 90.

15. Bartoli Langeli, "'Scripsi et publicavi,'" 58, 68.

16. Llop Jordana, "L'aljama de jueus de Vic," 15–18; Llop Jordana, "*Libri Iudeorum* de Castelló d'Empúries," 44.

17. Llop Jordana, "L'aljama de jueus de Vic," 13, 18–19.

18. Assis, *Jewish Economy*, 20–21; Winer, "Jews in and out of Latin Notarial Culture," 123–25.

19. Rich Abad, "Able and Available," 73–79; Ifft Decker, "Gender, Religious Difference, and the Notarial Economy," 167–68.

20. Winer, *Women, Wealth, and Community*, 87–88; Ifft Decker, "Jewish Women, Christian Women, and Credit," 166.

21. Courtemanche, "Femmes juives," 550; Reyerson, *Business, Banking, and Finance*, 73–74.

22. Winer, *Women, Wealth, and Community*, 99–103; Ifft Decker, "Public Economic Role," 48–50; Ifft Decker, "Gender, Religious Difference, and the Notarial Economy," 168–71.

23. Denjean, *Juifs et chrétiens*, 97–100.

24. Goig extended twenty-four extant loans in the 1250s, thirty-two in the 1260s, and twenty-six in the 1270s; she also extended six loans of indeterminate date, but probably from the 1260s or 1270s. Perhaps due to age, she gradually exited the credit market in the 1280s, when she made only five extant loans. She also extended one new loan in 1310, after a long period of inactivity. See Ifft Decker, "Gender, Religious Difference, and the Notarial Economy," 99, 173–76.

25. For a rare loan extended by David Canviador, see ACF 6, fol. 32v. For his assumed profession, see Llop i Jordana, "L'aljama de jueus de Vic," 60.

26. Guilleré, *Diner, poder, i societat*, 73, 77–78, 101–3.

27. Junyent, *Ciutat de Vic*, 111–14.

28. In one loan, the name of the debtor(s) cannot be identified.

29. See Emery, *Jews of Perpignan*, 61–66; Assis, *Jews of Santa Coloma de Queralt*, 49–50; Denjean, *Juifs et chrétiens*, 117; Colomer i Casamitjana, "El crèdit a Castelló," 59–60.

30. ACF 4583, fol. 3r.

31. ACF 4586, fol. 97v.

32. Howell, *Marriage Exchange*, 68–70; Smail, *Legal Plunder*, 66.

33. As Julie Mell has emphasized in a recent study, many Jews in both the Mediterranean and Northern Europe worked in professions other than moneylending. See Mell, *Myth of the Medieval Jewish Moneylender*, 1. 198–216, 2.120–38.

34. Ifft Decker, "Gender, Religious Difference, and the Notarial Economy," 201.

35. For Goig's will, see ACF 4583, fol. 8v. See also Llop i Jordana, "L'aljama de jueus de Vic," 61.

36. Burns, *Jews in the Notarial Culture*, 114–15; Reyerson, *Women's Networks*, 19–27.

37. Kuehn, *Heirs, Kin, and Creditors*, 128.

38. See Maimonides, *Mishneh Torah*, Hilkhot Nachalot 1.1–3.

39. ACF 4592, fol. 9v.

40. Klein, "Public Activities," 56–60; Winer, *Women, Wealth, and Community*, 97–98.

41. ACF 4593, fol. 17r.

42. ACF 4595, fol. 96r; ACF 4596, fol. 18r, 99r; ACF 4598, fol. 99v. See also Ifft Decker, "Public Economic Role," 61.

43. Winer, *Women, Wealth, and Community*, 98–99.

44. See Llop i Jordana, "L'aljama de jueus de Vic," 19. My sample yielded a paltry seventy-one loan repayment contracts, as compared with 2,663 new loans.

45. Ifft Decker, "Gender, Religious Difference, and the Notarial Economy," 60–62. Elka Klein, in contrast, argues that Jews and Christians had similar practices with regard to wives' control over conjugal property. See Klein, "Widow's Portion," 153–58.

46. See, for example, Solomon ibn Adret, *She'elot u-Teshuvot*, 6.4.

47. Lalinde Abadia, "Pactos matrimoniales catalanes," 144–49.

48. Lalinde Abadia, "Pactos matrimoniales catalanes," 183–86, 191–97.

49. Bensch, *Barcelona*, 268–69.

50. To Figueras, *Família i hereu*, 159.

51. Vinyoles, *Les barcelonines*, 89–90.

52. Winer, *Women, Wealth, and Community*, 94.

53. Emery, *Jews of Perpignan*, 17–25; Assis, *Golden Age*, 206–7, 238–39, 251–52; Assis, *Jewish Economy*, 15–16; Denjean, *Le loi de lucre*, 2.

54. Jordan, "Jews on Top," 50–55; Hoyle, "The Bonds That Bind," 122–24.

55. Courtemanche, "Femmes juives," 553; Ifft Decker, "Jewish Women, Christian Women, and Credit," 169–71.

56. Ifft Decker, "Gender, Religious Difference, and the Notarial Economy," 190.

57. Trivellato, *Familiarity of Strangers*, 275; Halevi, "Religion and Cross-Cultural Trade," 48–50.

58. See, for example, Jordan, "Jews on Top," 47–53; Cohen, *Under Crescent and Cross*, 82–87.

59. Shatzmiller, *Shylock Reconsidered*, 71–72, 104–18.

60. ACF 4591, fol. 3r; ACF 4592, fol. 26r.

61. ACF 4592, fol. 36v, 44r, 77v.

62. ACF 4592, fol. 30v.

63. ACF 4592, fol. 30r, 39r, 51r.

64. Llop i Jordana, "La fi de la comunitat jueva de Vic," 86–88; Llop i Jordana, "L'aljama de jueus de Vic," 39–48; Ollich i Castanyer and Llop i Jordana, "Espais publics i espais privats," 485–95.

65. Llop i Jordana, "La fi de la comunitat jueva de Vic," 87.

66. Llop i Jordana, "L'aljama de jueus de Vic," 54–59.

BIBLIOGRAPHY

Manuscripts and Archives

ACF Arxiu i Biblioteca Episcopal de Vic, Arxiu de la Curia Fumada. Llibres Generals, vols. 5, 6; Llibres Particulars, Comunitats, Judeorum, vols. 185, 4582–4607.

Ibn Adret, Solomon. *Sefer She'elot u-Teshuvot ha-R'ashb'a*. Jerusalem: Mekhon Tiferet ha-Torah, 1988–1990.

Maimonides, Moses. *Mishneh Torah*. Edited by Yohai Makbili, Yehiel Kara, and Hillel Gershuni. Haifa: Or Vishua, 2009.

Published Works

Assis, Yom Tov. *The Jews of Santa Coloma de Queralt: An Economic and Demographic Case Study of a Community at the End of the Thirteenth Century*. Jerusalem: Magnes, 1988.

———. *The Golden Age of Aragonese Jewry: Community and Society in the Crown of Aragon, 1213–1327*. Oxford: Littman Library of Jewish Civilization, 1997.

———. *Jewish Economy in the Medieval Crown of Aragon, 1213–1327: Money and Power*. Leiden: Brill, 1997.

Baiges i Jardí, Ignasi J. "El notariat català: Origen i evolució." In *Actes del I Congrès d'Història del Notariat Català: Barcelona, 11, 12, i 13 de novembre de 1993*, edited by Josep Maria Sans i Travé, 131–66. Barcelona: Fundació Noguera, 1994.

Bartoli Langeli, Attilio. "'Scripsi et publicavi': Il notaio come figura pubblica, l'instrumentum come documento pubblico." In *Notai, miracoli, e culto dei santi: Pubblicità e autenticazione del sacro tra XII e XV secolo*, edited by Raimondo Michetti, 55–71. Milan: Giuffrè, 2004.

Bensch, Stephen P. *Barcelona and Its Rulers, 1096–1291*. Cambridge: Cambridge University Press, 1995.

Burns, Robert I. *Jews in the Notarial Culture: Latinate Wills in Mediterranean Spain, 1250–1350*. Berkeley: University of California Press, 1996.

Carreras i Candi, Francesc. "Desenrotllament de la institació notarial a Catalunya en lo segle XIII." In *I Congrès d'història de la Corona d'Aragó*, vol. 2, 751–89. Barcelona: F. Altés, 1909–1913.

Cohen, Mark R. *Under Crescent and Cross: The Jews in the Middle Ages*. Princeton: Princeton University Press, 1994.

Colomer Casamitjana, Joel. "El crèdit a Castelló a principis del segle XIV: els Ravaia. La comunitat jueva de Castelló, cofre e tresor del comte." In *Jueus del rei i del comte: A l'entorn de les comunitats jueves de Girona a Castelló d'Empúries*, Girona Judaica 7, edited by Lídia Donat Perez, 53–72. Girona: Patronat Call de Girona, 2014.

Courtemanche, Andrée. "Les femmes juives et le credit a Manosque au tournant du XIVe siècle." *Provence Historique* 37 (1987): 545–58.

Denjean, Claude. *Juifs et Chrétiens: De Perpignan a Puigcerdà, XIIIe–XIVe siècles*. Canet: Editions Trabucaire, 2004.

———. *Le loi de lucre: L'usure en procès dans la Couronne d'Aragon à la fin du Moyen Âge*. Madrid: Casa de Velazquez, 2007.

Emery, Richard. *The Jews of Perpignan in the Thirteenth Century: An Economic Study Based on Notarial Registers*. New York: Columbia University Press, 1959.

Freedman, Paul. *The Diocese of Vic: Tradition and Regeneration in Medieval Catalonia*. New Brunswick NJ: Rutgers University Press, 1989.

Garcia i Sanz, Arcadi, "Precedents, origen, i evolució dels col.legis notarials." In *Actes del I Congrès d'Història del Notariat Català: Barcelona, 11, 12, i 13 de novembre de 1993*, edited by Josep Maria Sans i Travé, 167–87. Barcelona: Fundació Noguera, 1994.

Ginebra i Molins, Rafel. "Les escrivanies eclesiàstiques a Catalunya." In *Actes del II Congrès d'Història del Notariat Català*, edited by Juan José López Burniol and Josep Maria Sans i Travé, 89–160. Barcelona: Fundació Noguera, 2000.

Guilleré, Christian. *Diner, poder, i societat a la Girona del segle XIV*. Girona: Ajuntament de Girona, 1984.

Halevi, Leor. "Religion and Cross-Cultural Trade: A Framework for Interdisciplinary Inquiry." In *Religion and Trade: Cross-Cultural Exchanges in World History, 1000–1900*, edited by Francesca Trivellato, Leor Halevi, and Cátia Antunes, 24–61. Oxford: Oxford University Press, 2014.

Howell, Martha. *The Marriage Exchange: Property, Social Place, and Gender in the Cities of the Low Countries, 1300–1550*. Chicago: University of Chicago Press, 1998.

Hoyle, Victoria. "The Bonds that Bind: Money Lending between Anglo Jewish and Christian Women in the Plea Rolls of the Exchequer of the Jews, 1218–1280." *Journal of Medieval History* 34 (2008): 119–29.

Ifft Decker, Sarah. "The Public Economic Role of Catalan Jewish Wives, 1250–1350." *Tamid: Revista Catalana Anual d'Estudis Hebraics* 11 (2015): 45–66.

———. "Jewish Women, Christian Women, and Credit in Thirteenth-Century Catalonia." *Haskins Society Journal* 27 (2016): 161–78.

———. "Gender, Religious Difference, and the Notarial Economy in Medieval Catalonia, 1250–1350." PhD dissertation, Yale University, 2017.

Jordan, William Chester. "Jews on Top: Women and the Availability of Consumption Loans in Northern France in the Mid-Thirteenth Century." *Journal of Jewish Studies* 29, no. 1 (1978): 39–56.

Junyent, Eduard. *La ciutat de Vic i la seva història*. Barcelona: Curial Edicions Catalanes, 1976.

Klein, Elka. "The Widow's Portion: Law, Custom, and Marital Property among Medieval Catalan Jews." *Viator* 31 (2000): 147–63.

———. "Public Activities of Catalan Jewish Women." *Medieval Encounters* 12, no. 1 (2006): 48–61.

Kuehn, Thomas. *Heirs, Kin, and Creditors in Renaissance Florence*. Cambridge: Cambridge University Press, 2008.

Lalinde Abadia, Jesús. "Los pactos matrimoniales catalanes." *Anuario de historia del derecho español* 33 (1963): 133–266.

Llop i Jordana, Irene. "La fi de la comunitat jueva de Vic: Béns i conversió dels últims jueus (1391)." *Tamid: Revista Catalana Anual d'Estudis Hebraics* 9 (2013): 85–106.

———. "L'aljama de jueus de Vic al segle XIII (1231–1315): Orígens i consolidació de l'aljama." PhD dissertation, Universitat de Barcelona, 2016.

———. "Els *Libri Iudeorum* de Castelló d'Empúries." In *Jueus del rei i del comte: A l'entorn de les comunitats jueves de Girona a Castelló d'Empúries*, Girona Judaica 7, edited by Lídia Donat Perez, 43–51. Girona: Patronat Call de Girona, 2014.

Lynch, Katherine. *Individuals, Families, and Communities in Europe, 1200–1800: The Urban Foundations of Western Society.* Cambridge: Cambridge University Press, 2003.

Mell, Julie. *The Myth of the Medieval Jewish Moneylender,* 2 vols. New York: Palgrave Macmillan, 2017–2018.

Ogilvie, Sheilagh. "Guilds, Efficiency, and Social Capital: Evidence from German Proto-Industry." *Economic History Review* 57, no. 2 (2004): 286–333.

Ollich i Castanyer, Imma and Irene Llop i Jordana. "Espais públics i espais privats del call jueu de Vic: Evidències documentals i arqueològiques." *Ausa* 27:177 (2016): 481–506.

Reyerson, Kathryn L. *Business, Banking, and Finance in Medieval Montpellier.* Toronto: Pontifical Institute of Mediaeval Studies, 1985.

———. *Women's Networks in Medieval France: Gender and Community in Montpellier, 1300–1350.* New York: Palgrave Macmillan, 2016.

Rich Abad, Anna. "Able and Available: Jewish Women in Medieval Barcelona and Their Economic Activities." *Journal of Medieval Iberian Studies* 6, no. 1 (2014): 71–86.

Shatzmiller, Joseph. *Shylock Reconsidered: Jews, Moneylending, and Medieval Society.* Berkeley: University of California Press, 1989.

Smail, Daniel Lord. *Legal Plunder: Households and Debt Collection in Late Medieval Europe.* Cambridge: Harvard University Press, 2016.

To Figueras, Lluís. *Família i hereu a la Catalunya nord-oriental (segles 10–13).* Barcelona: Publicacions de l'Abadia de Montserrat, 1997.

Trivellato, Francesca. *The Familiarity of Strangers: The Sephardic Diaspora, Livorno, and Cross-Cultural Trade in the Early Modern Period.* New Haven: Yale University Press, 2009.

Vinyoles, Teresa-Maria. *Les barcelonines a les darreries de l'edat mitjana (1370–1410).* Barcelona: Fundació Salvador Vives Casajuana, 1976.

Winer, Rebecca Lynn. "Jews in and out of Latin Notarial Culture: Analyzing Hebrew Notations on Latin Contracts in Thirteenth-Century Perpignan and Barcelona." In *Entangled Histories: Knowledge, Authority, and Jewish Culture in the Thirteenth Century,* edited by Elisheva Baumgarten, Ruth Mazo Karras, and Katelyn Mesler, 113–33. Philadelphia: University of Pennsylvania Press, 2017.

———. *Women, Wealth, and Community in Perpignan, c. 1250–1300: Christians, Jews, and Enslaved Muslims in a Medieval Mediterranean Town.* Burlington VT: Ashgate, 2006.

2

Challenges Facing Mallorcan Conversas after 1391

NATALIE OELTJEN

In the early morning hours of August 2, 1391, a Jewish woman in the city of Mallorca was woken by screams a few streets away.[1] An angry mob of country folk had stormed past the city walls, rioting and attacking houses of elites before converging upon the Jewish quarter. They were fed up with the city magistrates over decades of political underrepresentation, and a fiscal exploitation that had driven many of them into debt with Jewish creditors. The woman, fearful that the mob would either slay her or force her to convert, ran to take shelter in the royal castle nearby, but there was no protecting her house from the ensuing plunder.[2] Her husband, on the other hand, fled to the port and found a ship willing to take him across the Mediterranean to Algiers, where he had relatives and business contacts who could help him settle there. He was not alone on that ship: many Jews managed to benefit from opportunist ship captains who agreed to ferry them across the sea to safety, for a good fee. He left his wife in the castle with the intention that she would find some way to liquidate their assets and join him in the future. These assets, which included her dowry, were invested in a combination of real estate, loans, and merchandise stored in warehouses. The woman stayed in the castle for over three months, crowded together with half of her community, and with the families of the ruling Christian citizens, all hoping to be spared the fury of the rebels who camped outside its walls. Ultimately, she was baptized—along with all the Jews that had taken shelter there—before she could safely return home. Her once-bustling neighborhood now seemed devastated and desolate. The streets were emptier. Buildings had been burned and plundered. The grand houses renowned for their splendor had been partly dismantled and were missing their beautifully carved lintel pieces and doors. Her own home was turned upside down. Many of its contents had been stolen and parchments with contracts and credit notes ripped apart—including the dowry contract which stipulated all the assets owed to her.

Fearful of a repeat attack, with unrest still fomenting outside the city walls and in the rural towns, financially insecure and eager to reconnect with her husband, the woman abandoned her remaining possessions the instant she heard of a ship that was preparing to take conversos across the sea, despite the fact that carrying conversos offshore had been strictly outlawed by the king. Given these stakes, she paid a high price to get on that ship. Lack of time, and royal decrees that prohibited anyone from purchasing property or merchandise from conversos, prevented her from acquiring portable currency to smuggle away with her (conversos were also officially forbidden to take any valuables off the island). She lacked the fortune of better-connected conversos who did manage to take with them a modicum of wealth by selling their houses surreptitiously—for a fraction of the worth—to buyers willing to risk the penalties.

It seemed a miracle—after the stories of conversos attacked and robbed at sea—that the woman made it to the port of Algiers relatively unscathed. The Jewish community there was small enough that she could quickly locate her husband once she arrived. However, what should have brought her relief after a long and arduous journey sadly brought her more grief. Her husband rejected her, furious that she had abandoned all their property, which the Crown was quick to confiscate in their absence. With rabbinical authority on his side, not only did he divorce her on the grounds that she should have stayed in Mallorca to protect their property, but he also refused to pay her the equivalent of her dowry, which typically would have been invested in property back on the island.

The story of this unnamed woman is taken from a *responsum* of Rabbi Simon ben Zemach Duran, an important Jewish legal authority of the period who continued to advise his native Mallorcan community after he fled the anti-Jewish violence in 1391 and settled in Algiers.[3] Duran's legal conclusion was that the husband should be permitted to divorce his wife on the grounds that she failed to protect their estate, and for this same reason he was not obligated to pay her dowry. This rabbinic ruling illustrates the particular vulnerability of both Jewish women and conversas in the wake of the 1391 violence in terms of their property and economic security.

This essay examines the threat to conversa property and dowries during the aftermath of the violence posed by two particular developments: the marked exile of so many Jews and conversos, and the reconstitution of the former Jewish *aljama* (the corporate, institutional body of the Jewish community that could tax, be taxed, and own property) into a distinct converso fiscal entity from 1390 through 1410. The post-1391 archival records in Mallorca, particularly those issued by King Joan and his administrators, focus overwhelmingly on the various fiscal implications of the rebellion: for the Crown, for the creditors of the former Jewish aljama, for the surviving Jews, and for the incipient converso community. A systematic analysis of these records reveals the establishment of a converso community, a *comunitas conversorum*,[4] founded upon fiscal exigencies in two respects. Firstly, it was quickly apparent that the conversos needed to band together in order to defend their collective interests. Secondly, when the Crown enforced the repayment of the aljama's corporate debts, and payment of de facto royal taxes from the newly converted Jews *as a collective*, the latter were forced to organize themselves as a single fiscal unit. It was most natural and efficient to maintain the former aljama's administrative structures and methods of tax collection.

As an integral part of these communities, women's property and their dowries became vulnerable to the same claims of creditors and extraordinary royal fiscal demands that were levied on converso households after 1391. The effective taxation of conversa dowries contrasts what recent studies suggest about the property of Christian women in the Crown of Aragon, where women's dowries were immune to the claims of tax collectors or the husbands' creditors. The notarial and royal administrative records consulted for this study reveal some attempts on the part of male kin or community representatives to defend conversa dowries through petitioning the Crown. Kings Joan (d. 1396) and Martí (d. 1410) did tend to protect women's economic security when complaints were explicitly brought before them, as long as those women were not themselves *relapsas*, that is, conversas who continued to observe Jewish practices, or who fled the island. Any converso or conversa who left the island was considered a renegade, and instantly lost all his or her property to the Crown.

Some Jewish communities survived through the tumult of 1391 relatively intact, while others, particularly in the major cities of the Crown of Aragon, were significantly or completely diminished. King Joan officially "dissolved" at least three of the largest Jewish aljamas ostensibly because of their depopulation, although the cessation of these corporate bodies conveniently entailed the reversion of communal assets to the Crown—assets which consisted of valuable real estate and annuity investments. In Barcelona, Valencia, and Mallorca, the Jewish aljamas ceased to exist *qua* semiautonomous corporate institutions, and new communities of conversos came into being.[5] These converso communities quickly organized in order to be able to petition and defend their collective interests before the Crown—mimicking the leadership of the former Jewish aljama, adopting and adapting many of its institutions with respect to communal administration, fiscal organization, welfare, and relations with the Crown.

The closure of the aljamas of Mallorca, Barcelona, and Valencia had far-reaching fiscal repercussions owing to the fact that these aljamas, like their cities, had amassed significant corporate debts. The kings had always heavily taxed their Jewish "treasure," but in the latter half of the fourteenth century, the emergence of a new kind of credit mechanism, the *censal*, enabled the Crown to solicit greater funds from its aljamas.[6] The censal was a kind of annuity that the creditor would purchase from the debtor for a large sum (the principal loan), while the debtor made yearly interest payments without paying off the principal for long periods of time. In the years leading up to 1391, the kings repeatedly requested that aljama leaders borrow money by means of *censals* and advance the funds to the royal fisc. Usually the aljama raised the funds required for the annual interest payments through imposing additional communal taxes, which became increasingly burdensome. By August 1391, the Mallorcan aljama had accrued a total debt of 24,000 pounds through *censals*, paying 1,500 Barcelonan pounds, or about 6.75 percent, in annual interest payments to its *censaler* investors in Mallorca and Barcelona.[7]

Early in 1392, aware of the former aljama's "dissolution," its creditors in Barcelona and in Mallorca collectively petitioned the king about reclaiming their investments from the individuals who had once comprised the aljama. This had to be done urgently while the members of the former aljama could still be identified and located. The Crown reacted quickly in brokering negotiations between representatives of the converso community and the creditors to establish a series of repayment plans, whereby every converso and Jewish household had to contribute over half of the total value of their assets, as a kind of debt repayment tax. Converso representatives mimicked the protocols of their former aljama in organizing major tax assessments and collections in order to carry out the debt repayment, which also entailed the transfer, to individual creditors, of various properties as well as rights to collect certain rents and debts.

Carrying out these agreements generated a flurry of administrative correspondence. The royal governor sent numerous letters to rural bailiffs ordering them to execute payment from the substantive number of Christians in their districts who were indebted to Jews (most now conversos) often with the end goal of directing these payments to the creditors of the aljama. In addition, royal officials were instructed to collect 20 percent of all debts owing to conversos, which comprised a "donation" that the latter had promised to the Crown.[8] These letters reflect a relatively low proportion of women actively engaged in moneylending—lending small amounts when they did, and rarely independently.[9] Nevertheless, women would have had debts allocated to them as part of their dowries. Whether the debts were owing to women or men, however, did not impact their collection by royal officials.

In 1393 the converso *taxadors* began their work of assessing personal property and determining the required contributions of each member, (or household), of the community. Royal letters refer to account books in which the taxation was recorded by the converso administrators, but not having discovered those, it is difficult to know with certainty how the tax was carried out and whether women were directly taxed at the outset. The agreement with the creditors refers to the taxation of "all the conversos," which may have indicated women as well as men, such that no converso-owned property would have been immune. The *taxadors* certainly had no qualms about demanding payments from women's dowries when the former could not access the property of their husbands. Judging from the complaints iterated by the converso administrators to the king, there were a number of cases in which the husbands' property was impossible to assess or access. In what would seem to be an attempt at tax evasion, conversos would conceal their property through various devices, sometimes shipping valuables or merchandise off the island (where they could not be assessed, and were technically outside of the tax jurisdiction), or personally leaving the island and taking their property with them, usually to North Africa, but also to other jurisdictions within the kingdom, such as Valencia.

Early in 1394, the converso Jaume Ribes, the son of the well-known Mallorcan Jewish mapmaker Abraham Cresques, petitioned the Crown in defense of his sister, Francisca, also a conversa. The converso *taxadors* were claiming her dowry to pay the debt-tax owing on property her husband held outside of Mallorca, which they could not access.[10] They claimed that Francisca should pay from her dowry since her still-Jewish husband, Marzoch Madini, could not be located, most likely because he had fled the island.[11] Her brother Jaume had informed the king that he had money owing to him from her dowry and offered to pay the tax in question if her dowry be "kept intact," to which the king acquiesced. Interestingly, Jaume does not argue that his sister's dowry should be kept intact based on any legal rights of hers, but rather as a kind of royal favor to protect *his* own property. Regardless of Jaume's justification on the basis of personal interest, it was in fact typical for Jewish males to protect their sisters' welfare.[12] Francisca's case comes before us because she had the fortune of belonging to a family with an established relationship to the king, who had commissioned maps from her famous father as well as her brother. However, other women in a similar bind may have gone unrecorded for lack of a defender like Jaume, or because they lacked access to the king's intervention; and their dowries may have been significantly depleted as a result of communal fiscal obligations.

The case of Francisca is particularly important because normally dowries should not have been subject to taxes. Local Christian law, based on Roman jurisprudence, protected women's dowries entirely from creditors and tax collectors.[13] While Jewish practices appear to have been less fixed, on the whole dowries were similarly protected. However, there was precedent in rabbinic responsa to suggest that women's dowries were not altogether immune. A responsum of the early fourteenth-century Saragossan rabbi, Yom Tov Ishbili, indicates that if a woman's husband did not pay communal taxes, she should make a contribution from her dowry.[14] Although the responsum does not explicitly state that she should "pay tax" from her dowry, it establishes a legal precedent to support tax collectors who endeavored to collect from wives what they could not collect from their husbands. The converso administrators in Mallorca, who were formerly aljama secretaries, may well have been familiar with this precedent and relied on it to justify their course of action with Francisca. That the king acquiesced to protect her dowry was in keeping with Christian legal precedents, as was his tendency to support Jewish and conversa women's dowries, in general. In 1393, for instance, King Joan issued a letter permitting Jewish (and conversa) women to reconstruct dowry contracts or *ketubot* that had been lost in the 1391 violence on the basis of legal witnesses.[15] Unfortunately I have not found examples of this privilege being put into practice, since this would likely appear in judicial records, but if Guerson and Wessell Lightfoot's essay is reflective of trends among Jewish women in the Crown of Aragon, it is likely that widows and abandoned conversas in Mallorca, too, claimed their rights before local Christian courts.

The situation of Jewish women and conversas whose husbands had left them behind on the island is another question that requires further investigation. Early medieval rabbinic texts advocate that traveling husbands either return to their wives within a finite period of time or grant them a divorce—but this was an entirely different context.[16] Francisca's husband was one of many Jewish men who fled Mallorca and left behind family members, trusted friends, or a wife, ostensibly to safeguard their property. Such a scenario is illustrated in the responsum of Rabbi Duran that introduced this essay.[17] Duran reports that the husband deliberately left his wife in charge of his property, which was subsequently plundered, and his wife was forced to convert, but that some property remained untouched in a warehouse. Duran writes that, "the Gentiles said to her that if she stayed there they would pay her *ketubbah* [her dowry] from what had remained in the ware-houses."[18] Bearing in mind that the responsa genre is problematic as a historical source, this text indicates that King Joan's decree allowing Jewish and conversa women to reconstruct (and claim) their dowries was conveyed to the community. However, it would have required painstaking efforts for the woman to claim and acquire her dotal rights, particularly since her husband's assets would have been confiscated once royal administrators determined that he was absent. She would have had to continue living in fear—perhaps without relatives to protect her—as a nominal Christian for a longer period of time; and even if she did reclaim her property, there was little hope of carrying any of its worth off the island with her. We can only make an educated guess about her motivations; perhaps she concluded it was not worth the risk to remain on the island in case she could not find another ship captain willing to take her to Algiers later. With all these doubts, she seized the opportunity to flee, which gave royal administrators license to confiscate the rest of her marital property.

Sadly, Duran's nameless female protagonist has no voice in his text. We cannot know her personal circumstances. She may well have had relatives or even children in Algiers who are not mentioned in the text, or perhaps she was pregnant and wanted to travel before she gave birth. Ultimately for Duran, however, her personal situation appears to have been irrelevant. What mattered most were the legal facts and contractual obligations; even the woman's adherence to Judaism (her ostensible if not actual motivation for exile) should not have taken precedence over her duty to safeguard both her husband's and her dotal property. Since she breached this aspect of the *ketubah*, the contract was rendered invalid and she forfeited the right to reclaim her dowry upon divorce. Thus the woman was left without any financial support and without a husband in a strange land. Admittedly, responsa must be used with caution, if they are to be employed as historical sources, and the stories generally should not be taken as referring to actual events but rather crafted to illustrate legal problems. This particular tale, however, illustrates a realistic scenario for the first generation of Mallorcan exiles, and appears plausible from the perspective of the royal correspondence and archival records.

Conversa exiles appear in royal correspondence often in relation to the confiscation of their property. For instance, it is through the sale of her confiscated house that we learn about Blanca, formerly Astruga, daughter of the deceased Mallorcan Jew Master Salamon de Paralada. Her house was confiscated by the Crown once she had fled "with all her sons to Barbary, where she lives with Samuel Faquim, Jew, her husband, and has rejected Christianity and returned to Jewish practices."[19] Blanca held legal title to one of the principal houses of the Jewish quarter or *call*, perhaps as a widow or heir and as a member of one of the former aljama's principal families. The royal treasurer sold her house to another administrator, Antoni Rexach, who had been buying up the most valuable real estate of the former *call*.[20] The letter does not state that Blanca fled *with her husband*, only that she was living with him, suggesting that she fled without him, possibly traveling on her own, like the woman in Duran's responsum. It is not clear whether her husband, Samuel, traveled separately, or whether she traveled as a widow and remarried in North Africa. If she did remarry, had she been released from the rabbinic obligation of levirate marriage to marry her deceased husband's brother? At least textually, contemporary rabbinic authorities ruled that even a conversa widow was obligated, according to Jewish law, to marry her husband's brother, unless he released her through the ritual of *halitza*, but I have not found such a case among the archival records.[21]

Royal confiscation of property belonging to conversa exiles like Blanca had repercussions among the wider community as well. Seizing the property of *relapsas* entailed tracking down the various assets that comprised their dowries, which frequently consisted of outstanding debts (owing to the dowry). Officials were quick to demand repayment of debts from anyone owing money to confiscated dowries, no doubt in order to seize these funds before creditors or converso *taxadors* might get to them, as conflict tended to break out between these three parties vying over converso assets during this period.[22] Many of the debtors to these dowries were conversos themselves and already in financial straits as a result of communal fiscal burdens, not to mention individual losses resulting from the violence. The threat posed by royal officials executing dotal debts became such a pressing concern among the converso community that its representatives raised the problem among their petitions to King Joan during his visit to the island in 1395. Although the king reiterated in no uncertain terms that *relapsas* would have their dowries seized, he did concede a pardon which released conversos who resided on the island from paying debts owing to confiscated dowries.[23] The text of King Joan's letter refers to the "confiscation of dowries . . . of the conversos' wives," suggesting the possibility that even the resident wives of exiles were having their property seized, leaving those women without financial support. The converso representatives committed to pay 460 gold florins for this pardon. That they were willing to levy yet another tax to raise these funds reflects the importance and centrality of dotal assets, which were deeply woven into the economic fabric of the wider community.[24]

For well over a decade following the revolt, conversos had to obtain special licenses and provide guarantors to legally leave the island, which was most commonly documented for commercial purposes. In some cases they could circumvent the guarantor requirement by obtaining a letter of safe conduct directly from the king. If the converso named in the license did not inform officials of his return to the island within the prescribed time, usually three months, it was concluded that he had gone to the Maghreb where conversos could live openly as Jews, and this "relapse" warranted the confiscation of all his goods by the Crown, as well as a large fine levied against the guarantor. The constant stream of exiles implicated an increasing number of converso guarantors condemned to pay heavy fines, another burden that converso representatives petitioned against during the 1395 royal visit. In response, the king, wanting to encourage the converso community to remain on the island, issued a pardon that exempted resident converso guarantors from paying those fines.

Among the sources consulted for this paper, there are many examples of travel licenses and letters of safe conduct issued to individual conversos, but none issued directly to a female traveler. This is not surprising given that the primary purpose of these licenses was to enable and regulate maritime trade, not facilitate the relocation of families outside the boundaries of the kingdom. A woman traveling independently would have had to bribe a ship captain at the port, like the protagonist of Duran's responsum. Both rabbinic and archival sources attest to this kind of "unlicensed" flight of conversas.

Sometimes, conversas (and conversos, for that matter) made the arduous trip twice: later returning to the island they had called home, where they would have to live ostensibly as Christians. Two conversa sisters, Alienor and Antonia, fled Mallorca around 1391 and had been living in Algiers with their three children for some time when their father, the converso Joan Riera, obtained a letter of safe conduct from King Joan to go to Algiers and bring his daughters back to the island where they would "preserve the Christian faith." It is no coincidence that this letter of safe conduct was issued on the same date as another pardon conceded to the converso community in 1395, which offered legal immunities to all conversos living in North Africa if they returned to the island, regardless of whether they had left illegally.[25] The letter makes no mention of husbands, who may have perished during the 1391 violence, or during the perilous voyage across the sea, or who may abandoned their wives; or perhaps daughters fled as single women so had no husbands.

We know of Joan Riera's case because in 1401 his wife, Margesia, brought the royal letter, dated six years earlier, before the local governor.[26] Evidently it took Joan a long time to retrieve his daughters—up to six years—and it is possible that they were detained in Mallorca, prompting Margesia to defend them—a situation not uncommon in this period; a woman left in charge of the household and left to act on behalf of her husband or other family members who traveled across the Mediterranean. We might imagine her at one point a mother who sent her children to a strange land in hope of a better, safer, and Jewish life for them.

There are other examples of mothers, parents, and grandparents who sent their converted sons and daughters to North Africa, themselves staying behind, perhaps to maintain the family patrimony. For instance, King Martí was furious to learn, in 1407, that the converso Pere Morro had sent his granddaughter, the child of his widowed daughter who still lived in his house in Mallorca, to Algiers, presumably to live and marry as a Jew.[27] Unfortunately these snippets of stories come to us with little context. How did these women travel in the first place? The few references to conversos on ships among the archival records, often reporting piratic attacks, would suggest that women traveling without the direct protection of male kin did so in a larger group with other members of their community.[28] Conversos traveling at sea were not only targets of piracy but also of attacks by Christian sailors—also subjects of the Crown of Aragon—seeking to vindicate the Christian faith by attacking "renegades." What happened to these women and children when their ships were overtaken by pirates specifically seeking to plunder the goods of renegade conversos?[29] The sources tell us little about the victims, and less still about any women who may have been on board.

In conclusion, although the royal correspondence and notarial records for Mallorca allow us to reconstruct little of conversa experience in the wake of 1391, they demonstrate ways in which conversas were distinctly affected by royal and fiscal policies. The destruction of the Jewish aljama with its concomitant emigration had destabilized the ownership of Jewish and converso property in the *ciutat*, and this affected conversa property too, particularly the dowries to which they held specific rights. This essay has outlined two major threats to dowries after 1391: first, the communal taxes imposed to repay the former aljama's debt, and second, the royal policy of confiscating property belonging to converso exiles. The extent to which women fended for themselves in local Mallorcan courts remains unknown since the records that would hold that information have not yet been located or excavated. Protecting Jewish women and conversas was—or should have been—an imperative for the Crown given royal anxieties around the loss of both Jews and conversos to exile. Despite their initial fiscal exploitation of conversos, both Kings Joan and Martí made explicit overtures to maintain these communities on the island with the understanding that they played an integral role in the island's economy and maritime trade and seem to have understood that building a community necessitated supporting its women.[30]

How did the *comunitas conversorum* respond to the threats against conversas dowries? In the first few years, in the fray of executing the repayment of the former aljama's debts in addition to collective financial commitments to the Crown, communal representatives do not appear to have acted in defense of conversas per se, but rather petitioned against communal burdens that resulted from royal confiscations of their dowries. The petitions of converso representatives demonstrate how conversa property was woven in to the economic fabric of the wider converso community. By the turn of the century there is evidence of community support of women's economic well-being, in the sense of providing dowries that allowed poor women to marry. The dynamic of converso representatives lobbying for the interests of communal welfare translated into the creation of a converso confraternity in 1404, which institutionalized communal welfare just as the Jewish aljama had done previously. Providing for poor women was a typical component of many Christian and Jewish confraternal statutes of the period, including the converso confraternity of San Miguel. Among its 1410 statutes was a clause stipulating confraternal assistance of up to forty florins (the equivalent of about three pounds) toward the dowry of a poor member's daughter.[31] In the absence of an official Jewish confraternity after 1391, unbaptized Jews, too, continued to provide dowries for poor Jewish girls in their wills—a custom that was also practiced by Christians. For instance, in his 1396 will, the prominent merchant and communal leader Samuel Fazuati left ten pounds to be directed toward the marrying of poor Jewish girls of Mostaganem, where he had close familial ties.[32] These were very modest amounts compared to some other dowries I have found—such as a 1403 notarial record of marriage between a conversa and converso, in which the stipulated dowry was forty-five florins, or about thirty-three pounds.[33]

This essay presents a very small part of the first-generation conversa experience in Mallorca. With time, scholars might flesh out this picture by combing through additional notarial —especially judicial—registers in the

Archive of the Kingdom of Mallorca. The picture of post-1391 conversas in general might be sketched out through comparative local studies and excavating the archives of other towns that house documents that more vividly reflect the experiences of Jewish and conversa women in this formative period.

1. This introductory vignette is a reconstruction of a likely scenario based on multiple records in the archives of Mallorca and Barcelona; various reports and events are used to flesh out the experience of one woman as told in a responsum of Rabbi Simon ben Zemach Duran. See note 3 for details. No names are given for women in these particular sources.

2. For a more detailed account of the attack on the Jewish quarter in Mallorca see Gampel, *Anti-Jewish Riots in the Crown of Aragon*, 68–91; Oeltjen, "Kings, Creditors and Converts," 135–43; see also Quadrado, *Forenses*, 97 and Pons, *Los Judíos de Mallorca*, vol. 2, 165. In the early morning of August 2nd 1391, the peasant and artisan classes in Mallorca stormed past the city walls and attacked the houses of elite citizens with whom they had political grievances then were redirected to attack the Jewish quarter. The riot lasted a few hours. The social rebellion, rooted in conflicts that had been fomenting for decades between the *forans* (country inhabitants) and *jurats* (local, urban ruling class) lasted another two months. Contemporary sources describing the violence are limited to two brief accounts written by notaries. Out of a Jewish population that modern scholars estimate to have been about 3,000 (Margalida Bernat i Roca, *El call*, 38–40; Sevillano Colom, "La demografía," 247), one wrote that 300 Christians and 180 Jews were killed (ARM rp 2048, cited by López Bonet in "La revolta de 1391," 122), which only makes sense when we consider that the violence was just one part of a citywide revolt. Another notary, Mateu Salzet, reported 300 Jews killed, and three Christians (see Campaner's *Cronicon Mayoricense*, 126–27). There may well have been some forced baptisms during the violence, as occurred in other cities, but for Mallorca none are documented; we only know that two months later, the alleged 800 Jews who had taken shelter in the royal castle were baptized.

3. I have filled in the lacunae of Duran's text with the help of archival records that tell us more of the local context and women's experiences: that 800 Jews took shelter in the royal castle before converting en masse, that many Jews bribed port officials and ship captains to be able to leave the island, selling their property at a discount to be able to take some wealth with them, and that any converso who

left the kingdom was considered to be an apostate and renegade, condemned to have all his property confiscated.

4. A term employed in royal letters. See ACA CR 2269: 152r–v (July 1, 1407).

5. In Mallorca a small and much less significant Jewish community did survive alongside the conversos, unlike in Valencia and Barcelona. The Mallorcan conversos maintained close ties to the smaller Jewish community until it was entirely converted in 1435, following a ritual murder trial that resulted in further anti-Jewish violence, the execution of community leaders, and the baptism of the rest of the community. Soon afterward the queen issued a ban against Jews living on the island altogether (Cortès i Cortès, 95–98; Isaacs, 110–15).

6. On the censal see, García Sanz, Arcadio. "El censal," 281–310; Riu, Manuel. "Banking and Society."

7. On the aljama's corporate debt and its creditors see Oeltjen, "Kings, Creditors and Converts," 151–57.

8. The conversos paid King Joan 20 percent of all the debts owed to them to secure the assistance of royal officials in executing their repayment. This "four sous per pound" was referred to as a "donatio" and was taken immediately by the officials when they collected the loan, and the remainder of the payment was, for the most part, transferred to the aljama's creditors as part of the collective debt repayment. For details on the donatio see Oeltjen, "Kings, Creditors and Converts," 147–51.

9. ARM AH 64 Lletres Comunes (1392). As a sample: in one register containing 181 letters about debts, dated between January and July 1392, seven out of the sixty-three Jewish or converso creditors seeking repayment were women; four of them were widows, and two had made the loans jointly with a husband or son. One was acting as her husband's procurator. Only one loan was made by a woman independently of any male relative, and it was for a notably small amount. The creditor was Dona Blanca, the wife of one of the most active moneylenders prior to 1391, called Miguel de Sent Pere after his baptism. One might anticipate that the number of widows soliciting the repayment of loans owed to their deceased husbands would have been greater right after 1391, but that was not the case in my sample; nor is there a significant number of widows in my wider collection of the archival records.

10. ACA CR 1997: 59r–v (March 22, 1394).

11. A certain Struch Madini had all his property confiscated in 1392 because he had fled the island (AH 64: 52r: March 22, 1392). It is quite possible that Struch and Marzoch were the same person. The name Struch comes from the old Catalan Estruc, meaning lucky (as if a lucky star); Marzuq is an Arabic name also meaning fortunate. Many of the Mallorcan Jewish families had cultural, linguistic, and familial ties to North African communities and had arabicized names. It is possible that he would have been known as Marzoch among peers and Astruc (or Struch)

in Catalan legal documents. Alternatively, it is possible that Struch and Marzoch were two different but related men who traveled together to North Africa.

12. In her study of women in Perpignan, Rebecca Winer also found that brothers protected their sisters' financial security.

13. On Christian women's dowries in the Crown of Aragon see Dana Wessell Light-foot, *Women, Dowries and Agency.*

14. Responsa of Yom Tov Ishbili, No. 134 (ed. Kapah, Jerusalem, 1959). An alternative precedent exists in Talmudic law as well as thirteenth-century French and German responsum, which state that landed estates that were part of a Jewish woman's dowry were not subject to the claims of creditors of her deceased husband, but any goods or chattel that were part of her ketubah could be taken by them (Cheryl Tallan, *Medieval Jewish Widows*, 68). Alternatively, Luciano Allegra has shown that in early modern Italy, Jews used the dowry to protect family wealth from potential claims of creditors or taxation, as it was inviolable under *ius commune*; and under *halakha* creditors could only claim the husband's debts that pre-existed the dowry (Allegra, *A Model of Jewish Devolution*, 49).

15. ACA CR 1996: 163r (September 16, 1393).

16. See Baskin, "Mobility and Marriage."

17. Simon ben Zemah Duran, Responsum 2:176, cited in Zsom, *Conversos in the Responsa*, 120; Epstein, *Responsa of Rabbi Simon*, 31–32.

18. Quotation cited and translated in Zsom, *Conversos in the Responsa*, 120. The woman then managed to get onto a boat "for 150 doblones."

19. ACA CR 1996: 121v–124v

20. ACA CR 1996: 121v–124v (April 10, 1393).

21. On responsa regarding Jews, conversos and levirate marriage in the post-1391 context see Zsom, 83–100.

22. Regarding the competing demands on Jewish property see Oeltjen, "Crisis and Regeneration," chapter four.

23. ACA CR 1998: 118v–120r (October 11, 1395); 1999: 151v–152r (October 15, 1395).

24. ACA CR 2000: 124r–v (December 18, 1395).

25. ARM AH G6 *llicencies i guiatges* 24r–v (January 21, 1401); the original letter is dated October 11, 1395.

26. ACA CR 1998: 118v–120r (October 11, 1395); 1999: 151v–152r (October 15, 1395); 2000: 124r–v (December 18, 1395). He absolved the conversos of "all cases held against them."

27. ACA CR 2269: 151v–152r (June 30, 1407).

28. On women and children who traveled independently (without male kin) after the Expulsion of 1492 see Meyerson, "Aragonese and Catalan Converts."

29. For examples of piratic attacks against conversos on ships at sea, see ACA CR 1996: 183r–v (November 16, 1393) and ARM AH 64: 81r–82r (April 8, 1392), also

published in BSAL 7:446 and cited in Pons, *Los Judíos de Mallorca*, 184; ARM
AH 64: 133r–v. Some of these "pirates" managed to be forgiven when they were
caught, since they were capturing traitors to the Christian faith.

30. In her introduction to *Daughters of the Reconquest*, Heath Dillard discusses the
necessity of women in creating community.

31. ACA CR 2271: 54r–57r (January 8, 1410) published also in BSAL 21 (1926–1927):
361–64. On the converso confraternity of Mallorca and a comparison of Jewish and
Christian confraternal welfare statutes see Oeltjen, *A converso confraternity in Mallorca*.

32. ACM Prot. Not. 14751 (July 23, 1396).

33. ACM Prot. Not. 14676 (August 3, 1403).

BIBLIOGRAPHY

Primary Sources

ACA. Arxiu de la Corona d'Aragó
    CR. Cancellería Real
    LR. Lletres Reials

ACM. Arxiu Capitular de Mallorca
    Protocols Notarials

ARM. Arxiu del Regne de Mallorca

BSAL. Bolletí de la Societat Arqueològica Lulliana

Campaner y Fuertes, Alvaro. *Cronicon mayoricense: Noticias y relaciones históricas de
    Mallorca desde 1220 á 1800*. Palma de Mallorca: Estab. tip. de J. Colomar y Salas, 1881.

Ishbili, Yom Tov. *Responsa*. Edited by Yosef Kapah. Jerusalem: HaRav Kook Institute, 1958.

Secondary Sources

Allegra, Luciano. "A Model of Jewish Devolution Turin in the Eighteenth Century."
    Jewish History 7, no. 2 (1993): 29–58.

Baer, Yitzhak. *A History of the Jews in Christian Spain*. Vol. 2. Philadelphia: Jewish
    Publication Society of America, 1961.

Baskin, Judith R. "Mobility and Marriage in Two Medieval Jewish Societies." *Jewish
    History* 22, no. 1/2, (2008): 223–43.

Bernat i Roca, Margalida. *El call de ciutat de Mallorca a l'entorn de 1350*. Palma de
    Mallorca: Lleonard Muntaner, 2005.

Cortès i Cortès, Gabriel. *Historia de los Judíos mallorquines y de sus descendientes Cris-
    tianos*. Palma de Mallorca: Miquel Font, 1985.

Dillard, Heath. *Daughters of the Reconquest: Women in Castilian Town Society, 1100–1300*.
    Cambridge: Cambridge University Press, 1984.

Epstein, Isidore. *Studies in the Communal Life of the Jews of Spain: As Reflected in the
    Responsa of Rabbi Solomon Ben Adreth and Rabbi Simon Ben Zemach Duran*. New
    York: Hermon, 1968.

Gampel, Benjamin R. *Anti-Jewish Riots in the Crown of Aragon and the Royal Response, 1391–1392*. New York: Cambridge University Press, 2016.

García Sanz, Arcadio. "El censal." *Boletín de la Sociedad Castellonense de Cultura,* 37 (1961): 281–310.

Isaacs, Abraham Lionel. *The Jews of Majorca*. London: Methuen, 1936.

López Bonet, Josep Francesc. "La revolta de 1391." XIII *Congrés d'Història de la Corona d'Aragó* (Palma de Mallorca, 27 setembre–1 octubre 1987), Vol. 2: 111–23. Palma de Mallorca: Institut d'Estudis Baleàrics, 1989.

Meyerson, Mark D. *A Jewish Renaissance in Fifteenth-Century Spain*. Princeton: Princeton University Press, 2004.

———. "Aragonese and Catalan Jewish Converts at the Time of the Expulsion." *Jewish History* 6, nos. 1–2, *Frank Talmage Memorial Volume* (1992): 131–49.

Oeltjen, Natalie. "A Converso Confraternity in Majorca: La Novella Confraria de Sant Miquel." *Jewish History* 24, no. 1, (March 2010): 53–85.

———. "Crisis and Regeneration: The Conversos of Majorca, 1391–1416." PhD dissertation, University of Toronto, 2012.

———. "Kings, Creditors and Converts: The Impact of Royal Policy and Corporate Debt on the Collective Identity of Majorcan Conversos after 1391." *Sefarad* 73, no. 1, (2013): 33–164.

Pons Pastor, Antoni. *Los Judíos del reino de Mallorca durante los siglos 13 y 14*. Madrid: Consejo Superior de Investigaciones Científicas, Instituto Jerónimo Zurita, 1958.

Quadrado, José María. *Forenses y ciudadanos: Historia de las disensiones civiles de Mallorca en el siglo XV*. Estevan Trias, 1847.

Riu, Manuel. "Banking and Society in Late Medieval and Early Modern Aragon." In *The Dawn of Modern Banking*, 131–67. New Haven: Yale University Press, 1979.

Sevillano Colom, Francisco. "La demografía de Mallorca a través del impuesto del morabatí: siglos XIV, XV, XVI," *Boletín de la Sociedad Arqueológica Luliana* 34: 233–73.

Tallan, Cheryl. "Medieval Jewish Widows: Their Control of Resources." *Jewish History* 5, no. 1 (1991): 63–74.

Wessell Lightfoot, Dana. *Women, Dowries and Agency. Marriage in Fifteenth-Century Valencia*. New York: Manchester University Press, 2013.

Winer, Rebecca. *Women, Wealth, and Community in Perpignan c.1250–1300: Christians, Jews, and Enslaved Muslims in a Medieval Mediterranean Town*. Burlington: Ashgate, 2006.

Zsom, Dora. *Conversos in the Responsa of Sephardic Halakhic Authorities in the Fifteenth Century*. Piscataway: Gorgias Press, 2014.

3

Death and Gender in Late Sixteenth-Century Toledo

GRACE E. COOLIDGE

In the Castilian city of Toledo in 1600, three women at different points of the life cycle summoned a notary and wrote their wills. Isabel Rodríguez was single and employed as a maidservant; doña Cebriana Ruiz was married to a notary and pregnant with her seventh child; and Catalina López was the childless widow of a master builder.[1] The wills they wrote were deeply religious[2] but also left meticulous instructions for the distribution of their private property. Taken individually, these three wills provide glimpses into the lives of three early modern women who were of different social classes and at different points in the life cycle, but taken together, these three wills reveal a pattern. Single, married, or widowed, each of these women had command of some economic resources and could, with the help of a notary, make careful decisions about what was to happen to their property after their death.

Research has demonstrated that widowed women (who are often the most easily visible in the records) could be economically and politically active in early modern Spain across the social spectrum.[3] Two widows from a wealthy Toledo *converso* family exemplify the importance of widows in defining and perpetuating their families. Inés de Vargas and her sister Catalina dominated a family that suffered from a lack of adult male heirs, appearing between 1600 and 1603 in notarial records such as "dowry contracts, foundation of chapels, placement of children in religious orders, litigation, and loaning and securing money borrowed by other family members."[4] In 1600, Catalina organized a legal defense of the family estate that defeated the challenger in Toledo and then again in the Valladolid chancery court. Inés and Catalina provided a lavish dowry to facilitate the marriage of Catalina's younger daughter Petronila, and when Petronila and her husband both died young, Inés stepped in and raised their two surviving boys. She paid the elder boy's entry into the monastery of San Augustín in Toledo but forced the younger boy to abandon the clerical career he aspired to and arranged his marriage at the young age of fifteen "to conserve and augment the ancestry and nobility" of the family.[5] In her eighties, Inés was still litigating to preserve her patrimony.[6] The activities of these two women demonstrate how the specific economic powers of widowed women could be combined into a powerful family strategy that ultimately benefited and supported their male relatives. Before his death, Catalina's grandson appointed his mother, his wife, and his mother-in-law as the executors of his will, suggesting his trust in the women of his family.[7]

The question arises: how did widows gain the experience needed to wield authority and influence the way Inés and Catalina de Vargas so successfully did? Recent research on women's education has helped address this issue,[8] but in Spain even uneducated widows who give no evidence of being able to sign their names were chosen by their husbands to execute their wills, be guardians of their children, and administer family resources.[9] How did widows gain the skills necessary to carry out the economic roles (executor, guardian of children, head of household) that they were often asked to fill after their husbands' deaths? How did women's marital status and place in the life cycle affect their access to and control over economic resources? How did access to economic resources affect women's relationships with their husbands, families, and other women in their communities?

Under Spanish law, widows regained control over their dowries and their personal property, were entitled to half of the couple's community property, and (if guardians) had temporary control over the property of their children. This essay argues that the economic power of widows was embedded in a culture where women of almost every social status and station in life had access to resources and the ability to make fiscal decisions at every point in the life cycle. Widows, therefore, were not unique. They gained economic skills by practicing them all through their lives in a society that expected women to have and exercise economic power throughout their life cycle. Single women were most likely to be in expectation of economic resources that they could claim in the future such as wages, dowries, or inheritances. Married women were involved in a more complex array of economic concerns with more immediate control over their assets, while widows had the most economic assets and the most control over their own and their family's property. Widows were the logical peak of a continuum, and they had the knowledge to exercise their authority because they had been involved in economic activities and communities in different ways throughout their adult lives. Like Inés and Catalina, women provided dowries for their daughters, chose careers for their sons, founded chapels, loaned and borrowed money, and above all, litigated throughout their lives.

In terms of methodology, this essay draws on a sample of twenty-one male testators and thirty female testators who wrote wills in the city of Toledo between 1600 and 1605. The fifty-one testators left bequests to fifty male beneficiaries and to more than twice that number (one hundred and twenty-two) female beneficiaries. The social class of the testators ranges from some of the leading citizens of Toledo (councilmen and their wives and widows) to day laborers and maid servants. In early modern Castile, will writing was a spiritual exercise, regulated by the Roman Catholic Church in the decrees of the Synod of Zaragoza (1357), as well as an important issue of heredity, succession, and distribution of property regulated in the thirteenth century by King Alfonso X's *Siete Partidas* and subsequently by the *Leyes de Toro* (1505).[10] All Spaniards (male and female) were theoretically required to make wills and dying intestate could cause spiritual and legal problems for the testator and his or her heirs.[11]

These wills also fit the shift in Castilian values that Teofilo Ruiz argues took place in will writing after 1200. They are written in Castilian by lay scribes, and they divide their legacies between diverse ecclesiastical institutions (usually parish churches, convents, and monasteries within Toledo) and family members, with the family being the main beneficiary, rather than the church.[12] Ruiz argues that after the early thirteenth century, Castilian wills "included elaborate provisions to ensure that the testator's property remained in the hands of the family," with the "preservation of property for the benefit of family and friends" being "the overriding concern."[13] I contend that this new focus inadvertently benefited lay women because inheritances to women, especially in the form of dowries, could be a crucial tool to the new project of increasing and strengthening the lineage that began to absorb the financial energies of what Ruiz calls the "middling sorts" in Castilian cities like Toledo.[14]

In the historiography on women's power, historians have defined power as the "ability to act effectively, to influence people or decisions, and to achieve goals" in their families and communities.[15] Scholars of Spain have focused on access to economic resources as a source of that power. Helen Nader states that "much of the matriarchal power in Castilian society derived from women's inheritance rights and married women's property law," and Elizabeth Lehfeldt argues that cloistered women in Valladolid were empowered by their legal rights to dowries and maintenance allowances.[16] Allyson Poska argues that further down the social scale, Galician peasant women's "domestic power derives from a variety of sources, the most important of which is access to and control of economic resources," and Scott Taylor contends that "by maintaining their own networks of debt and credit outside their houses, women also possessed an autonomous area of economic activity in the public marketplace."[17] The wills in this study demonstrate that women from a range of backgrounds in late sixteenth-century Toledo exercised control over economic resources throughout their lives and were able to use those resources to achieve their own goals.

SINGLE WOMEN

By using the wills of both men and women in late sixteenth-century Toledo, it is possible to trace the economic assets that women had access to at different points in their life cycle (single, married, widowed). Most single women in this sample appear in men's and women's wills as beneficiaries, and most of them received legacies designed to help them amass a dowry that would enable them to either marry or join a convent. These women were potentially what Judith Bennett and Amy Froide have designated as "life-cycle singlewomen," because the expectation was that they would marry or join a convent where they would be "brides of Christ."[18] For example, Pedro de Alcázar dowered his three granddaughters, Madalena, María, and Ana, using the formulaic phrase "in order to help with their marriage or to enter in religion."[19] While some bequests came from uncles, grandfathers, or other male relatives (the twenty-one male testators in the sample named thirty-two female beneficiaries), single women were more likely to receive legacies from other women (the thirty female testators named ninety female beneficiaries) even if those women were not their relatives. For example, Juana López, who was married when she wrote her will, left a dowry of ten thousand *maravedís* to María, whom she identified only as "the daughter of Manuel de Montenegro."[20] Single women in this sample benefited from a community of (usually) older women, some of whom may themselves have amassed dowries in this way at earlier points in their life cycles.

Another group of single women that figured in wills as beneficiaries was domestic servants, who could also fit into the category of life cycle single women. Men and women specified in their wills that their maids needed to be paid either in money or in kind. Apolonya Hernández's employer left her four thousand maravedís and a set of bedclothes in return for her service.[21] Often legacies to maids also included something to help with their dowries, emphasizing the expectation that maid servants would be single while in service but would marry later when they had worked long enough to amass a dowry.[22] María Ortiz left one maid the salary she owed her and something extra "in order to help her to take an estate."[23]

Despite social expectations, however, not all women married or joined convents—and five of the thirty female testators in this sample were single when they wrote their wills. If these women died while still single, they would fit into Bennett and Froide's second category of "lifelong single-women," for whom the single state was a permanent one.[24] Of those five testators, four identified themselves as being in service. Single women in service had access to a range of economic resources. María de Tenayda left only one skirt, maidservant Isabel Sánchez had only the expectation of future wages and a debt of two *maravedís*,[25] but Isabel Rodríguez stated in her will in May of 1600 that she owned some land and half a house in the nearby town of Las Ventas, as well as some dresses, and wages from her service.[26] Isabel demonstrated the most secure economic situation in this small sample with a mixture of assets that she currently had control over (the land, her half of the house, and her clothes) and resources that she was in expectation of receiving in the future (her wages from her service). In turn, following the pattern of women giving legacies to other women, her will specified that her three nieces (probably also single, since they are described as the daughters of her brother and sister) were to be her universal heirs.[27] Isabel's will again demonstrates how single women functioned as part of a community, because even with relatively modest economic resources Isabel provided economic help to her nieces.

Another single female testator, Ursula Bravo, wrote a will that illustrates how the lack of a community could create social situations that undermined a single woman's control over economic resources. Ursula was ill with venereal disease in Toledo's Hospital de Santiago when she wrote her will.[28] She had inherited some land and other goods in the town of Roca, outside of Madrid, but her property was currently under the guardianship of her brother. She stipulated that after the expenses of the guardianship had been paid, all these properties should go to the hospital on her death, and she appointed two hospital officials as the executors of her will, suggesting that she had no functional family ties at the time she wrote her will.[29] Ursula's case illustrates the tenuous nature of single women's control over economic resources. Young, single women who stood to inherit a dowry when the testator died at some point in the future did not have much, if any, control over that property in the moment. Unmarried, away from her hometown, and suffering from venereal disease, which may have been the result of prostitution or a sexual relationship that did not result in marriage, Ursula seems to have been estranged from the brother and guardian who should have been looking after her and whom she did not name as an heir in her will.[30] Even a single woman with a dubious reputation dying away from home had the promise of future economic assets, but in this case, Ursula had no female community to remember in her will. Instead, fulfilling her obligation to make economic decisions about her property, she left her assets to an institution, the hospital that had provided her care. Ursula was, however, the exception. Single women were more economically vulnerable than either their married or widowed sisters. While they may have benefited the most from communities of women, many of them also managed to participate in and help form those communities.

MARRIED WOMEN

Married women's wills reflected a more complex array of economic concerns and more immediate control over economic assets than those of their single sisters.[31] While they were, in general, legally subject to their husbands, Castilian law contained specific protections for married women that dated back to Visigothic times. These protections allowed married women to own, bequeath, and inherit property, including dowry property that was legally owned by the wife, even though it was usually administered by her husband.[32] Married women also participated actively in managing property and businesses owned by the couple, often serving as surrogates for absent husbands.[33] In these sixteenth-century wills, married women appear in a variety of economic roles, sometimes in conjunction with their husbands and other times acting more independently.

Married women's bequests can give examples of family ties, households, daily communities, and economic activities and suggest the importance of other women in these daily communities. Some of their legacies illuminate the ties between mothers and daughters. Cara de la Paz, married and mother of three, had the support of her own mother to whom she left a cloak and an underskirt "in recompense for the help she has given me in my illness."[34] Many other female testators were concerned with the future well-being of their daughters. Doña Cebriana Ruiz, making her will in anticipation of the birth of her seventh child, left all her silk dresses and her personal jewelry to her eldest daughter Marcela.[35] Ana de Aquilera, mother of eight, and doña Geronima de la Peña, mother of five, both used the additional bequest allowed by the law (*mejora del tercio*) to benefit their daughters.[36]

Married female testators also recognized ties to daughters-in-law. María de Elas left a bequest to her daughter-in-law Catalina, whom she appointed as one of the executors of her will.[37] Catalina, then, is an example of a married woman who would own some resources of her own after her mother-in-law's death and would also play an active role in her community as one of the executors of her mother-in-law's will.

The bequests in doña Elvira Davalos Jofre's will reveal a community of women in her life and household. Married at the time she made her will, doña Elvira had control over extensive resources about which she made detailed decisions. She left a writing desk and a gold and coral rosary to her sister María who was a nun, and a chess set and a gold and crystal cross to her married sister Isabel. She also left two of her maidservants money for their dowries (six *ducados* for Ursula and two *ducados* for María), and made a more personal bequest to a third maid, Martina, of shirts, ruffs, headdresses, and various other textiles as well as the chest they were kept in, "because she has served me well and this is in addition to her salary." Extending her network of women heavenward, doña Elvira then left clothing to the image of the Virgin Mary "the one they take in the procession . . . of St. Augustine."[38] Doña Elvira also had a husband in whom she expressed confidence and two sons who were her heirs, but the detailed bequests to women conjure up an image of the female community who probably provided the companionship of her daily life. Her will recognized the bonds of that community with economic bequests of treasured possessions for her sisters, substantial financial help towards dowries for her maids, and even an acknowledgement of the feminine aspects of her local religious procession.

Married women also acted as religious patrons in Toledo, a role more usually associated with the independence of widows.[39] Catherine King argues that female patronage "always destabilized conventional notions of the good feminine to some extent," because it placed women (in these cases wives) in a decision-making capacity.[40] Patronage in the wills of married women can reveal how women balanced this ability to make decisions with the power their husbands had in relation to their property. Doña Elvira Davalos Jofre had an agreement with her husband about the terms of her will. Under Castilian law, four-fifths of a parent's estate (mother or father) had to go to their direct descendants (legitimate children). The mother or father could allocate the remaining one-fifth (called the *quinto*) for funeral expenses, pious works, and free bequests to any person.[41] Doña Elvira directed that the *quinto* from her dowry be used to endow a chantry that required the incumbent to say three masses a week for her soul in a chapel built by her parents. She stated in her will, "I have communicated the entire content of this, my last will and testament, to don Pedro de Ysasaga, my lord and husband, and so he has promised me and given his word as a gentleman (*hijosdalgo*) that if my dowry and arras are not sufficient for what I have directed he will complete it from his estate."[42]

This kind of explicit statement of the conversations that husbands and wives had over money and property is rare, but many married women (including doña Elvira) left their husbands as executors, signaling that they were not expecting conflict with their husbands over the terms of their wills. Francisca Vélez endowed a chapel in the Church of the Magdalene in Toledo and left money to a local confraternity. She left her husband, along with a local priest, as executor of her will.[43] Francisca Vélez had no children and her husband was her universal heir. In contrast, after using the *quinto* to endow her chaplaincy, doña Elvira left her two sons as her heirs. She used the additional bequest allowed by the law (*mejora del tercio*) to augment her eldest son's inheritance.[44] While both these women made very explicit choices about where their property should go after their deaths, those choices were not overtly subversive since the bulk of their property ultimately benefitted male family members. This outcome might explain their confidence that their husbands would support choices that benefitted their families and their local churches. Other female testators made choices that suggest a desire to benefit other women. Elvira de Orozco was married but childless when she wrote her will. With no children of her own, Elvira left a legacy of two hundred *ducados* and her dresses and shirts to her stepdaughter, Juana de Espinosa. If Juana died before her father did, Elvira stipulated that her husband Martin (Juana's father) got a life interest in this property, but after his death it went to Elvira's niece, Petronila.[45] So Elvira used her will to enrich her stepdaughter, a girl she may have helped raise, and finally, to benefit her niece. While she also supported her husband, Elvira ultimately left her property to her female relatives.

Indeed, married women did not always act in conjunction with their husbands. While many women left their husbands as executors of their wills—like merchant's wife Juana López who bound her husband to donate her clothes to the local Franciscan monastery and give money to feed the poor—other women did not choose their husbands as executors.[46] Lady Geronima de la Peña requested that her husband choose her burial site, but she did not leave him as an executor of her will, choosing her brother and her nephew to carry out that task instead.[47] Lady Geronima may have had an excellent and uncontroversial reason for not choosing her husband as an executor, but Sebastiana López complained that during her marriage the majority of her dowry of 200 *ducados* "had been consumed" and all she retained was part ownership of several houses in a nearby town, about 8,000 square meters of land, and a suit of clothes. She left the clothes to her sister, the land to her stepfather, the houses to her cousin and named the hospital where she lay dying as her residual heir, a division of her property that completely excluded her husband, town councilman André Barrios.[48] Sebastiana used her legal control over her dowry property to act independently of her husband, leaving him as neither an heir nor an executor since in her eyes he had clearly demonstrated his inability to be a competent administrator.

WIDOWS

Across the female life cycle, widows had the most independent control over their assets, but their economic activities followed many of the same patterns that characterized those of single and married women. Under the Castilian *fueros*, "the urban charters and liberties" that had been granted to Castilian towns during the Reconquest, widows had more rights than married women, but fewer than men.[49] They were not legally allowed to be *vecinos*, or citizens, but "they were recognized as heads of households; they controlled property, operated productive enterprises, participated in communal activities and paid taxes."[50] Among the nobility and propertied classes, a high percentage of men appointed their wives (future widows) as guardians of their children and executors of their wills.[51] Widows "played a key role in creating, defining and perpetuating their families and, in turn, the social fabric of the urban environment."[52]

Widows, therefore, had more formal authority in the urban community than single women or wives did, but examining their actual economic activities reveals similarities in women's experiences across the life cycle. In early modern Spain, a wife's estate, owed to her on her husband's death, consisted of one half of their community property, her wedding gift from her husband (*arras*), her dowry, and any supplementary parental inheritance or gifts that she had acquired prior to her marriage.[53] While her husband might administer much of this property during the marriage, once he died it came back under the control of the widow. This independence and range of activities is reflected in widows' wills. María Ortiz stated confidently, "I do state and declare that after the death of the aforementioned my husband I bought some houses in the parish of San Bartolomé . . . in the street of San Rocaz" in Toledo. María was clarifying that her husband's heirs had no claim on these houses because "I have bought them with my own money after his death."[54] Her words emphasize the economic basis for her independent actions. She had her own money, she was a widow, and so she could both buy houses and stipulate who would inherit them after her death.

As well as having extensive control over their own property, widows were often in charge of their children's inheritance or assets. In 1600 the merchant Pedro de Alcázar left his wife the task of administering the dowries he was leaving to their three granddaughters after his death (when she would be widowed), and the widowed Lady Catalina de Ortiz stated in her will in 1605 that she was administering a legacy of 350 *ducados* that her brother had left to her daughter.[55] Another role that was technically reserved for widows was guardianship. Women could not be legal guardians of their children if their husbands were still alive, but men across the social scale chose their wives to be guardians of their children after their deaths. In 1600 Toledan confectioner Asencío Ramírez named his wife (and future widow) guardian of their four-month-old son and one of the two executors of his will; and that same year the widowed doña María de Barrionuevo appeared in the notarial documents as the guardian of her four daughters.[56]

This neat division between widows and wives is complicated by the fluidity of women's lives. If widowed guardians remarried and became wives again, the law dictated that they lose their guardianship, a condition that many husbands made explicit when they appointed their wives as guardians.[57] In practice, however, a woman who wished to keep her guardianship after her remarriage could use a legal mechanism known as a *cedula de gracias al sacar* to petition the king for a special license to continue her guardianship in spite of having contracted a second marriage.[58] The fluid marital status of María Gómez, guardian of her nine-year-old son, was thus stated in the notarial records in Toledo in 1600 as "wife as she first was of Diego Ruiz, deceased, and wife as she now is of Juan Gonzalo."[59] Technically, María was both a widow and a wife and she had apparently retained the widow's privilege of guardianship of her son from her first marriage. Other wives might also have had the prior experience of being a widow, thus fitting them for tasks usually associated with widowhood, such as serving as an executor or a guardian. While most female executors were widows, single and married women could technically still carry out this task. Doña María de Ramírez left her eldest daughters, Catalina and Francisca, both of whom were still single, as two of her executors, and María de Elas appointed her daughter-in-law, the wife of her son Juan, as one of her executors.[60] This overlapping of status between married and widowed expands the idea of women's experiences, since some women would have experienced both multiple marriages and widowhood.

Moreover, the wills of married and widowed women reveal similar concerns and communities. Like married women, widowed mothers left bequests that illuminate their ties to family and often focused on the future well-being of their daughters. The widowed doña Catalina de Ortiz left both the *mejora del tercio* and the remnant of the *quinto* to her single daughter, Ana. These bequests, along with the legacy Ana had already received from her uncle, probably provided a substantial dowry to help secure Ana's future.[61] Also like married women, widows lived their lives in the context of a female community. María Ortiz's lengthy will suggests that while she was a widow with no surviving children, she did have a network of women at various stages of life that she was close to or, at least, who depended on her economically. María dowered her maids, left her widowed daughter-in-law, Inés, a legacy of 40,000 *maravedís*, and gave six nieces dowries of 100 *ducados* each, in addition to remembering her housekeeper, her sister, and her sister's granddaughter.[62] Even women whose wills did not reveal the presence of close relatives usually had other women whom they depended on. Widowed with no children, Catalina López did have a brother, a niece, and a nephew, but her will suggests that she had depended on women who were not related to her when she fell ill. She left twelve *ducados*, a skirt, a cloak, and some bed linens to Ana Sánchez, a resident of Toledo "in satisfaction and payment for the cure and what she has given me" and four *ducados* to Isabel, a widow, "who has served and benefited me during this illness."[63]

The least conventional female community can be found in the will of Isabel de Covaz, a widow who was sick in the Hospital de la Misercordia in Toledo in 1600.[64] Isabel made no mention of any relative, but left "the wife of Alonso López" some clothes, asking her to "pray to God for me"; left a bequest to "Catalina who lives in las Tendillas"; bequeathed a coral necklace to the wife of Francisco Ramírez; a gold ring to Isabel Gómez; and paid a debt ("whatever she says I owe her") to Catalina Carranza.[65] It is not possible to tell what relationship these women had with each other from this list, but the legacies imply a community of economic interests even though no blood ties are stated in the description. The combination of legacies and repayment of debts suggests that Isabel's business dealings with other women may have been rooted in friendship or at least daily companionship. Every woman mentioned in this will (single, married, or widowed) would have had access to some economic resources, however modest, after Isabel de Covaz's death.

CONCLUSION

A woman making her will in the urban center of Toledo in the late sixteenth century could have passed through a variety of life stages before being forced to bed by "an illness which God has brought me," as the wills formulaically state. If she had access to any property or means of making a living, if she was even one step above destitute, she would have taken part in a series of socially expected economic activities that had the potential to connect her to a community of other women and that gave her the space to develop her management abilities. Spanish society expected women to have economic skills and depended on their ability to use them. By the time a woman became a widow, her husband could feel confident that she had the skills necessary to take on management of the family's resources because these were skills most women in Toledo used throughout their lives, from their first step towards accumulating a dowry to their deathbed bequests. These skills could be a powerful protection for women dealing with life's disasters and uncertainties. Young women left orphaned might receive dowries from their aunts or grandmothers, married women could augment the dowries of the young daughters they were leaving motherless, and widows could use their resources to maintain family structure and help launch their children in the world. Even women with no living family could create communities in which they did business with each other, cared for each other in times of illness, and formed economic networks with other women.

Single, married, and widowed women, from the urban elite down to serving maids, all took part in economic activities throughout their lives, and all had resources (however limited) over which they could exercise control. Women from a range of social class backgrounds and life stages demonstrated a similar agency in economic decisions even though the resources involved varied widely between resources controlled in the present (property that widows had inherited and did control) and the expectation of resources to be received in the future (wages owed to a single woman in domestic service). Nevertheless, similarities between the economic activities undertaken by women of different marital statuses stand out more than the differences do. Expectations for the future did sometimes materialize. Some single women did receive dowries, get paid for their service, or live to the age of majority so they could receive their inheritance. The social ideal was that women's economic resources be controlled by men, but the reality of women's lives meant that this was not always the case. Young girls raised in the expectation of a dowry or sent out to work for wages were in a position to begin to understand the implications of fiscal decisions they and others made about the economic resources available to them. These activities and resources as they appear in wills reveal the presence of strong economic ties between women of different social stations and at all stages of the life cycle, (often centering around the accumulation of dowries), and create a narrative of female economic agency that is remarkably consistent across class and marital status. The answer to the question of how widows gained the skills to be executors, guardians, and heads of households is that they had been practicing those skills in various forms in all the previous stages of their lives.

NOTES

1. Archivo Histórico Provincial [hereafter AHP], Toledo, protocolo 15790; protocolo 15782; protocolo 15790.

2. For more on the religious implications of wills in early modern Spain, see Martínez Gil, "Actitudes ante la muerte"; Eire, *From Madrid to Purgatory*.

3. For widows in peasant communities in Galicia see Poska, *Women and Authority*, 163–92 and Poska, "Gender, Property, and Retirement Strategies"; for widows from a range of social backgrounds in the city of Toledo see Fink De Backer, *Widowhood*, 122–47; for noble widows in Spain, see Coolidge, *Guardianship*. Widows could also be vulnerable, especially if they were poor: see Vassberg, "The Status of Widows"; French, "Loving Friends," 22–24; McCants, "The Not-So-Merry Widows"; Chabot, "Widowhood and Poverty." For widows across Europe see Cavallo and Warner, *Widowhood*; Levy, *Widowhood and Visual Culture*.

4. Martz, *Network of Converso Families*, 322. Martz cites the Archivo Histórico Provincial, Toledo, protocolos 2506, 2509, and 2510.

5. Martz, *Network of Converso Families*, 328.

6. Martz, *Network of Converso Families*, 322–28.

7. AHP, Toledo, protocolo 31038.

8. For work on women's education in Spain, see Howe, *Education and Women*; Cruz and Hernández, *Women's Literacy*; Baranda Leturio, "L'éducation des femmes"; Mar Graña Cid, *Las sabias mujeres*; Hoffman, *Raised to Rule*.

9. For more on the connection between literacy and the ability to sign one's name, see Nalle, "Literacy and Culture," 67.

10. Eire, *From Madrid to Purgatory*, 22; The sixth partida deals specifically with wills and will writing, see Burns, *Underworlds*, 1175–1302; for the influence of the *Leyes de Toro* on wills in a family context see García Fernández, *Herencia*, 24–30.

11. Eire, *From Madrid to Purgatory*, 20.

12. Ruiz argues that after 1200 testators in Castile left less property to the church and put more restrictions on those legacies. Ruiz, *From Heaven to Earth*, 2–3.

13. Ruiz, *From Heaven to Earth*, 57.

14. Ruiz, *From Heaven to Earth*, 57, 3.

15. For the definition of power, see Erler and Kowaleski, "Introduction," 2.

16. Lehfeldt, "Convents as Litigants," 645; Nader, "Introduction," 4.

17. Poska, *Women and Authority*, 11; Taylor, *Honor and Violence*, 167.

18. Bennett and Froide, "A Singular Past," 2, 11.

19. "para ayuda a su casamiento o entrar en religion," AHP Toledo, protocolo 15790.

20. AHP, Toledo, protocolo 15790.

21. AHP, Toledo, protocolo 31038.

22. For an in-depth study of this pattern in fifteenth-century Valencia and its implications for women's agency, see Wessell Lightfoot, *Women, Dowries, and Agency*. For domestic service and dowries in sixteenth-century Toledo, see Fink De Backer, *Widowhood*, 181–83.

23. AHP, Toledo, protocolo 15790.

24. Bennett and Froide, "A Singular Past," 2.

25. AHP, Toledo, protocolo 15783.

26. AHP, Toledo, protocolo 15790; protocolo 15783; protocolo 15790.

27. AHP, Toledo, protocolo 15790 (2.52); Bennett and Froide found that across early modern Europe, singlewomen often forged especially close relationships with siblings, nieces, and nephews. Bennett and Froide, "A Singular Past," 23.

28. Martz, *Poverty and Welfare*, 36; Berco, "Textiles as Social Texts," 786.

29. AHP, Toledo, protocolo 31038. There is a possibility that she was pressured by hospital officials to leave the institution as her heir, although official guidelines stated that priests working for the hospital were to help a dying patient draw up a will but were strictly forbidden to "influence the patient to leave anything to the hospital." Martz, *Poverty and Welfare*, 180.

30. Female patients at the Hospital Santiago were not necessarily prostitutes, but syphilis severely limited a woman's marriage options and even damaged her employment opportunities. Berco, "Textiles as Social Texts," 797.

31. Married women also make up the largest category of women making wills (fifteen out of thirty), perhaps suggesting that their economic concerns were complex and needed a will.

32. These rights were contained in various law codes including the *Fuero Juzgo*, and the *Leyes de Toro*. Korth and Flusche, 397, 400.

33. Borrero Fernández, "Peasant and Aristocratic Women," 24–25; Coolidge, *Guardianship*, 61–62; Poska, "Elusive Virtue," 141; Crabb, *The Merchant of Prato's Wife*.

34. AHP, Toledo, protocolo 15782.

35. AHP, Toledo, protocolo 15783. For women's fears about childbirth in early modern Spain, see Díaz Balsera, "Mujer-Águila," 253–54.

36. AHP, Toledo, protocolo 15790; protocolo 31308. Under Castilian law, a parent could divide his or her property equally between all his or her children or the parent could take out a fifth of the value of the estate to pay for funeral expenses, pious works, and bequests. If all of those expenses didn't come out to a fifth of the estate, the remainder could be designated as a special bequest to one or more of the heirs (*quinto*). The remaining four-fifths of the estate had to be divided among direct heirs, but from the four-fifths, a parent could remove a third of the value (*mejora del tercio*) and assign it to an heir or heirs as an additional bequest. Korth and Flusche, "Dowry and Inheritance," 398.

37. AHP, Toledo, protocolo 15782.

38. AHP, Toledo, protocolo 16505. Susan James found this type of "overlapping circles of support" in English women's wills also. James, *Women's Voices*, 152.

39. One example of the important role that widowed women played as patrons in Toledo is doña Luisa de la Cerda who served as the patron of the Hospital de Tavera from the death of her husband in 1561 to her own death in 1596. Martz, *Poverty and Welfare*, 170. The women of the Mendoza family (married and widowed) were also noted patrons of the arts. See, for example, Alegre Carvajal, "Utopía y realidad."

40. King, "Lay Patronage and Religious Art," 96.

41. Korth and Flusche, 398.

42. AHP, Toledo, protocolo 16505.

43. AHP, Toledo, protocolo 31038.

44. AHP, Toledo, protocolo 16505; Korth and Flusche, 398.

45. AHP, Toledo, protocolo 16505.

46. AHP, Toledo, protocolo 15790.

47. AHP, Toledo, protocolo 31038.

48. AHP, Toledo, protocolo 15790.

49. For more on the *fueros* and their importance in medieval Castilian will writing, see Ruiz, *From Heaven to Earth*, 60–65; Heath Dillard uses the *fueros* to analyze the role of widows in medieval Castile. Dillard, *Daughters of the Reconquest*, 96–126; for the role of widows in sixteenth-century Castile, see Vassberg, "The Status of Widows," 180.

50. Vassberg, "The Status of Widows," 182.

51. Coolidge, *Guardianship*, 111–18; Fink De Backer, *Widowhood*, 148–84.

52. Fink De Backer, "Constructing Convents," 177.

53. Korth and Flusche, 399; Fink DeBacker, *Widowhood*, 111–12.

54. AHP, Toledo, protocolo 15790.

55. AHP, Toledo, protocolo 31038; protocolo 15790.

56. AHP, Toledo, protocolo 15790.

57. Coolidge, *Guardianship*, 111–18.

58. The Spanish monarchs used the power of the *gracias al sacar* to remedy a wide variety of legal problems that Spaniards were willing to pay to have addressed. Petitioners to the Crown could purchase legitimacy, citizenship, a title of nobility, and even whiteness (in the Americas). Twinam, *Public Lives*, 43.

59. "muger que primero fue de Diego Ruiz, difunto, e muger que agora es de Juan Gonzalo" AHP, Toledo, protocolo 15790.

60. AHP, Toledo, protocolo 15790; protocolo 15782.

61. AHP, Toledo, protocolo 31038.

62. AHP, Toledo, protocolo 15790.

63. AHP, Toledo, protocolo 15790.

64. For Toledan hospitals and their clientele, see Martz, *Poverty and Welfare*, 9–44.

65. AHP, Toledo, protocolo 15790. Her heir was her soul and her executors the hospital staff.

BIBLIOGRAPHY

Primary Sources

AHP. Archivo Histórico Provincial de Toledo
    Protocolos Notariales

Burns, Robert I., SJ, ed. *Las Siete Partidas*, Vol. 5, *Underworlds: The Dead, the Criminal, and the Marginalized*. Translated by Samuel Parsons Scott. Philadelphia: University of Pennsylvania Press, 2001.

Secondary Sources

Alegre Carvajal, Esther. "Utopía y realidad: Mujeres Mendoza constructoras de la ciudad renacentista." In *Retrato de la mujer renacentista*, edited by A. Serrano de Haro Sorioano and Esther Alegre Carvajal, 45–66. Madrid: UNED, 2012.

Baranda Leturio, Nieves. "L'éducation des femmes dans l'Espagne post-tridentine." In *Genre et identities aux Pays-Bas Méridionaux. L'éducation religieuse des femmes après le concile de Trente*, 29–63. Louvain-la-Neuve: Bruylant-Academia, 2010.

Bennett, Judith M., and Amy M. Froide. "A Singular Past." In *Singlewomen in the European Past, 1250–1800*, edited by Judith M. Bennett and Amy M. Froide, 1–37. Philadelphia: University of Pennsylvania Press, 1999.

Berco, Christian. "Textiles as Social Texts: Syphilis, Material Culture and Gender in Golden Age Spain." *Journal of Social History* 44.3 (2011): 785–810.

Borrero Fernández, Mercedes. "Peasant and Aristocratic Women: Their Role in the Rural Economy of Seville at the End of the Middle Ages." In *Women at Work in Spain: From the Middle Ages to Early Modern Times*, edited by Marilyn Stone and Carme Benito-Vessels, 11–31. New York: Peter Lang, 1998.

Carlé, María del Carmen. *Una sociedad del siglo XV: Los castellanos en sus testamentos.* Buenos Aires: Instituto de Historia de España, 1993.

Cavallo, Sandra, and Lyndan Warner, eds. *Widowhood in Medieval and Early Modern Europe.* Harlow: Pearson, 1999.

Chabot, Isabell. "Widowhood and Poverty in Late Medieval Florence." *Continuity and Change* 3.2 (1988): 291–311.

Coolidge, Grace E. *Guardianship, Gender, and the Nobility in Early Modern Spain.* Farnham: Ashgate, 2011.

Crabb, Ann. *The Merchant of Prato's Wife: Margherita Datini and Her World, 1360–1423.* Ann Arbor: University of Michigan Press, 2015.

Cruz, Anne J., and Rosilie Hernández, eds. *Women's Literacy in Early Modern Spain and the New World.* Farnham: Ashgate, 2011.

Díaz Balsera, Viviana. "Mujer-Águila, polvo espiritado y un conejo boca arriba: Oraciones y conjuros para el parto en el México pre-hispánico y colonial." In *Perspectives on Early Modern Women in Iberia and the Americas: Studies in Law, Society, Art and Literature in Honor of Anne J. Cruz,* edited by Adrienne L. Martín and María Cristina Quintero, 253–68. New York: Escribana, 2015.

Dillard, Heath. *Daughters of the Reconquest: Women in Castilian Town Society, 1100–1300.* Cambridge: Cambridge University Press, 1984.

Eire, Carlos. *From Madrid to Purgatory: The Art and Craft of Dying in Sixteenth-Century Spain.* Cambridge: Cambridge University Press, 1995.

Erler, Mary, and Maryanne Kowaleski. "Introduction." In *Women and Power in the Middle Ages,* edited by Mary Erler and Maryanne Kowaleski. Athens: University of Georgia Press, 1988.

Fink De Backer, Stephanie. *Widowhood in Early Modern Spain: Protectors, Proprietors, and Patrons.* Leiden: Brill, 2010.

———. "Constructing Convents in Sixteenth-Century Castile: Toledan Widows and Patterns of Patronage." In *Widowhood and Visual Culture in Early Modern Europe,* edited by Allison Levy, 177–94. Aldershot: Ashgate, 2003.

French, Katherine L. "Loving Friends: Surviving Widowhood in Late Medieval Westminster." *Gender and History* 22, no. 1 (April 2010): 21–37.

García Fernández, Máximo. *Herencia y patrimonio familiar en la Castilla del antiguo régimen (1650–1834): Efectos socioeconómicos de la muerte y la partición de bienes.* Valladolid: Universidad de Valladolid, 1995.

Hoffman, Martha. *Raised to Rule: Educating Royalty at the Court of the Spanish Habsburgs, 1601–1634.* Baton Rouge: Louisiana State University Press, 2011.

Howe, Elizabeth Teresa. *Education and Women in the Early Modern Hispanic World.* Aldershot: Ashgate, 2008.

James, Susan F. *Women's Voices in Tudor Wills, 1485–1603*. Farnham: Ashgate, 2015.

King, Catherine E. "Lay Patronage and Religious Art." In *The Ashgate Companion to Women and Gender in Early Modern Europe*, edited by Allyson Poska and Katherine McIver, 95–113. Farnham: Ashgate, 2013.

Kolpacoff Dean, Jennifer, Julie A. Eckerle, Michelle M. Dowd, and Megan Matchinske, "Women's Kinship Networks: A Meditation on Creative Genealogies and Historical Labor." In *Mapping Gendered Routes and Spaces in the Early Modern World*, edited by Merry Wiesner-Hanks, 229–50. Farnham, UK: Ashgate, 2015.

Korth, Eugene H., and Della M. Flusche. "Dowry and Inheritance in Colonial Spanish America: Peninsular Law and Chilean Practice." *The Americas* 43, no. 4 (1987): 395–410.

Lehfeldt, Elizabeth A. "Convents as Litigants: Dowry and Inheritance Disputes in Early-Modern Spain." *Journal of Social History* 33.3 (2000): 645–64.

Levy, Allison, ed. *Widowhood and Visual Culture in Early Modern Europe*. Aldershot: Ashgate, 2003.

Mar Graña Cid, María de, ed. *Las sabias mujeres: educación, saber, y autoria (Siglos III–XVII)*. Madrid: Asociación Cultural Al-Mudanya, 1994.

Martínez Gil, Fernando. "Actitudes ante la muerte e historia social en la España Moderna." *Historia Social* 16 (1993): 19–32.

Martz, Linda. *A Network of Converso Families in Early Modern Toledo: Assimilating a Minority*. Ann Arbor: University of Michigan Press, 2003.

——— . *Poverty and Welfare in Habsburg Spain*. Cambridge: Cambridge University Press, 1983.

McCants, Anne EC. "The Not-So-Merry Widows of Amsterdam, 1740–1782." *Journal of Family History* 24.4 (1999): 441–67.

Nader, Helen. "Introduction." In *Power and Gender in Renaissance Spain: Eight Women of the Mendoza Family, 1450–1650*, edited by Helen Nader, 1–26. Urbana and Chicago: University of Illinois Press, 2004.

Nalle, Sara T. "Literacy and Culture in Early Modern Castile." *Past and Present* 125 (1989): 69–96.

Poska, Allyson. *Women and Authority in Early Modern Spain: The Peasants of Galicia*. Oxford: Oxford University Press, 2005.

——— . "Elusive Virtue: Rethinking the Role of Female Chastity in Early Modern Spain." *Journal of Early Modern History* 8.1–2 (2004): 135–46.

——— . "Gender, Property, and Retirement Strategies in Early Modern Northwestern Spain." *Journal of Family History* 25.3 (2000): 313–25.

Ruiz, Teofilo F. *From Heaven to Earth: The Reordering of Castilian Society, 1150–1350*. Princeton: Princeton University Press, 2004.

Taylor, Scott K. *Honor and Violence in Golden Age Spain.* New Haven: Yale University Press, 2008.

Twinam, Ann. *Public Lives, Private Secrets: Gender, Honor, Sexuality, and Illegitimacy in Colonial Spanish America.* Stanford: Stanford University Press, 1999.

Vassberg, David. "The Status of Widows in Sixteenth-Century Rural Castile." In *Poor Women and Children in the European Past,* edited by John Henderson and Richard Wall, 180–95. London: Routledge, 1994.

Wessell Lightfoot, Dana. *Women, Dowries and Agency: Marriage in Fifteenth-Century Valencia.* Manchester: Manchester University Press, 2013.

Part 2

Challenging Communal Ties

4

Women, Injurious Words, and Clerical Violence in Fourteenth-Century Catalunya

MICHELLE ARMSTRONG-PARTIDA

In the village of Lledó, the woman Na Oliva returned home one July afternoon in 1323 from collecting wood in the forest to discover her mother crying and consoling her infant daughter. She learned that their neighbor, the priest Joan, had entered their home and had accused her mother Guillema of killing his chicken, rubbing the dead animal in Guillema's face and punching her repeatedly. Na Oliva, enraged by the attack on her mother, began cursing the priest Joan so loudly that he heard the insults and entered Na Oliva's home armed with a staff. Calling her a whore, the priest Joan hit Na Oliva in the head with his staff so forcefully that the baby in her arms fell to the ground. Fearing her child dead, crying for help and trying to escape, Na Oliva ran out into the street where the priest caught and repeatedly beat her with his staff until she remained prostrate and nearly dead.[1]

While the brutality of this attack is certainly astonishing by modern day standards, parish priests in late medieval Catalunya regularly committed crimes and acts of violence against their parishioners. Like the laymen they lived among, secular clergymen fell prey to the same feelings that provoked violence, such as anger, shame, pride, a desire for revenge, and the need to protect one's honor.[2] Fourteenth-century episcopal records from the dioceses of Girona and Barcelona show that conflict commonly occurred between the priest and a male parishioner in which the outcome was a brawl, sword fighting, or acts of retribution that in some cases resulted in murder.[3] Clergymen, however, also committed acts of violence against the women in their parishes. The beating, harassing, and raping of female parishioners is indicative of the more inter-personal violence women experienced in their communities at the hands of a known assailant.[4] The interpersonal violence that women faced could greatly affect their relationship to and their status within the community. When men employed acts of brutality against women, it was not only a form of retribution, but was also meant to humiliate them, to put them in their place within the parish hierarchy. The kinds of violent behaviors aimed at women at the parish level give us insight into how violence could function in rural communities among the lower levels of Catalan society, and what it meant for women who were vulnerable to these attacks. The aim of this essay is threefold. First, to explore why women were the targets of clerical violence; second, to understand what prompted clergymen to show brute force against women; and third, to show how the community responded to protect or forsake vulnerable members of their parish.

It is difficult to fully recover the experiences of women who endured violence at the hands of clergymen because ecclesiastical sources, such as court cases and visitation records, show that episcopal authorities were more concerned with enumerating the crimes of the clergy to determine their validity—meaning that officials recorded the most basic information relating to the crime and were not overly concerned with documenting the most intimate aspects of an attack. In a number of cases the statement of the female victim is absent and the details of the incident can only be found in the testimonies of people who either witnessed the violence itself or testified to the physical and emotional state of the woman. How villagers, friends, and family presented and perceived an assault is easier to glean from the sources than the thoughts or feelings of the victim, which at the very least give us insight into how the community regulated notions of acceptable and unacceptable behavior.[5] The community, made up of village men, women, and their friends and kin living in the immediate surrounding of the parish church, set the standards of behavior deemed appropriate for men and women in their village society.

The circumstances and motives that prompted an assault are not always clearly identified in the sources either. This is particularly true when what little survives of the case brought against the cleric in the bishop's court is simply a list of charges with brief descriptions of the alleged crimes. The testimonies of witnesses, as well as the final judgement on the case, no longer exist. In pastoral visitation records, accounts of violence appear regularly. A visitor's initial inquiry into a claim depended upon the gravity of the attack, and it is clear that they were less inclined to investigate accusations of petty violence that did not shed significant blood or physically incapacitate an individual.[6] Moreover, the amount of energy invested in investigating violent conflict was also affected by the fact that these episcopal officials were following a set travel itinerary that required visitations to several parishes in one day. Church law in the thirteenth century obliged a bishop or his official to visit each parish in a diocese to correct the moral failings of the clergy and laity, but in reality, visitations to parishes were driven in part by the collection of the procuration fee, which villagers were obligated to pay to the bishop's official for the visitation. While episcopal visitors noted the violent and sexual deeds of the clergy and laity in their records, the incentive to visit as many parishes as possible to collect the procuration fee generally outweighed a thorough investigation of lower levels of violence between clergymen and parishioners in the community. Notwithstanding these difficulties and the lacunae in the sources, it is worth attempting to reconstruct the experiences of women and uncover the behaviors that made women the focus of male violence. It is not surprising that adult women without male protection, or those who were seen as insolent meddlers in their villages, could easily become the targets of male violence. In particular, parish priests felt entitled, as pastoral leaders imbued with the privilege and status of their clerical office, to correct and physically beat women who insulted them and who they perceived to be troublesome. Understanding the circumstances in which women received support from their male or female parish members in the face of such attacks gives us insight into the dynamics of gender in the community.

In spite of the culture of violence that existed in medieval society,[7] the physical aggression aimed at women was not random, particularly when perpetrated by men known to the victim, her family, and neighbors. Women like Na Oliva, who were without the protection of a male family member, could become the focus of clerical aggression. Testimonies reveal that Na Oliva and her mother were women of little means who lived together in a rented house next door to the priest Joan. Although never stated in the court documents, it is clear that these women were on their own with no male figure in their household. Only once is Na Oliva identified as the wife of Pere Mescla, but in the ninety-four folios of this case, the testimony of her husband is absent, and he is never mentioned by the sixteen witnesses who testified. Since Na Oliva is not identified as a widow, it is probable that she was an abandoned wife as well as a single mother. Na Oliva was likely part of a group of women often unnoticed by historians—married but essentially on their own. We forget that a married woman could be easily dismissed by her spouse, or that she could be solely responsible for her own survival because her husband left to find work elsewhere and returned infrequently or not at all.[8] There were also degrees of marriage in medieval society, which meant some married women lived on the margins of "singleness."[9] Interestingly, Guillema, Na Oliva's mother, is identified as neither a wife nor a widow, suggesting that she had at some point in her life entered into an informal union and never married. Both women likely lived together as a means of support and as a way to survive economically, which reveals that mother and daughter were vulnerable members of the village community. In a patriarchal society, single women were often mistrusted when they did not live under the moral authority or control of a man, and thus were often suspected of participating in the sex trade.[10] This may explain why the priest Joan labeled Na Oliva to be a whore (*bagassa*), although none of the witnesses in the case assigned such label or profession to Na Oliva. Joan probably assigned this descriptor to Na Oliva to justify his assault, because the beating of a sexually promiscuous woman was not necessarily viewed as a reprehensible act.[11]

Women who lacked the protection of a male relative or who were suspect due to their reputations for sexual misconduct, were easy targets of clerical violence because of their outlier status in the community, which also made it easier for clergymen to justify their actions against women who lived on the margins of respectable society. The beating of a reputable married woman whose husband could protect and represent her in court was seen as a far more serious act than the thrashing of a woman of ill repute, whether single or married, who deserved, according to these clerics, to be put in her place. Marie Kelleher, in her work on women and the law in the Crown of Aragon, has noted that women deemed to be whores by the community "could be subjected to brutal treatment in public," and argues that both communities and the courts "understood whores to be different."[12] These public beatings served to marginalize women as suspect members of the community that deserved to be disciplined and publicly humiliated for their shameful lifestyles. Such women could also be used as examples of male privilege, whereby a man could publicly denounce a woman and beat her, as a show of his authority to correct and discipline a disreputable woman.

The reaction of fellow villagers to the assault on Na Oliva and her mother Guillema, however, indicates that both women were considered part of the community and received help from female neighbors during a most drastic situation. Three married women, all neighbors to Na Oliva and Guillema, risked their own safety by standing in front of the priest Joan to prevent him from continuing the beating. Neighbors carried Na Oliva's body into her home, and two women washed the blood away and poured broth in her mouth to sustain her during her days of unconsciousness. Raimunda and three other neighbor women helped care for Na Oliva during the days they feared she would die from her wounds and gave aid to Na Oliva's mother throughout the time (more than three weeks) it took Na Oliva to recover from the beating and rise from her bed. These same women, after the attack, inspected the baby for injuries, because she had been dropped, and looked after the child. The married woman Dolça comforted Na Oliva's baby girl while she cried from the scare and nursed the infant with her own breast milk until Na Oliva regained consciousness.[13] The ties that Na Oliva and her mother Guillema had to their community were such that their immediate neighbors came to their aid, offered support, and even some protection, and testified on their behalf before the bishop's court. In spite of their marginalized status as two women who were perhaps suspect for living without the support or guidance of a male relative, the married women of the neighborhood offered help in a time of crisis and appear to have been on friendly terms, if not friends, with Na Oliva and her mother. The care and support provided by these married women speaks at the very least to a sense of neighborliness in this community, to help out its women in need. For women, maintaining good relations with neighbors was just another way of navigating community and creating social bonds that had the potential to enhance women's lives.[14]

The beating and subsequent death of the single woman Margarida Baborera similarly shows the role of neighborhood women in taking care of one of their own. Five women attended to Margarida as she was ravaged by fever on her death bed and testified to hearing Margarida's request that the cleric Berenguer Ollers be absolved of her attack, even though she had initially identified him as her assailant to the local sheriff.[15] As a single woman, Margarida lived among other unmarried women and was employed dyeing wool in the textile industry of Banyoles. It is possible that Margarida, like her single and married neighbors, clustered together, united in their poverty, and shared an occupation in Banyoles's wool industry. Monica Chojnacka has noted that unmarried women in Venice lived near one another and often "shared a common set of economic activities" that created a sense of community.[16] She observes that, "For people with few personal, immediate resources of money or family, neighborliness surely formed a crucial barrier between the individual and disaster in moments of personal difficulty."[17] Both Margarida and the previously mentioned Na Oliva, who apparently did not have a family with male relatives to depend upon, relied on a community of women who may have shared an identity based on their struggles to survive, their close physical proximity to one another in the neighborhood, and their participation in the woolen cloth industry.[18]

Historian Sharon Farmer has also shown, in her study of the poor in late medieval Paris, that women without husbands provided economic and emotional support to each other in order to survive the harsh realities of poverty in a big city.[19] Mireia Comas-Via's essay in this collection similarly reveals how impoverished widows in late medieval Barcelona relied on the assistance of other widows to make ends meet, often living together or in the same neighborhood, and creating bonds of solidarity that were strengthened by their desperate circumstances.[20] In Na Oliva's situation, we see that her mother helped provide childcare while Na Oliva collected wood in the forest, and that their neighbors, most of them married women, came to their aid to provide food, comfort, and care. The close-knit ties of a village community and the help of female neighbors were essential to the survival of single and widowed women in need, especially during an emergency. Other men and women of the village also took interest in the attack on Na Oliva and her mother Guillema. Na Oliva's mother testified that for many days after the assault around forty villagers stopped by their home to see Na Oliva's condition, and that even the monks of the monastery of Santa Maria de Lledó, where the priest Joan served, came to see her daughter and proclaimed that the priest had done a very "bad deed."[21]

It is not surprising that women of low status, who were poor, and above all those who lacked a male family member to defend them, were more likely than married women (with a husband present) to be the targets of clerical physical aggression. Na Oliva and her mother were vulnerable because they had no male figure to exact revenge on their behalf, or even defend them against further harassment. Considering these women's inferior social status within the community, the priest Joan may have believed that his reputation as a man and his standing as a canon at the monastery could not tolerate the insults of such a woman, and the he could, moreover, easily retaliate with impunity.[22] He certainly felt the incident with Na Oliva was worth advertising, since he reportedly bragged about the beating he administered to this mother and daughter to many in the parish and in nearby villages.[23] It is interesting too that the two laymen who witnessed the attack did not intercede even after the women of the neighborhood physically intervened to stop the beating. On the one hand, the priest Joan went about the parish armed with a sword and various other weapons, often in the company of two other heavily armed canons, which likely caused village men to fear engaging with a man known for his bellicosity.[24] On the other hand, these laymen may have been reluctant to interfere in what they considered the priest's authority to correct errant women who were not under the guidance of a paterfamilias, and perhaps believed the priest had a right to defend himself from the insults of women, particularly those that might have been viewed as suspect due to their independence from men. Nevertheless, at risk to themselves, Na Oliva's female neighbors felt the need to interfere, suggesting that these women viewed the perpetrator and the vicious attack on Na Oliva differently than the men viewed it.

While the testimonies of villagers and canons reveal a consensus in that they considered the beating of Na Oliva to have been excessive in the extreme because it was nearly fatal, no one questioned the priest's right to physically chastise a female parishioner or his right to avenge an insult. Indeed, the priest Joan had felt entitled to beat two other women in nearby villages. Once again, it appears that the issue at hand was not the act of striking two women, but that Joan had beaten them "atrociously."[25] Even though it is clear that the priest Joan had a reputation for being a hothead, and villagers were wary of his wrath, the act of assaulting a parishioner was not all that uncommon. Visitation records are rife with accounts of parish priests who beat their male or female parishioners for offending them; and in fact, the priest Joan defended his actions on the grounds that Na Oliva had spoken "injurious words" to him (*quia mulier predicta dicebat ei verba injuriosa*).[26] The leniency the bishop's court extended to the priest Joan illustrates how priests were frequently absolved for committing acts of violence against their parishioners that did not reach the level of homicide. Although the priest Joan ultimately confessed and was found guilty of severely beating Na Oliva and her mother, he received absolution for his crime once he paid 200 sous to the court. He was also instructed to do penance in the form of fasting and ordered to pay fifty sous as restitution to Na Oliva.

Considering that complaints about clerical aggression appear regularly in visitation records, it is noteworthy that episcopal officials were largely unconcerned with these encounters, unless the cleric had crossed the line and had seriously injured a parishioner. The injuries that appear in these court cases deal with the life-threatening cuts and dismemberment due to a sword fight, the loss of a great amount of blood, severe head trauma that resulted in the loss of speech or consciousness for days and weeks that meant a parishioner was unable to perform labor for a lengthy period of time, or death that resulted from the altercation.[27] The most common justification that clergymen offered to episcopal authorities for their violent confrontations with parishioners involved verbal or physical affronts that were disrespectful to the status of the clerics. For example, in 1330 the tonsured cleric Berenguer Collell defended his beating of the married woman Guillema Metge with the explanation that she had many times scorned him (*vilipendisset*) publicly with insulting words aimed at his family.[28] Rather than catch Guillema alone, the cleric made sure to strike her with his staff multiple times in the presence of more than ten villagers to ensure that his retribution and Guillema's humiliation took place publicly. According to Berenguer, he had not drawn blood but had mostly hit Guillema in the arms and body. The four local men who offered testimony in the case did not defend Guillema or mention the severity of her injuries—as witnesses who testified in favor of the victim typically did—but instead simply stated that they knew nothing more than that they had heard that Berenguer had beaten Guillema.[29] Such testimony reveals that these men did not view the cleric's actions as unreasonable. Although Guillema was married, it appears that she too may have been a deserted wife because her husband is never mentioned in witnesses' testimonies and he did not appear at the bishop's court to give a statement. In Catalonia, the 1330s were a time of poor harvests and economic upheaval, and it is likely that a great number of poor women saw their husbands leave to find work.[30]

Men in the community viewed women like Guillema, who scolded and belittled them, as troublemakers who needed to be reined in. That fellow villagers did not intervene in the beating, that the four male witnesses called to court did not underscore the excessiveness of the beating, and that her husband's absence rendered Guillema a woman without the protection of a husband are factors that help us understand why no one testified in Guillema's favor. In fact, not one witness who contradicted the cleric's account, or who had actually been present during the attack, showed up to bear witness on her behalf—not even the wife of En Cabrerra whose home Guillema had hidden in to avoid further blows from Berenguer's staff. Village men likely understood the cleric Berenguer's need to retaliate against a woman's scornful speech and restore his family's honor by degrading Guillema on the public street of the village, which explains why they did not criticize the cleric in their testimonies. The actions of Pere de Vic, the prior of the monastery of Sant Thomàs, reveal as much when he explained to the episcopal visitor that he had beaten Guillema Blanca because she was "disparaging him" (*vituperabat eum*). In this case, the men of the parish reported the conflict to the episcopal visitor but at the same time dismissed the culpability of the prior because they described the single woman Guillema as known for her "intemperance."[31]

Within the parish community, then, men determined when it was acceptable to beat a woman and influenced the proceedings with their testimony, casting some women as culpable in their own beating. Because a woman's contemptuous words could be considered annoying and troublesome, particularly when delivered by poor women without standing in the community, village men were often unsympathetic to the beating. The disdain for women's speech can be seen in the writings of the famous fourteenth-century Franciscan Francesc Eiximenis, who wrote that girls and maidens "should always remain silent and speak but little," and that a woman "should avoid saying anything foul or bad mannered." He added that "she should not shout when she speaks" and "if she has anything to say to a person, she should say it graciously and using few words."[32]

Catalan culture tolerated the beating of women to a certain degree, especially if they were considered impertinent. A priest's manual written in the Crown of Aragon during the fourteenth century condoned the striking or beating of a parishioner as long as it was administered to correct and chastise a penitent.[33] The Valencian friar Francesc Eiximenis advocated that husbands beat their wives to curtail "feminine wickedness" and to "make a good woman of her."[34] Eiximenis encouraged men to reprimand women who lacked a sense of shame, as well as to ensure their subordination and obedience by "means of fear and dread" if necessary.[35] Given the acceptance of the physical punishment of women, a parish priest might have taken to heart the responsibility to discipline and keep women in check, particularly with women who were not under the supervision of a male relative. The entitlement to beat offending women was strengthened by the authority that accompanied their priestly profession and position within the parish. In the village of Beuda, the priest Arnau de Quera was known for insulting the women of the parish, calling them *bagassas* (whores). The male parishioners of the village objected to the manner in which Arnau spoke to their wives and applied the term whore to all the women in the village. In addition, parishioners recounted to the episcopal visitor that during his fifteen-year tenure in the village, the priest had beaten his sister Saurina, along with three other female parishioners. While these beatings were not characterized as an affront to the good men of the village, as was the label of whore to their wives, two of these assaults were disturbing enough to be brought to the attention of local officials. Three out of the four women the priest Arnau had physically beaten were not described as the daughters or wives of men. The priest, then, administered beatings to women in the parish that were without the protection of a husband or father, or in another case, a daughter, described as belonging only to her mother.[36] When women lacked a male head of household, priests like Arnau believed they had the authority to physically correct these women, or if offended, retaliate against them. Considering there is evidence of priests beating their own sisters, sisters-in-law, daughters-in-law, and concubines, as the paterfamilias of their families these men may have seen the beating of women who were not under the direct supervision of a male as an extension of their responsibility in their role as parish priests.[37] Such cases illustrate that women did not need to be considered whores to receive physical discipline from men; it extended to any woman living outside the control of a male relative.

While cases of priests beating female parishioners who were married or identified as the daughters of parish men are noted in the records, in these situations, the husbands, fathers, or men of the community were less accepting of the cleric's overreach and are recorded as condemning the cleric's actions, taking the cases to court, or testifying against the clergyman's behavior.[38] For example, when the rector of Porqueroles beat the wife of Arnau Tarrat from a neighboring parish, the men of the village reported to the visitor that the rector had broken her arm and had "treated her vilely."[39]

Married women seem to have had more success when taking their assailants to court. The episcopal court of Girona punished the priest Bonant Bonet for "gravely" beating Brunissenda, the wife of Bernat Mateo. The court also punished the priest Berenguer Mir, who beat the wife of Guillem de Matamala so severely that she miscarried.[40] It is likely, too, that many incidents against women went unreported when the level of violence or correction was not considered harsh to the point of serious physical injury. In other situations where a cleric acted violently against a woman, such as the priest Pere d'Alda's scolding and beating of Na Cortona, it is clear that episcopal officials punished a parish priest for his egregious bellicosity against numerous parishioners and not simply for targeting a woman.[41]

Returning to the case of Na Oliva, the testimonies of parishioners in the suit against the priest Joan further reveal a history of conflict that was very much gendered. The priest resented the nosiness of his female neighbors and found ways of causing trouble for Na Oliva and her mother. There had been quarrels over some windows recently made between the two houses, which the priest Joan later objected to. The priest had petitioned the owner of Na Oliva and Guillema's home to expel the women for observing and eavesdropping on the priest in his home with his friends.[42] Given that the priest Joan was accused of accepting armed men described as "evildoers" into his home, he had cause to be worried about what Na Oliva and Guillema witnessed and heard through the window. What is more, the priest Joan was known to gather in his home with the canon Pere de Pahols, and both were known to be "enemies" of the prior and rebellious to his authority.[43] The priest may have feared what testimony both women could offer against him, or that they would gossip about the goings-on in his home to fellow villagers. Late medieval literary texts and legal commentaries show that people living in homes with thin walls were worried about their neighbors eavesdropping and anxious that women in particular would blab about their business.[44]

A concern that women could cause trouble with their gossiping seems to have prompted some clergymen to intimidate and teach a woman they perceived to be meddlesome a lesson. For example, the priest Guillem de Tor, in a fit of fury, savagely beat the young woman Francesca with his staff for telling the noblewoman Ricolesse that he had entered the home of Romia on more than one occasion and in her husband's absence. As a result, Romia's husband beat her and the lady Ricolesse criticized the priest to other clerics.[45] Guillem's beating of Francesca was a lesson meant to impart that he would not endure the gossiping and disapproval of a servant, particularly when it affected his reputation with a patron and the community. In another example, Astruga, the servant of the lady Cília de Gornallo, was attacked by the canon Baldrà de Soler, who sliced her face and nose at least six times with his knife as a warning to keep her quiet. According to Astruga, the canon Baldrà and the lady Cília feared that she would reveal their sexual affair. The lady Cília had even threatened Astruga and had made her swear by the holy gospels of God not to expose her secret.[46] Only Astruga's deposition survives in this instance, so the canon Baldrà's version of the attack is unknown to us. However, it is worth noting that the judge asked Astruga if she had insulted, reproached, or shown any contempt toward Baldrà, indicating that the court viewed the insults of a woman, particularly one of a lower status, as a mitigating factor for a cleric's violence.[47] The assault on Astruga reveals that clerics felt entitled to enact violence against lower-level working women that could damage their reputation with their gossip, especially if these women were perceived to be a threat to an ongoing love affair. The abuse of servant women like Astruga was not exceptional.[48] The scars on her face, however, were permanent and directly affected Astruga's future because obtaining employment would now be a challenge, and the scars might even affect her prospects of finding a husband. Mutilation by attacking the face was very much a gendered crime against women meant to disfigure their person, which served as a constant reminder of their humiliation and the attacker's triumph. Cutting off the nose and slicing women's faces disfigured them to such a degree that "the entire human being is deformed" and renders "the entire person a hideous monster."[49] Privy to the secrets and affairs of their employers, the attacks on female servants underscores their delicate position in the household. Their beating and mutilation sent a clear message—discretion was important and an act of garrulousness could mean paying a heavy price.

Writing in Catalan, the friar Francesc Eiximenis cautioned parents against raising a maiden who was not humble or discrete in her speech. Not only did Eiximenis instruct parents to beat their daughters for swearing and speaking disrespectfully, but he also warned that if a daughter had not been beaten to avoid such speech, then by the time she had reached maidenhood, she "will be punished by someone who has no pity on her."[50] Eiximenis' advice rings true for lower status women whose thrashing received little sympathy from male community members. The beatings of women who scorned and insulted clerics, in addition to Eiximenis' writings, reveal a Catalan culture where women were disciplined for insolent speech aimed at men. While single women were especially at risk, the absence of a husband meant that married women were also vulnerable. A female servant who meddled in the affairs of a cleric could easily become a target too. The privileged standing of clergymen meant that they did not accept lower status women disrespecting their authority and position in the community and believed their pastoral duties allowed them to physically reprimand women who were not under the immediate charge of a man. As long as the clergyman did not kill or brutally discipline a woman without a husband, or target a married woman whose husband was present, village men did not condemn the cleric. Men and women in the community determined when the violence had exceeded acceptable limits. Ties of friendship among poor, single, and married women meant that they looked after each other when a severe beating incapacitated a female neighbor.

In England and in other European cities, the fourteenth and fifteenth centuries saw a rise in the prosecution of speech crimes, and women, more often than men, were likely to be indicted in either secular or ecclesiastical courts for scolding and defamation.[51] As a response, late medieval devotional texts instructed women that their silence was pious and virtuous. These cleric-authored didactic works very clearly equated women's intemperate speech with sin.[52] The social anxiety over women's verbal expressions and increased involvement in parish affairs in late medieval society was not unique to Catalunya, but a clerical culture that dealt so harshly with sharp-tongued women may have been, to some degree, unique. It is significant that in late medieval Catalunya clergymen did not respond by taking their verbal slayers to court for their insulting speech.[53] In his study of 3,000 criminal court cases, Flocel Sabaté found that in 63 percent of the cases women were the victims of male violence and that women were charged with causing verbal injuries in only 4 percent of the cases, indicating that in fourteenth-century Catalunya men chose to settle their disputes with women through violence rather than pursue a legal solution.[54] The dearth of Catalan court records charging women with verbal crimes reveals that pursuing an enemy in court was a far less popular option and that the culture of vengeance in rural communities demanded violent retribution. Moreover, for clergymen who enjoyed the protection of their clerical status and the privilege of being tried in an ecclesiastical court that tended to be lenient with crimes of the clergy, their manhood and reputation benefitted more from physically punishing a shrew or insolent woman before the community than the effort and expense to take a woman of little consequence to a town court.[55] From their point of view, a beating solved the problem.

The following essay in this volume, written by Mark Meyerson, illustrates how Valencian women participated in the culture of vengeance and honor in their neighborhood and were physically targeted as a means to impugn the masculinity of men. Meyerson's essay highlights the role of women's belligerent speech in defending the family's honor and in inciting their male family members to enact violence against their enemies. Our essays show that in defense of personal or family honor, women in fourteenth-century Catalunya and women in fifteenth-century Valencia used insults and scornful speech to confront men in their communities at great physical risk to themselves. Similarly, the perception that women were gossipy and could easily betray the secrets of men's private lives made it easy for men to justify their violence. Low status women without the protection of a male family member and married women too, by proxy, experienced violence as an act of retribution or as an act of degradation that was meant to put them in their place. If anything, our findings indicate that women in both rural and urban landscapes frequently encountered violence at the hands of men they personally knew in their communities. It seems likely, therefore, that many women experienced violence when they tested the limits of speech appropriate for women or when violence was directed at a woman in order to indirectly humiliate her male relative. While the community could offer women support, a culture of enmity amongst neighbors could also foster a surprising level of violence at women.

NOTES

1. ADG Processos, no. 66, 25rv–26rv, 42rv–43rv (1323). Joan Oliver's list of crimes is extensive, including carrying various arms, gambling, and engaging in rebellious activities against the prior of the monastery of Lledó, whom he considered to be his "enemy." However, the main charges dealt with Joan's nearly fatal beating of Na Oliva.
2. Brown, *Violence in Medieval Europe*, 1–2, 7, 288.
3. Armstrong-Partida, *Defiant Priests*. See also Marquès, "Processos anteriors," 145–77; Marquès, *Processos Medievals*.
4. Flocel Sabaté estimates that family members were responsible for physically assaulting a woman in 15 percent of the cases brought to court, and that 25 percent of murdered women were victims of marital violence. See Sabaté, "Orden y desorden," 1399.
5. I am following Susan Alice McDonough's lead, which uses the testimony of witnesses in court records to study the "ways in which women and men cooperated or contended with each other to create and regulate notions of community, family, and morality." See McDonough, *Witnesses, Neighbors, and Community*, 7, 134, 143.
6. Episcopal visitors also paid particularly attention to physical attacks perpetrated by laymen against clergymen because it was a crime. Church law, specifically the canon known as *privilegium canonis*, dictated excommunication for anyone who lay violent hands upon a cleric or monk.
7. See Brown, *Violence in Medieval Europe*; Serra Ruiz, *Honor, honra e injuria*; Meyerson, "A Great Effusion of Blood"; Hyams, *Rancor and Reconciliation*; Skoda, *Medieval Violence*.
8. Teresa Vinyoles i Vidal also notes that the wives of mariners and soldiers were left to survive on their own during their husbands' prolonged absences. See Vinyoles i Vidal, "Respuestas de mujeres medievales," 81. Bernard Capp, in his study of early modern English women, has remarked how women with absent husbands, who were in essence surviving as single women, have received little scholarly attention. Capp, *When Gossips Meet*, 38–41.
9. Cordelia Beattie has argued that marital status in late medieval England was "a performance that had to be acted out in order to be visible," and that there was

"a grey area between singleness and marriage" where a married woman could be "living as a single person." See Beattie, "'Living as a Single Person,'" 337.

10. Karras, *Common Women*, 52; Farmer, *Surviving Poverty in Medieval Paris*, 37–38, 108, 114–15; Farmer, "'It Is Not Good,'" 87.

11. Marie Kelleher finds that terms such as *vilis mulier*, *bagassa*, and *puta* were used in the Crown of Aragon's courts to denote a woman's unacceptable sexual promiscuity. These women were often treated as prostitutes or "public" women. See Kelleher, *Measure of Woman*, 99–100, 102.

12. Kelleher, *Measure of Woman*, 108. Keller notes the vicious beating of a woman denounced as a whore in the Catalan village of Cabanes d'Arc where no one from the community came to her aid.

13. ADG, Processos, no. 66, 33rv, 37rv–41rv (1323).

14. McDonough, "Being a Neighbor," 3–5.

15. ADG, Processos, no. 96, 12 folios (1327). Margarida Baborera is identified as "condam filiam de Na Dolça habitatricis" of Banyoles. Neither mother nor daughter is identified as married or a widow. Three married women, the widow of a weaver, and one single woman took care of Margarida during her last days. In total, seven neighborhood women and three men testified to hearing Margarida identify the cleric Berenguer as her attacker before recanting her claim. According to the single woman Ermesenda Frigola, Margarida worked dying wool in Banyoles. It is possible that Margarida may have migrated to Banyoles to find work. In the end, Margarida's wish came true; the bishop's court cleared the cleric Berenguer of any wrongdoing. Although the reasons are not specified, it appears that the court absolved the cleric because no one could testify to witnessing Berenguer beat Margarida, and her dying wish that he not stand accused of the crime probably went a long way in casting doubt on his guilt.

16. Chojnacka, *Working Women*, 54.

17. Chojnacka, *Working Women*, 54, 55.

18. Banyoles, along with other Catalan towns such as Lleida, Perpinyà, Puigcerdà, Berga, Bagà, and Barcelona were important producers of mid-quality woolen cloth in the fourteenth and fifteenth centuries that sent their wool to markets in Genoa, Pisa, Naples, and Palermo. See Riu, "The Woollen Industry," 213, 225; Ferrer, "Catalan Commerce," 31.

19. Farmer, *Surviving Poverty in Medieval Paris*.

20. Comas-Via, "Looking for a Way to Survive: Community and Institutional Assistance to Widows in Medieval Barcelona," 177–94 herein.

21. ADG, Processos, no. 66, 40v–41rv (1323).

22. The culture of honor in medieval society pressured men to verbally and physically respond to insults or else they suffered a "loss of face" that affected their

reputation and social standing in the community. See Strochia, "Gender and the Rites of Honour," 52–53.

23. ADG, Processos, no. 66, 3r (1323). "Item quod ipse Johannes pluries et in pluribus locis dixit gloriando se sive jactando de dicta percussione quod ipse eam fecerat et volebat eam fecisse."

24. ADG, Processos, no. 66, 3v–4r, 5r, 29v (1323).

25. ADG, Processos, no. 66, 3rv, 28r, 41v, 45v, 58v–59v (1323).

26. ADG, Processos, no. 66, 1v (1323). See also chapter 4, "'Quarrelsome' Men," in Armstrong-Partida, *Defiant Priests*.

27. See, for example, ADG, Processos, no. 16 (1308); ADG, Processos, no. 25 (1317); ADG, Processos, no. 39 (1320); ADG, Processos, no. 33 (ca. 1320); ADG, Processos, no. 96 (1327); ADG, Processos, no. 125 (1333); ADG, Processos, no. 198 (1338); ADG, Processos, no. 276 (1354).

28. ADG, Processos, no. 106, 1rv (1330).

29. ADG, Processos, no. 106, 1v–2r.

30. Catalunya suffered from a shortage of grains in 1315–1318 and 1322–1327 prior to the years of the 1331 crisis. See Batlle i Gallart, *La crisis social y económica*, 44–46.

31. ADG, Visites Pastorals, no. 6, 37v–38rv (1338). Given that episcopal records regularly identify the marital status of women, I believe Guillema Blanca was a single woman because neither the four male parishioners nor the prior Pere de Vic labeled her a married or widowed woman.

32. Renedo and Guixeras, eds., *Francesc Eiximenis*, 118. Eiximenis's view falls in line with legal codes in Valencia and Catalunya that permitted a husband to beat his wife for "palabras deshonestas." See Vinyoles, "Respuestas de mujeres medievales," 86.

33. Guido of Monte Rochen, *Handbook of Curates*, 224–25.

34. Renedo and Guixeras, eds., *Francesc Eiximenis*, 93, 95, 98, 99–100.

35. Renedo and Guixeras, eds., *Francesc Eiximenis*, 93, 95, 98, 99–100. Marie Kelleher also observes that "some violence was expected as part of the marriage relationship," and cites cases that were brought to the court because the level of violence was alleged to be extraordinary. She argues that both the courts and the community determined what was considered abusive and beyond reasonable. See Kelleher, *Measure of Woman*, 112, 116.

36. ADG, Visites fragmentaris, P-171, 39rv–40r (1364).

37. Armstrong-Partida, *Defiant Priests*, 193, 195–96.

38. Examples include the priest Jaume Floris for injuring the wife of Guillem Mercadell in a fight, and the cleric Pere de Montoliu who was found guilty in a civil court for injuring the daughter of En Brugués in the face. Episcopal officials, however, pardoned the cleric and granted him absolution. ADG, Remissions de Penes, no. 1, 32rv (1352); Arxiu Diocesà de Barcelona, Visites Pastorals, no. 5, 23v (1341).

39. AEV, Visites Pastorals, no. 1200/2, 44v (1331).

40. ADG, Remissions de Penes, no. 1, 37rv, 38v (1352). The priest Andreu Maioll also beat, on two separate occasions, two pregnant parish women who both miscarried due to the severity of the attack. See ADB, Registra Communium, no. 4, 162r (1328).

41. ADB, Registra Communium, no. 4, 161v (1327). In the priest Pere's case, he had attacked the parishioner Arnau Mascarello and dragged him from his home at night, he had wielded weapons against three laymen from the village, had participated in a feud against two other laymen, and had attacked with his sword another cleric in the parish church. While the priest was fined 200 *lliures* for his pugnacious behavior, he continued to serve the parish of Caldes de Montbuí as before. Another example is that of a cleric serving in the monastery of Sant Esteve de Banyoles, who was found guilty by the bishop's court for carrying arms and for treating two villagers badly, a weaver whom he wounded in the head and the servant Berengaria whom he beat with his staff. See ADG, Remissions de Penes, no. 1, 5rv (1346).

42. ADG, Processos, no. 66, 4v, 46r (1323).

43. ADG, Processos, no. 66, 5rv (1323).

44. Bardsley, *Venomous Tongues*, 11–12, 108, 112, 139, 146.

45. ADG, Processos, no. 73, 10v–11rv (1323). The priest Guillem de Tor was brought before the bishop's court for a number of crimes, the beating of Francesca was just one among many instances of violence that were mostly aimed at men.

46. ADG, Processos, no. 89, 3rv (1325).

47. ADG, Processos, no. 89, 2v (1325).

48. Other servant women, such as Berengaria, who worked for Na Coloma, and the daughter of En Frigola de Seguero, were also severely beaten by priests. See ADG, Remissions de Penes, 5rv (1346); 35r (1352). Galceran de Queralt, the rector of Sant Vicenç de Jonqueres, beat his own "*ancilla*" (female servant) and was fined thirty sous by episcopal officials. See ADB, Registra Communium, no. 9, 141r (1341).

49. Groebner, "Losing Face, Saving Face," 6. Jonathan Ray mentions a case in which Jewish officials insisted that the nose of a Jewish woman be cut off to "disfigure her" in an attempt to dissuade "her Christian lover from pursing the relationship." See Ray, *Sephardic Frontier*, 173. Examples of men cutting the faces of women can also be found in Taylor, *Honor and Violence*, 210.

50. Renedo and Guixeras, eds., *Francesc Eiximenis*, 120, 121–22.

51. See Bardsley, *Venomous Tongues*, 16–18, 70, 77–78, 80–82, 84–85, 122–25; Gowing, *Domestic Dangers*, 32–38, 61, 111; Dean, "Gender and Insult," 217–31; Smail, *Consumption of Justice*, 20, 130; Juan Miquel Mendoza Garrido, Clara Almagro Vidal,

Maria de los Ángeles Martín Romera, and Luís Rafael Villegas Díaz, "Delincuencia y justicia en la Chancillería de Ciudad Real y Granada (1495–1510). Primera parte. Estudio," 423–25.

52. French, *Good Women of the Parish*, 4–5, 180–81, 184.

53. Neither the ecclesiastical court records of Girona and Barcelona, nor the account registers of bailiffs (Llibres de Batlle or Llibre de Cùria), show that women were regularly prosecuted for scolding or defamation. I have looked through various fourteenth century registers of the Llibre de Cùria for the villages of Peralada and Sant Feliu de Guixols in the Arxiu Històric de Girona (Pe, no. 1034, 1286–1389; Pe, no. 1317, 1338; Pe, no. 100, 1339–1442; sFe, no. 884, 1308–1319; sFe, no. 1035, 1309–1316) and the Llibres de Cort del Batlle de Terrassa in the Arxiu Històric de Terrassa (years 1298, 1321–1323, 1325–1326) and have not found any cases.

54. Sabaté, "Femmes et violence dans la Catalogne du XIVe siècle," 279, 280, 294. Sabaté notes that 16 percent of the cases of male violence against women dealt with sexual violence; the rest was "general violence."

55. Daniel Lord Smail has argued that in the city of Marseille litigation was a useful vehicle to humiliate an enemy and that people chose to invest in litigation because of its publicity. Smail, *The Consumption of Justice*, 94–95, 132.

BIBLIOGRAPHY

Primary Sources

ADB. Arxiu Diocesà de Barcelona

    Registra Communium

    Visites Pastorals

ADG. Arxiu Diocesà de Girona

    Processos

    Remissions de Penes

    Visites Pastorals and Visites fragmentaris

AEV. Arxiu Episcopal de Vic

    Guido of Monte Rochen. *Handbook for Curates: A Late Medieval Manual on Pastoral Ministry*. Translated by Anne T. Thayer. Edited by Anne T. Thayer and Katherine J. Lualdi. Washington DC: Catholic University of America Press, 2011.

    Renedo, Xavier, and David Guixeras, eds. *Francesc Eiximenis: An Anthology*. Translated by Robert D. Hughes. Barcelona: Barcino-Tamesis, 2008.

    Visites Pastorals

Secondary Sources

Armstrong-Partida, M. *Defiant Priests: Domestic Unions, Violence, and Clerical Masculinity in Fourteenth-Century Catalonia*. Ithaca: Cornell University Press, 2017.

Bardsley, Sandy. *Venomous Tongues: Speech and Gender in Late Medieval England.* Philadelphia: University of Pennsylvania Press, 2006.

Batlle i Gallart, Carmen. *La crisis social y económica de Barcelona a mediados del siglo XV.* Barcelona: Institución Milá i Fontanals, 1973.

Beattie, Cordelia. "'Living as a Single Person': Marital Status, Performance and the Law in Late Medieval England." *Women's History Review* 17, no. 3 (2008): 327–40.

Brown, Warren C. *Violence in Medieval Europe.* Harlow: Pearson Education, 2011.

Capp, Bernard. *When Gossips Meet: Women, Family, and Neighbourhood in Early Modern England.* Oxford: Oxford University Press, 2003.

Chojnacka, Monica. *Working Women of Early Modern Venice.* Baltimore: Johns Hopkins University Press, 2001.

Dean, Trevor. "Gender and Insult in an Italian City: Bologna in the Later Middle Ages." *Social History* 29, no. 2 (2004): 217–31.

Farmer, Sharon. *Surviving Poverty in Medieval Paris. Gender, Ideology, and the Daily Lives of the Poor.* Ithaca: Cornell University Press, 2002.

———."It Is Not Good That [Wo]man Should be Alone': Elite Responses to Singlewomen in High Medieval Paris." In *Singlewomen in the European Past,* edited by Judith M. Bennett and Amy M. Froide, 82–105. Philadelphia: University of Pennsylvania Press, 1999.

Ferrer, Maria Teresa. "Catalan Commerce in the Late Middle Ages." *Catalan Historical Review* 5 (2012): 29–65.

French, Katherine L. *The Good Women of the Parish: Gender and Religion After the Black Death.* Philadelphia: University of Pennsylvania Press, 2008.

Gowing, Laura. *Domestic Dangers: Women, Words, and Sex in Early Modern London.* Oxford: Oxford University Press, 1996.

Groebner, Valentin. "Losing Face, Saving Face: Noses and Honour in a Late Medieval Town." *History Workshop Journal* 40 (1995): 1–15.

Hyams, Paul R. *Rancor and Reconciliation in Medieval England.* Ithaca: Cornell University Press, 2003.

Karras, Ruth Mazo. *Common Women: Prostitution and Sexuality in Medieval England.* Oxford: Oxford University Press, 1996.

Kelleher, Marie. *The Measure of Woman: Law and Female Identity in the Crown of Aragon.* Philadelphia: University of Pennsylvania Press, 2010.

Marquès, Josep M. "Processos anteriors al 1500 de l'Arxiu Diocesà de Girona." *Annals de l'Institut d'Estudis Gironins* 44 (2003): 145–77.

——— . *Arxiu Diocesà de Girona. Processos Medievals.* Girona, 1999.

Mendoza Garrido, Juan Miguel., Clara Almagro Vidal, Maria de los Ángeles Martín Romera, and Luís Rafael Villegas Díaz. "Delincuencia y justicia en la Chancillería de Ciudad Real y Granada (1495–1510). Primera parte. Estudio."

Clío & Crímen: Revista del Centro de Historia del Crimen de Durango, no. 4 (2007): 353–488.

McDonough, Susan Alice. *Witnesses, Neighbors, and Community in Late Medieval Marseille*. New York: Palgrave Macmillan, 2013.

———. "Being a Neighbor: Ideas and Ideals of Neighborliness in the Medieval West." *History Compass* 15, no. 9 (2017): 1–11.

Meyerson, Mark D., Daniel Thiery, and Oren Falk, eds. *"A Great Effusion of Blood"? Interpreting Medieval Violence*. Toronto: University of Toronto Press, 2004.

Ray, Jonathan. *The Sephardic Frontier: The Reconquista and the Jewish Community in Medieval Iberia*. Ithaca: Cornell University Press, 2006.

Riu, Manuel. "The Woollen Industry in Catalonia in the Later Middle Ages" in *Cloth and Clothing in Medieval Europe*. Edited by N. B. Harte, Eleanora Mary Carus-Wilson, and Kenneth G. Ponting, 205–9. London: Heinemann Educational, 1983.

Sabaté, Flocel. "Orden y desorden. La violencia en la cotidianidad bajomedieval Catalana." *Aragón en la Edad Media* 14–15, no. 2 (1999): 1389–1408.

———. "Femmes et violence dans la Catalogne du XIVe siècle." *Annales du Midi: revue archéologique, historique et philologique de la France méridionale*, Tome 106, no. 207 (1977): 277–316.

Serra Ruiz, Rafael. *Honor, honra e injuria en el Derecho medieval español*. Murcia: Sucesores de Nogués, 1969.

Skoda, Hannah. *Medieval Violence: Physical Brutality in Northern France, 1270–1330*. Oxford: Oxford University Press, 2013.

Smail, Daniel Lord. *The Consumption of Justice: Emotions, Publicity, and Legal Culture in Marseille, 1264–1423*. Ithaca: Cornell University Press, 2003.

Strochia, Sharon T. "Gender and the Rites of Honour in Italian Cities" in *Gender and Society in Renaissance Italy*, ed. Judith C. Brown and Robert C. Davis, 39–60. London: Longman, 1998.

Taylor, Scott K. *Honor and Violence in Golden Age Spain*. New Haven: Yale University Press, 2008.

Vinyoles i Vidal, Teresa. "Respuestas de mujeres medievales ante la pobreza, la marginación y la violencia." *Clío & Crímen: Revista del Centro de Historia del Crimen de Durango*, no. 5 (2008): 72–93.

5

Women, Violence, and Community
in Late Medieval Valencia

MARK MEYERSON

Valencians . . . are impulsive, putting their hand to their sword for little and killing without much difficulty . . . There is no city in all of Spain where one encounters more death . . . The majority of their murders are caused by the women, who are boisterous from being, because of the climate, of a very passionate temperament.

—Barthélemy Joly, "Voyage en Espagne" (1603–1604)

While Joly's impression of Valencians as touchier and more prone to shedding blood than other peoples in seventeenth-century Spain might be dismissed as mere hyperbole, his assertion that most homicides in Valencia were caused by the city's loud, passionate women warrants closer consideration. In this essay I will show that women indeed played visible and vociferous roles in the violent contests for honor and status around which social life in late medieval Valencia revolved, and that their sexualized bodies often were, symbolically and really, the focus of violence. The social logic of the behaviors that Joly observed had medieval roots.

A denunciation made before the court of the Criminal Justice on May 30, 1440, by Damiata, the pregnant wife of the merchant Daniel Forcadell, captures the symbolic function of the female body in the violent encounters that punctuated life in Valencia's neighborhoods as well as the assertive verbal role that women assumed in defending their family's honor against aggressive challengers—in this instance, in court.[1] Damiata had already voiced a complaint (*clam*), on May 25, that armed men of the Castellar family—a broker, a scribe, and a bookbinder—and their friends—a tailor, a hosier, and a doublet-maker—"assaulted her house" in an attempt to kill her husband. They wounded him on the right thigh with a sword. Such acts of household assault (*combatiment de alberch*) were intended, as will be explained, to dishonor the inhabitants of the targeted house (*alberch*). Having decided that her initial *clam* had not adequately conveyed her and her husband's feelings of humiliation, Damiata reappeared before the justice and included in her formal denunciation details that witnesses corroborated, as well as an embellishment that they did not. When the attack took place, Damiata maintained, she was "inside her said house weaving on a loom." The "denounced threw a lance at her; it landed between the loom and her thighs . . . and if it [the lance] had gone a little farther, it would have killed her and the fetus that she had in [. . .] her womb."[2] The assailants had not only sullied the purity of the Forcadell household by penetrating it and shedding Daniel's blood inside, they had also symbolically violated Damiata with the phallic lance and impugned the paternity of her offspring. Damiata intimated the gravity of the affront through this fiction that she and her unborn child, the present and future of the family whom the house embodied and was supposed to protect, had been mortally threatened.

In her embellishment, Damiata articulated the meaning of a social practice that, to all appearances, would have been destructive of community. Yet, paradoxical as it may seem, violent contests for honor, in which household assaults were a central element, contributed to a sense of community in Valencia's neighborhoods precisely because all of the neighbors participated in them, whether as assailants, victims, or all-too-interested bystanders. Community cohesion was strengthened through the neighbors' common acceptance of the social norms underlying the practice of violence and their common concern about the impact of violence on the local competition for social status.[3] Women in particular, through their actions as victims, observers, inciters, and perpetrators of violence, played a key part in this competition and in promoting the values of the local community that household assaults made manifest.

As is evident in Michelle Armstrong-Partida's contribution to this volume, women were also very much involved in the agonistic politics of rural Catalan communities, as verbal aggressors insulting their enemies, male and female, and as targets of the violence of clerics and laymen who beat them in retaliation for their insults or for having transgressed community values.[4] What is striking in both rural Catalonia and urban Valencia is the acceptability and frequency of male violence against women, whether the perpetrators were clergy or laymen. It is not clear, however, that the physical abuse of women inside their own houses in rural Catalonia conveyed the same meaning as in Valencia, or that such invasions of domestic space were ritualized as they were in both the cities and the villages of the kingdom of Valencia.[5]

Household assaults, above all, reminded Valencian Christian women and men of the necessity of preserving female chastity for the future of the family, community, and kingdom. These violent performances focused the attention of Christian communities on women on account of the metaphorical association of the house with the female body, the control and protection of which were deemed crucial for the proper ordering and perpetuation of Christian society.[6] The house, the *alberch*, functioned as a "root metaphor," a symbol which "provide[d] a set of categories for conceptualizing other aspects of experience. . . . [B]y establishing a certain view of the world, [it] implicitly suggest[ed] certain valid and effective ways of acting upon it."[7] The salience of the symbol of the house in Valencian Christian culture originated in the wake of the thirteenth-century conquest (1232–1245), when a fundamental linkage was established between the colonizers' Christian identity and their possession of a house appropriated from the vanquished Muslims. Christian settlers, however, never felt secure living amidst a large, restive Muslim population who rebelled repeatedly from the 1240s through the 1270s.[8] Their structuring of the quotidian politics of their own communities around ritual household assaults stemmed from their fear that their houses and the women within might be violated and polluted by Muslim or Jewish men.[9] Rituals that emphasized the necessity of defending the integrity of the *alberch* against inimical Christian neighbors served to distance Muslims and Jews even further from Christian houses and women. The house became a fortress meant to shield Christian women from all men, infidels or coreligionists.[10]

As Valencia expanded in later centuries through the absorption of immigrants, many of whom had no ties to the conquering families, the house became less the victor's prize and stronghold and more a symbol, or material manifestation, of an immigrant family's settlement and membership in local society. The newcomer's establishment of himself as an honorable member of a Valencian neighborhood entailed possessing a house—even by lease—and defending it against the attacks of Christian neighbors. Through the act of *combatiment de alberch* the neighborly assailants marked the targeted house as a distinct domestic space that was in the possession of its inhabitants while implicitly acknowledging that the inhabitants were honorable—that they possessed honor worth taking. Household assaults remained crucial for the creation and perpetuation of community.[11]

The house was such a potent symbol because it concretized a dichotomous world view which drew sharp distinctions between inside and outside, female and male, the private and the public, the intimate and the inimical, shame and honor.[12] "Spatial arrangements," anthropologists observe, "institutionalize one of the primary means by which society's order is communicated to individuals and 'felt' by them. The power of space semiotically is that it functions as . . . a primary means by which society is both interpreted and experienced by its members."[13] In Valencians' ideal gendered geography, the interior of the *alberch* was the domain of women, an inviolable space where their sexual purity would be safeguarded.[14] A "good woman" therefore was supposed to be inside or at the threshold of her house.[15] The world outside was the sphere of men; there, through their professional and political activities, they could contribute to the wealth and prestige of the family and violently defend its honor, when necessary. Yet social, economic, and political realities hardly accorded with these ideals. Valencian women often worked outside the house attending to household chores or engaging in other forms of employment.[16] In this exterior domain of men, moreover, women were neither silent nor submissive; they were vociferous and assertive political actors who did not shy away from aggressively pursuing the interests of their families. Even with this marked disjunction between ideal and reality, the idealized dichotomous, architectonic frame of reference inspired and lent meaning and moral force to the practice of *combatiment de alberch*.[17]

The neighborhood theaters where household assaults were enacted encompassed roughly a city block. When Alfonso V ruled, in 1428, that neighbors should suffer no more than a fine for committing such offenses against each other, he defined as the "neighbors" of an assaulted house those who resided in the five houses on either side of it, or in the five houses on either side of the house directly across the street from it.[18] Such neighborhoods (*vehinats*) were the pulsating cells of a constantly growing urban organism, perhaps the most populous in Christian Spain by the late fifteenth century.[19] The neighborhoods on which my research has focused were composed of the nuclear households of artisans, agricultural workers, and professionals, that is, members of the non-elite classes whose precise social status was always open to challenge.

The composition and informal power structure of these neighborhoods were perpetually in flux, as a steady stream of immigrants peopled the houses that plague or other misfortunes periodically emptied.[20] A family's status in the *vehinat*'s rough pecking order rested on the possession of material wealth and honor. Honor was a moral commodity, basically "the value of a person in his or her own eyes, but also in the eyes of society";[21] it was a "condition of integrity, of being 'untouched'" by the verbal or physical injuries that neighbors might inflict.[22] Honor also constituted an informal code, "a system of symbols and values in terms of which phenomena were conceptualized and interpreted," and which guided social action.[23] Although economic competition frequently generated violence, as evinced in the many conflicts between artisans practicing the same craft, neither the clashing artisans nor the neighbors observing their conduct spoke of economic issues. Instead, they consistently rationalized violence as involving the acquisition or defense of "honor" through "dishonoring" another.

In the contests for honor in the *vehinat*, neighbors were the audience and the judges, and women, because they stayed in and around the house more than men, played a crucial role in observing, discussing, and evaluating the comportment of others in accordance with communal norms. Valencians were nosy and loath to miss a good fight, especially when their neighbors were involved. In her eyewitness testimony about an armed clash between her neighbors Miquel Ducles and Francesc Gomar, Dolçeta, the spouse of Martí de Ribes, mentioned that she was not the only spectator: "the neighbors—men and women—ran [there] since the said brawlers were likewise neighbors."[24] If they had not been present, women could quickly learn about notable happenings through the gossip network. When Pasqualla, the wife of Johan de Sison, entered the house of the widow Caterina and kicked and punched her, leaving her with a bloody face, Francesca, a silversmith's wife, only heard "great cries" coming from Caterina's house. Francesca soon discovered what had occurred since "everyone in the neighborhood was talking about it."[25] The political necessity of keeping informed about who had done what to whom enabled women to offer frank assessments of a neighbor's character in court. After recounting how a married couple, the Bonets, had beaten up their neighbor the widow Marieta, Clara, a cutler's wife, added that "she knows well and is certain that the said Na Marieta is a good woman and woman of integrity with a good reputation, but it is true that the said Na Marieta in her day has had a strong personality and a strong tongue."[26]

Women were in a position to see and hear about the politicking on their streets because they frequently situated themselves at the doors of their *alberchs*. One female plaintiff described herself as "simply" sitting at the door of her house "just as other good women do."[27] By boldly placing their bodies at the entrance of the domicile that was supposed to shield them, women reaffirmed the symbolic connection of the house to a woman's body and, in effect, dared their neighbors to dishonor them and their household.[28] The gendered geography of the *vehinat*, where each *alberch* had its women sitting on the threshold observing, gossiping, and challenging, gave household assaults a scripted quality and symbolic resonance.

Conflict between households can, for purposes of analysis, be divided into distinct phases. The first phase involved verbally and publicly insulting an adversary. Insults hurt because other people, the neighbors on whose opinions the target's prestige hinged, heard them. Women were the principal, though not the only, perpetrators of insult. In regard to matters of family honor, there was a gendered division of labor. Men were responsible for physically defending the honor of the household and often wielded arms—daggers, swords, and lances—for this purpose. Women resorted to physical violence far less frequently than men, and when they did, they punched, kicked, and scratched their opponents or hit them with tiles or brooms. Instead of stabbing with steel, women thrust verbal daggers at their enemies.[29] Their tongues left stinging wounds, as evinced in the behavior of men who assaulted women in retaliation for their cutting remarks. Martí Alvaro, a livestock dealer, made the mistake of trading insults with Beatriu, the wife of the farmer Berthomeu Pinyol. When Beatriu entered his godson's house, he exclaimed, "'By my faith, the *Carrer Blanch* was the best street in all of Valencia and of good reputation, and now I see that it has a bad reputation and that there are nothing but whores here.'" Beatriu shot back, "'And look how you have lived, you have a wife and a mistress.'" Martí responded defensively, "'I have lived well, so that my children don't have to lower their heads.'" Then Beatriu finished him off, saying with "great wrath" two or three times, "'Your granddaughters should watch their skirts,'" suggesting that their virginity was in question or that he himself had incestuous intentions. Martí could not contain his rage. He followed Beatriu outside and beat her on the back with the branch of an apricot tree in full view of the neighbors.[30]

So that their insults would most clearly register on the neighborhood scorecard of honor, women stood in front of their enemies' houses in broad daylight to hurl verbal abuse. They often repeated the insults many times in order to intensify the impact.[31] According to the notary Martí Garcia, a woman named Achnes accosted him as he was leaving his father's house, calling him traitor, thief, and murderer twenty times.[32] Barchinona Valls, a farmer's wife, complained that while she was at the door of her house doing her work, Caterina "the hunchbacked" appeared and cried out loudly nine or ten times that she was a "vile whore [and] pimp for chaplains . . . and friars."[33]

Insults were often of a sexual nature, especially when they were directed at women. Defamers, both female and male, called the women of opposing households "whore" (*bagassa* or *puta*); wives, daughters, and widows were all the objects of this insult. Male heads of household were correspondingly labelled "cuckold" (*cornut*) by their opponents.[34] Such insults implied that the men of a family could not protect their wives and daughters from violation or control their sexual behavior, thereby raising doubts about the integrity of the defamed family's household and the legitimacy of its offspring. Elaborations on the sexual theme played on Christians' primordial fears of the dangers posed by Muslims and Jews to the purity of their households, the fears which had given rise to the custom of *combatiment de alberch*. For example, Francesca, a squire's wife, slandered Johana, the spouse of Domingo Mascó, by calling her "whore, bitch . . . go-between who does it often with dogs, Muslims, and Jews."[35] Men, especially, were the targets of insults that impugned their professional integrity. While men often uttered them, women did too. "[D]efaming him in many places," Marieta, an esparto-worker's wife, asserted that the notary Anthoni Cavaller, "had falsified a will."[36] The common insult "traitor" (*traydor/a*), which suggested that the target was untrustworthy, was usually directed at men and only occasionally at women.[37]

The insults that women articulated were mostly conventional and standardized, but this did not detract from their efficacy since they drew on and reinforced accepted social values while harping on deeply rooted anxieties.[38] A vehicle for socialization, insults pointed Valencians, immigrants and native-born, toward ideals of conduct against which all were measured, the conduct that would make them honorable women and men in the eyes of their peers.

Another aspect of women's roles as wielders of verbal weapons was their appearance in court to level accusations against those responsible for aggression against them or members of their families. Wives performed this function more than their husbands, who perhaps deemed recourse to the authorities to be a sign of weakness on their part. Men were supposed to respond to violence with violence, with fists and daggers and not just words. Yet wives' filing suit against neighborhood enemies was no less significant than their husbands' physical attacks against them. Both were tactics in the contests between families, for the court was no less of a forum for the pursuit of private conflicts than was the neighborhood street.[39] Thus Pere Navasques complained that Francesca, wife of the notary Eximeno Sanxeç, had brought charges against him for assaulting her while she swept in front of her house "more out of a desire to exhaust and vex [him] . . . than out of a zeal for justice."[40]

Once contending parties publicly challenged each other with verbal insults, physical violence was the next and more serious phase of the conflict. Indeed, the resort to violence by the men of rival families often originated in the exchange of verbal or even physical injuries between the families' female members.[41] The animosity generated in clashes between women moved them to goad their menfolk into taking violent action against the women and men of opposing families.[42] Dolça, wife of the carter Bernat Rellà, described how after Miquel Torres clubbed and choked her in the street and "left her . . . for dead," his wife Caterina stood over her mocking, "'whore, bitch, beggar; didn't I tell you that I would see to it that you have a bad evening?'"[43] An argument between Maciana, wife of the squire Jacme de Monfort, and Maciana, wife of the farmer Joan Navarro, resulted in the justice compelling the two Macianas to swear not to harm each other. Nevertheless, Maciana Monfort subsequently insulted the Navarros and threatened the wife that she would have her face slashed and then have her killed. Her husband Jacme later entered the Navarros' house and cut Maciana's face with a dagger.[44]

Such violence gravely affronted the male kin of the victimized woman, for it was a public demonstration of their inability to protect their women from the brutal attentions of other men. It therefore exacerbated animosities and had the potential to transform a dispute between families into murderous battles between armed men. The exchange of words over some "matter of pasturage" between Francesca, the carter Pere Ledo's wife, and Simona, spouse of the tavern-keeper Arnau Punyet, moved Pere Ledo to strike Simona on the head with the shaft of his lance at the door of the

Punyets' house. Despite the peacemaking efforts of friends and neighbors, an armed melee eventually took place during which Pere Ledo and the Punyets' son-in-law were killed.[45]

Plaintiffs in the Criminal Justice's court often accused women of conspiring with and inciting their husbands, sons, and sons-in-law to perpetrate violence. After Johan de Sallas attacked him while he was sitting outside his house and cut off his hand, the wooldresser Beneyto Simó denounced both Sallas and his wife Marieta, describing her as the "plotter, performer, and instigator" of the crime.[46] It was women, however, who most often accused other women of responsibility for their men's bloodshed. On the basis of their own experience, they had no doubts about the voice that wives had in the nuclear family's political decision-making. In circumstances of uxorilocal residence, in which a wife's dowry had come with a house and her widowed mother, female plaintiffs presumed that a man's mother-in-law also weighed in, for she was still intent on maintaining the good name of her household. According to the widow Elionor, the mother-in-law and wife of the metalworker Gaspar Lopiç both persuaded him to beat her up because she had not spoken to them "with due reverence."[47] The widow Caterina alleged that Na Caneta, the mother-in-law of Beneyto de Campos, had admonished him to assault her with these words: "'I promise God that if you do not slash Na Caterina on the face ... you will not be worthy to enter this house.'"[48] Beneyto dutifully cut Caterina across the nose and cheeks.

Usually, however, a man did not have his mother-in-law living with him and his wife under the same roof, even if he still benefited from having affinal allies. In any case, his wife's substantial contribution to the household economy, through her dowry and through her labor, lent her political opinions considerable weight and made him amenable to her counsel.[49] Wives, after all, understood as well as their husbands what was good for the reputation of the family and how that reputation could best be enhanced or defended. Johana, wife of the esparto-worker Arnau Llorenç, accused Caterina, the baker Miquel Manyiques' wife, of threatening to dishonor her family and to pay her back after the Manyiques took umbrage at the Llorençs' refusal to marry their daughter Dolça to the Manyiques' friend Jacme Barrassa. Caterina and her husband then allegedly instructed their son and the spurned suitor to dishonor Dolça publicly by seizing her and kissing her as she exited Mass and to beat Johana with a stick as she stood at the door of her house.[50] In her account of the events that ended with the wounding of her son Johan, Francesca, the wife of Pere Domingo, described Caterina, the wife of their enemy, the notary Johan Gil, telling her husband that if he "was not [man] enough to punish . . . Pere and Johan Domingo, she would have them punished." Caterina and Gil often quarreled about this; she would nag at him, "'Why haven't you killed or punished Pere and Johan Domingo? . . . Already you have delayed much too long.'"[51] Plaintiffs like Francesca had little difficulty imagining such domestic dialogues because they themselves and their female relatives and friends were equally adept at goading their men into violence.

Upright wives depicted women involved in extramarital relationships as operating in a slightly different manner. These infamous and promiscuous *amigas* used their bodies to persuade their lovers to attack and dishonor their enemies. Johana, wife of the sailor Miquel de Moros, accused Caterina la Romana of telling her lover Eximo de Novalles, "'Cut the face of that vile whore Johana, or at least give her some good blows with your buckler inside her house . . . in a manner that the punishment will stand for all time, and then I will do what you want.'"[52] Johana would be left with a physical mark of dishonor equivalent to Caterina's own moral stain.

The price that women paid for playing such a vital role in their family's contests with rival households was being targeted by the men of the latter.[53] Men seem to have had little or no compunction about beating up or slashing enemy women, as a number of instances above suggest; among non-elites it was acceptable, if not normative male behavior. The Criminal Justice did not specifically condemn such violence, probably because he recognized that it was deliberately restrained, if not ritualized. When families were battling for precedence in the *vehinat*, assault on a woman of a rival family was a safer way of demoting her family. Since women did not carry and use weapons, there was minimal risk of such an assault immediately degenerating into a lethal armed encounter between men. Still, as has been seen, an attack on a woman could cause an escalation in the violence between families and factions.

Women's faces were the choice targets of the men and women of opposing households. Although men sometimes scarred each other's faces, in order to leave an indelible, visible mark of their triumph over an adversary,[54] their cuts to a woman's face were meant to denote the shameful violation of her chastity while disgracing the male relatives who had proved themselves unable to protect her.[55] Women's internalization of the social attitudes underlying a rather grisly practice that could make their own face a visible marker of their family's degradation led them, as has been seen, to incite men to slash the faces of their female foes. According to female plaintiffs in court, women who uttered threats about what was in store for them often used the phrase "*senyalar*" or "*marcar la cara*," that is, "to make a sign on" or "to mark the face."[56] Women literally had more face to save and more face to lose than their men. Their bodies were the real and symbolic field upon which Valencian households battled for prestige.

Violence was most resonant when it was perpetrated publicly inside or at the door of the adversary's *alberch*, which was thus the preferred site for the performance of violence, just as it was for the chanting of insults. Household assaults varied in intensity and in the amount of bodily damage the attackers inflicted, ranging from bloodless belligerent gesturing in the street outside to, rarely, homicide inside the house. Given the interchangeability of the *alberch* and the female body in the minds of Valencians, the *alberch*'s doors and windows were viewed, in certain circumstances, as orifices of a woman's body.[57] Jacme Carasquer assaulted the house of the merchant Bernat Sanç and his wife Mariana by showing up in front of it with a naked dagger and demonstratively unsheathing his sword. Carasquer screamed at Bernat, "'Come out traitor and I'll cut off your beard!'" Then, while shouting other insults, he "gave great stabs and blows to the door of the said plaintiff [Bernat]."[58] Carasquer, in short, threatened to emasculate Bernat by removing his beard, thus leaving the house—and Mariana—defenseless. His treatment of the door communicated what could happen to Mariana in an unguarded *alberch*.

Still, in the overwhelming majority of cases recorded in the Criminal Justice's registers, armed men committed *combatiment de alberch* by bursting through its doors; their targets were usually the men of the household.

Murder, however, was rarely the aim of these ritual acts of violence; dishonoring the victim was. For example, the broker Anthoni de la Barba and three of his friends, who were allegedly armed to the teeth, invaded the house of the broker Johan Climent and his wife Marieta as they sat down to dinner. They wounded Johan on the left hand and the left ear with a sword.[59] For the male victims, being bested and wounded anywhere by known enemies was degrading enough, but suffering such treatment inside their own abode, the embodiment of their family's honor, was particularly ignominious. Through breaching the boundaries of the house—the metaphorical female body—the invaders symbolically threatened the real bodies of the women within; and by bloodying the men of the house, they showed that the women were defenseless and at risk. Caterina, wife of the mason Johan Buixó, thus complained that the Martís, a father and three sons, one of whom was also a mason, not only "broke down the doors and entered the house and . . . wounded her husband on the right hand"; they also called him "cuckold."[60] The Martís suggested that Johan could neither protect himself and his household nor guard his wife.[61] The aforementioned denunciation of Damiata Forcadell clearly and creatively deciphered the message that her family's enemies sent when they spilled her husband Daniel's blood inside the walls of their house.

Women, as is obvious in a number of cases cited above, frequently suffered bodily harm during household assaults. It was not accidental. The male attackers were making the statement that if they could enter the house to beat and bloody a woman, they could have raped her as well.[62] Some of them expressed the meaning of their actions in the insults they shouted at their female victims while physically abusing them. When the weavers Domingo Guarcia and Pasquall Vicent pummeled Johana, the wife of Johan Sanxez, at the door of her house, they chanted ten times "slut, whore, go-between." Johana took care to contest this symbolic desecration of her house and body by maintaining publicly, in court, that she was a "good woman and a reputable woman."[63]

Perpetrators of household assaults took a more serious step when they slashed the face of a woman of the house, leaving a scar that judicial claims and testimonies as to the victim's sterling character could not erase. The squire

Martí Roiç complained to the justice that the weaver Pere Fogon had broken the "peace and truce" affirmed between them the previous year by coming into his house and wounding his wife Pasqualla with a knife "on the left side of her face."[64] Roiç would not likely have left avenging Pasqualla to the discretion of the Criminal Justice alone. Cutting a woman's face anywhere, as noted above, signified a violation of her chastity, but doing it inside her house was an iteration of symbolic rape, a still more graphic way of dishonoring a woman and her family through a ritual in which the woman's body, already violated symbolically through household invasion, or really, through physical assault, became the permanent register of her family's dishonor.

The many symbolic and actual assaults on women's bodies and the houses that were supposed to protect them repeatedly accentuated the necessity of safeguarding these same bodies, real and metaphorical, in order to ensure the legitimacy of each family's offspring and to preserve the social order of Christian community and kingdom. Violent, immoral chaos would ensue if houses were unguarded and women were promiscuous. A *demanda* presented by the notary Martí d'Alagó on behalf of his clients, four farmers and artisans, reflects the association that Valencians made between the house, the female body, and the social order. The four men were requesting that Guisabel, wife of the weaver Johan Guirau, be ejected from their neighborhood. The *demanda* described the plaintiffs as solid citizens "who have their domiciles or *alberchs* with their wives and companions [apprentices or employees], exercising . . . their crafts and trades simply and honestly."[65] Their wives and houses came together, as if interchangeable; they were clearly secure. Guisabel, on the other hand, was a quarrelsome woman with a foul mouth who "every day provokes rows and brawls with the neighbors . . . and with their wives and companions, and for no reason she abuses and dishonors them."[66] Because of her, "the whole neighborhood" was "roused"; armed, deadly fights erupted.[67] The ultimate source of all of this tumult was Guisabel's body and house. Guisabel, the plaintiffs claimed, "is a bad woman in regard to her body such that day and night she receives men in her house for the purpose of fornication . . . with the result that the neighbors do not dare to leave their houses without great mistrust . . . of the people who enter and exit the house of the said woman armed."[68] Guisabel's promiscuous and uncontrolled body, then, was like her unguarded house: men—armed men—had easy access to and could freely enter both. Open houses and female bodies opened neighborhoods to anarchic, murderous violence.

This description of Guisabel would seem to support Joly's assertion that women caused most murders in Valencia, but the plaintiffs' portrait of Guisabel was in all likelihood exaggerated, a pointed exception to the rule of how most Valencian wives, such as their own wives, conducted, or were supposed to conduct, themselves. Whether chaste and honorable like the plaintiffs' wives, or promiscuous and infamous like Guisabel, women and their bodies—real and metaphorical—were at the center of the violent contests that constituted political life in Valencia's Christian communities. No woman or man could imagine a future that did not involve defending or attacking women. Their honor depended on it.

NOTES

1. On the court of the Criminal Justice and violence in Valencia, see Roca Traver, *Justicia de Valencia*; Narbona Vizcaíno, *Malhechores, violencia y justicia*; Pérez García, *Comparsa de los malhechores*. My analysis of the court records has a significantly different emphasis than theirs; none of them deal with the role of women in violent conflict.

2. Archivo del Reino de Valencia [ARV]: Justicia Criminal [JC] 21: Manus [M] 4, no foliation (May 25, 1440); JC 97: case no. 29, no foliation (May 30). Case inconclusive.

3. Simmel, *Conflict*, 17–20, is the classic statement regarding "conflict as an integrative force in the group." See also Gilmore, *Aggression and Community*.

4. Clerical violence was also common in the kingdom of Valencia, though the extant fragmentary diocesan records do not contain many cases of the victimization of women specifically. See Meyerson, "Clerical Violence."

5. Escriche Rivas, "Injurias, amenazas," 129, mentions an assault on the house of the *jurat* Bartomeu Cardona in 1333 in rural Alcoi. Villages in the irrigated Horta of the city of Valencia, which fell under the Criminal Justice's jurisdiction, were also sites of household assaults. For example, in Campanar, Jaume Pasqual allegedly forced his way into the *alberch* of Bernat Pasqual, called his wife Guisabell "vile whore" four or five times and struck her with a club (ARV: JC 40: M 4, 40r–41r [July 15, 1377]).

6. For the house as a female body, see Dubisch, "Culture Enters through the Kitchen," 201–10; Giovannini, "Woman," 412–15, 420–21; Bahloul, *Architecture of Memory*, 22, 30–33, 51–53, 128–30; and Baker, "'Ordering the House,'" who notes (223) that "from . . . the fifth century BCE, and earlier, the equation of woman/wife with house/household becomes so familiar in literatures and images throughout the classical and late ancient Mediterranean as to be entirely unremarkable."

7. Ortner, "On Key Symbols," 1340–42.

8. On the Christian conquest, Muslim revolt, dispossession of Muslims, and allocation of their property to Christians through the process of *repartiment*, see Burns, *Islam under the Crusaders*; Guichard, *Musulmans de Valence*; Torró, *Naixement d'una colònia*; and Glick, *From Muslim Fortress to Christian Castle*, 92–166.

9. Das, *Life and Words*, 18–38, writes in regard to the violence occurring during the Partition of India and Pakistan in 1946–1947: "the imagination of a social contract that would inaugurate the nation-state saw men as heads of households—husbands and fathers—who became authorized to initiate the advent of the nation-state only after they had shown themselves capable of offering protection to women defined as 'their own women' from men of the enemy community."

10. My interpretation of the origins of *combatiment de alberch* in the kingdom of Valencia is inferential, based on the evidence of the kingdom's laws, the *Furs*, and court cases. King Jaume I (d. 1276), the Conqueror, addresses the practice in his laws; see *Furs*, 7: 115 (Llibre 9. Rúbrica 8.8). The commission of combatiment de alberch was certainly widespread in other Valencian towns. Viciano, "Violencia y sociedad," 856, found that one half of the acts of violence perpetrated within the walls of Castellón between 1416 and 1495 occurred within "the private sphere of the house." (Only one of these cases involved spousal abuse.) Viciano, however, does not comment on the social and cultural significance of the violent acts, and he incorrectly describes them as "spontaneous (854, 878)" when they were in fact deliberate performances of violence meant to dishonor the victims in the eyes of their neighbors. Sabaté, "Femmes et violence," 301–2, observes the relative frequency of household assaults and invasions in Catalonia without analyzing them, though he does point out, significantly, that conflicts between *bandos* often caused them (311). See also, Cohen, "Honor and Gender," who treats the less violent ritual of "house scorning," which involved the hurling of insults as well as garbage and excrement at the targeted house.

11. Extant *Cèdules* registers from 1401–1402, ARV: JC 15–16, which record the day-to-day activities of the Criminal Justice and his men, provide some sense of just how normative a practice combatiment de alberch was. In 1401 the justice received eighty-one complaints about acts of violence perpetrated inside or at the door of

the plaintiff's house; in 1402, seventy-four such complaints were heard. The city's intramural population at the time numbered less than 36,000, the total in 1418. These household assaults occurred only a few years after Martí I had attempted to outlaw them by threatening perpetrators with capital punishment, first in the city of Valencia in 1398 and then throughout the kingdom in 1403. See *Furs*, 7: 116–19 (Llibre 9. Rúbrica 8.9–10).

12. A good amount of anthropological scholarship treats this theme. For example, Gilmore, "Why Sexual Segregation?"; Delaney, *Seed and the Soil*, 39–40, 107; Delaney, "Seeds of Honor," 39–44; Wilson, *Feuding, Conflict and Banditry*, 211–15; Herzfeld, *Poetics of Manhood*, 66, 227–28.

13. Gilmore, "Why Sexual Segregation?" 119, summing up the scholarship on the subject.

14. As Maria Vazques put it, when she denounced the converso Aymerich Donat for attacking her inside her house: she should have been "secure inside her house, which is just like a castle to her." ARV: JC 42: M 1, 22r–23v (May 16, 1396). For relevant anthropological literature, see Pitt-Rivers, *Fate of Shechem*, 116–19; Bourdieu, "Sentiment of Honour in Kabyle Society," 216–24; Campbell, *Honour, Family and Patronage*, 292–93.

15. The *procurador* of Anthonia, Jacme Bernat's widow, argued that his client could not have struck the plaintiff Miquel Ducles on the nose with a rock on a particular winter evening in 1377 since she had been in her house "just like a good woman." ARV: JC 40: M 1, 38r (January 29, 1377).

16. Iradiel, "Familia y función de la mujer," which deals specifically with Valencia.

17. Herzfeld, "Within and Without," 215–33, emphasizes that the stereotypes of women as "interior" beings and men as "exterior" beings are at the same time highly evocative and manipulable. Bringa, *Being Muslim the Bosnian Way*, 87–91, while discussing "the house embodied," also notes the tension between the ideal and reality, between men's wishes and women's social and economic activities. In the medieval context, see Riddy, "Looking Closely," 220–27.

18. *Furs*, 7: 119 (Llibre 9. Rúbrica 8.11). The realization that household assaults were part and parcel of neighborhood politics moved Alfonso to annul Martí's harsh penalties (see n.11) in those cases in which only neighbors were involved.

19. Furió, *Història del País Valencià*, 124–28, 184–91. In 1489 the city had a population of 70,000.

20. Cruselles Gómez, "Población de la ciudad de Valencia"; and Navarro Espinach, Igual Luis, and Aparici Martí, "Los inmigrantes."

21. Pitt-Rivers, "Honour and Social Status," 21, 24, where he notes that in the competition for honor "the victor . . . finds his reputation enhanced by the humiliation of the vanquished."

22. Campbell, *Honour, Family and Patronage*, 269. There is no one definition of honor in the anthropological literature that precisely fits Christian society in late medieval Valencia. Valencians, in their many pleas and depositions, did not define or express what they meant by honor; rather, they frequently spoke of "dishonor" and of "injuries" to their honor. Honor was something that the individual and his or her family were presumed to possess; it could be sullied, damaged, or lost. The works that accord best with the Valencian situation are Campbell's, 268–72, 306–9, 320; and John Corbin's discussion of the politics of the calle in which "[e]ach man . . . defends his own honour, questions the integrity of his opponents and discusses that of others" in "Insurrections in Spain," 31–33, 47. Corbin also points out that the most serious acts of violence occurred at the "casa/calle boundary" when the boundary was transgressed.

23. Friedrich, "Sanity and the Myth of Honor," 284.

24. ARV: JC 40: M 1, 20r–v, 37r–48v; M 2, 18r–29v (January 29, 1377). In this case, Ducles, an agricultural laborer, was laying charges not against Gomar but against Anthonia, the widow of Jacme Bernat (see n.15). Though Ducles did not mention his fight with Gomar in his accusations, it is clear from the testimony of Dolçeta and other witnesses that Anthonia threw the stone at Ducles while he was occupied with Gomar. The justice acquitted Anthonia; Ducles appealed the decision.

25. ARV: JC 40: M 7, 4r–7v; M 9, 1r–4v, 27r–32v; M 10, 33r–38v (October 16, 1377). Pasqualla's attack was her response to Caterina's verbal insults and accusations that she had taken the feathers from a pillow that had been borrowed from Caterina for the use of a woman giving birth in the neighborhood. The justice fined Pasqualla thirty morabatíns for the assault and Caterina ten morabatíns for the insults. Pasqualla objected and pleaded poverty.

26. ARV: JC 40: M 10, 34r bis (October 24, 1377). Case inconclusive.

27. ARV: JC 41: M 1, 1r–v; M 2, 1r (January 2, 1395). The plaintiff, "G," was contrasting her 'Valencian' posture with that of Agnes, a Castilian or Portuguese woman and spouse of the squire Andrés López, who allegedly was "vile with her body and worse with her tongue . . . such that . . . she has hardly been able to find a place in Valencia to stay . . . for within the space of a year . . . her neighbors have thrown her out." G. accused Agnes of assaulting her. Case inconclusive.

28. Some other examples are ARV: JC 41: M 1, 20r–v; M 2, 31r (July 28, 1395): the sifter Matheu de Vallterra is accused of clubbing Johana, wife of the tile-maker Ramon Bonet, as she sat at the portal of her house; and JC 43: M 2, 26r–27r (June 16, 1397): Guillamona, wife of the sailor Pere Telleca, denounces the sailor Francesc Boyx for punching, kicking, and stabbing her when she was sitting "simply and honestly at the door of her house." Both cases inconclusive.

29. Viciano, "Violencia y sociedad," 858, 866; Sabaté, "Femmes et violence," 280; Lesnick, "Insults," 76; and Davis, *Fiction in the Archives*, 79–81.

30. ARV: JC 53: M 1, 24v–29v (1456).

31. Bremmer, "Insults Hurt," 96, asserts that insults said more than once were not impulsive but indicative of a premeditated intention to dishonor. Much more could be said about the meaning and efficacy of such repetitive, ritualized insults, which had the quality of an incantation. Suffice it to say here that I think that Dean, "Gender and Insult," 222, draws too sharp a distinction between "ritual insult" and "real insult." I agree with Spierenburg, "Knife Fighting," 111, as to the combination of ritual and deeply felt emotion in premodern aggressive exchanges. See also Neu, *Sticks and Stones*, 123–24.

32. ARV: JC 42: M 1, 43r–44v (July 7, 1396); just the demanda.

33. ARV: JC 41: M 1, 3r–v; M 2, 3r–4v, 7r–8r (February 13, 1395). Caterina responded in court to this *demanda* with the claim that, in fact, Barchinona had insulted her when she was at the door of her house, calling her, nine or ten times, "vile, old, hunchbacked whore, pimp." According to Caterina, the many neighbors and passersby who heard the insults were favorably impressed by the "great sufferance and patience with which she heard or bore the injurious words said to her."

34. Madero, *Manos violentas*, 65–68, 110–11; Sabaté, "Femmes et violence," 280; Córdoba de la Llave, "Violencia cotidiana," 417–18; Lesnick, "Insults," 76–78; and Ewan, "'Many Injurious Words,'" 166–69; Blok, "Rams and Billy-Goats," 428–31.

35. ARV: JC 42: M 4, 39r–40r (September 27, 1396). Johana dropped the charges the next day. Johana may have been a convert from Islam, for she was "alias appellada Mari Sarrana," perhaps meaning *Sarraina* or Saracen; it could also have meant *Serrana*, from the mountains. See also Sabaté, "Femmes et violence," 280, for insults regarding alleged Muslim lineage.

36. ARV: JC 16: M 7, 28r (July 1, 1402); Cavaller dropped the charges four days later.

37. For example, ARV: JC 39: M 2, 18r–20v (March 15, 1361): the prostitute Maria allegedly called Geralda, the daughter of Jacme Moner, a whore and *traydora* who acted as a procuress for her own daughter.

38. See the useful comments of Garrioch, "Verbal Insults," 113.

39. See Smail, *Consumption of Justice*, 90, who notes that there was "a basic equivalency between brawls, insults and lawsuits; they were all ways to instantiate and publicize existing animosities"; and Cohn, *Women in the Streets*, 16–38, who discusses the declining presence of women in Florence's criminal tribunals between the mid-fourteenth and mid-fifteenth centuries.

40. ARV: JC 46: M 1, 50r–v; M 3, 25r–28v; M 4, 16r–v (March 4, 1387); Pere's complaint is on M 3, 26v. Case inconclusive.

41. There are a number of cases in which women denounced other women for physical assault—for example, ARV: JC 39: M 1, 32r–v (February 20, 1361): Jacmeta, wife of Johan Ferrandez, accuses Maria, the wife of Domingo Gil, of punching her on the head and face and tearing out her hair. Case inconclusive.

42. Sabaté, "Femmes et violence," 310; compare Córdoba de la Llave, "Violencia cotidiana," 407–9, who emphasizes the role of women as mediators and peacemakers.

43. ARV: JC 39: M 2, 42r–45v; M 3, 8r–10v (May 13, 1361). Case inconclusive.

44. ARV: JC 39: M 5, 28r–29v (November 13, 1361). The justice evidently took with a grain of salt the Navarros' accusation that Jacme would have slit Maciana's throat if some neighbors had not stopped him. The Monforts appeared in court and were told to return four days later to respond to the *demanda*. Case inconclusive. When the two Macianas had sworn not to harm each other it was through a mutual "assurance" or *asegurament* administered by the justice. On this institution, see Ferrero Micó, "Pau e Treua en Valencia."

45. ARV: JC 47: M 1, 2r–v; M 2, 30r–36v, 39r–v, 43r–48v; M 3, 1r–4v, 12r–27v; M 4, 10r–11v; M 5, 24r–48v; M 6, 16r–48v; M 7, 1r–v (January 15, 1396). This inconclusive case is Francesca Ledo's denunciation of the Punyets and their accomplices for the murder of Pere Ledo. JC 47: M 1, 21r–v; M 5, 1r–6r (April 24, 1396) concerns the denunciation made by Catalina, the Punyets' daughter and widow of the slain silversmith Johan Lopez, against Nicholau Ledo, son of Pere Ledo, Miquel and Berenguer Pastor, Nicholau's in-laws, and others. On April 29 the lieutenant governor, Pere Morera, informed the Criminal Justice that he had just supervised a "final peace" between Nicholau Ledo and his accomplices and the guardian of the children of Johan Lopez.

46. ARV: JC 37: 22r–30v, 36r–38r (February 13, 1351). The justice arrested Marieta and released her on bail; her husband, however, was contumacious. The justice sentenced de Sallas to pay Simó 500 sous per year for the rest of the latter's life, since the wound had left him crippled and unable to work.

47. ARV: JC 52: M 1, 27r; M 5, 3r–4v, 4r bis (November 4, 1454).

48. ARV: JC 41: M 1, 23r–v; M 2, 36r–38v (August 16, 1395). Na Caneta's threat to Beneyto allegedly occurred after her daughter (and Beneyto's wife) Francesca "promised" Caterina that she would see to it that someone "slashed her face." The lieutenant Criminal Justice apprehended Beneyto holding the bloody knife and jailed him. His wife and mother-in-law were not at home when the justice's messenger summoned them to appear in court. Case inconclusive.

49. Wessell Lightfoot, *Women, Dowries and Agency.*

50. ARV: JC 52: M1, 14r; M 3, 14r–19v (June 8, 1454). It is interesting that when Caterina allegedly threatened Johana, Caterina's husband and son were present, but they were silent, only adding "heat and strength" to the words of Caterina,

who did all the talking. Johana also accused Caterina of trying to bring off the marriage through sorcery by attempting to procure some of Dolça's hair and knitting needles (she obtained the former but not the latter). The response of Caterina and Miquel Manyiques to Johana's accusations was that they themselves had nothing to do with either affront to the Llorenços. They heard about Barrassa kissing Dolça, though their son, Miquel Jr., was not involved. They admitted that Miquel Jr. had indeed beaten Johana for verbally dishonoring his mother, but Barrassa was not involved. The case file ends without either Barrassa or Miquel Jr. having appeared in court, though not enough time had passed for the justice to have declared them contumacious.

51. ARV: JC 52: M 1, 4v; M 2, 9r–20r (March 26, 1454). Animosity between the families apparently began when Johan Domingo sued Johan Gil in the episcopal court in regard to Gil's administration of his sister's will. The course of events is unclear. Francesca, the plaintiff, maintained that Gil, at Caterina's urging, hired laborers expressly to kill or wound her son and husband. There was in fact an armed clash between the laborers, who were spreading manure on Gil's fields, and Johan Domingo and his father, who were visiting their adjacent field. Johan Domingo suffered a wound to the head. Caterina, Gil, and the laborers, however, asserted that it was the Domingos' threats to assault her—for example, "'You vile, dirty woman, I'll break your face'"—that sparked the fight that led to Johan Domingo's wounding. Case inconclusive.

52. ARV: JC 49: M 11, 25r–v; M 12, 29r–31r (November 15, 1399). According to Johana, Caterina, who lived in the house behind hers, had first come to her house as she sat in front chatting with a neighbor and insulted her ("shitty whore, brothel-keeper") and threatened to have Eximo assault her. Eximo indeed burst into her house when she and her husband were eating dinner. Eximo struck Johana five times on the head with his buckler and wounded her on the left hand with his sword, which he also used to take a swipe at her husband. Johana dropped the charges three days later, out of a stated desire to have peace and concord with Caterina. A similar example is JC 52: M 1, 27r; M 3, 42r–46r (October 3, 1454): Ysabel, wife of the "citizen" Johan de Monblanch, accuses Ysabel Munyoç, amiga of the mason Jaume Vilaplana, of persuading her lover and at least five other men to ambush Monblanch by offering them her body and other gifts. After wounding Monblanch severely on the leg, the assailants fled the city. The justice sentenced Vilaplana and the mason Pere Gombau, the principal attackers, to death by hanging should they be captured.

53. Viciano, "Violencia y sociedad," 865–66, notes, with little explanation, the victimization of women, often by their neighbors.

54. For example, ARV: JC 99: no. 8, no foliation: the broker Bernat Jaqua accuses one Bernat Blanch of slashing his face. Some other discussions of attacks on the faces of men and women in premodern times are Skinner, *Living with Disfigurement*, 41–101, and 133–58 regarding women; Groebner, "Losing Face, Saving Face"; Groebner, *Defaced*, 67–86; Cohen, "Lay Liturgy of Affront," 863. Valencians, however, seem not to have targeted women's noses in particular, as was the case in the societies discussed by Skinner and Groebner, and in the Bible.

55. Kelleher, *The Measure of Woman*, 133, points out that many law codes "required a raped woman to demonstrate distress and anguish . . . by raking her cheeks with her nails until she drew blood"; see also Dillard, *Daughters of the Reconquest*, 181–85; and Madero, *Manos violentas*, 51–53, 113–16. In Valencia, then, in cases of both real and symbolic rape, women's faces would bear the scars of their anguish. It is important to note, however, that in the aggressive status competition and occasional blood feuds between Valencian Christian families, men did not employ rape—real rape—against the women of rival families as a means of dishonoring them; in this context, rape was always symbolic. See also Blok, "Rams and Billy Goats," 433, who notes that the Sicilian practice of *sfregio*—disfiguring someone by cutting her or his cheek—is also used to denote any willful infringement of property rights, including the violation of a woman's chastity.

56. For example, ARV: JC 40: M 4, 12r–13v; M 5, 9r–11v (May 25, 1377): Pasquala, the daughter of Jacme Vidal, maintains that when she had words with two women, Alichsen and Benvenguda, they threatened to have someone "make a sign on her face" (*senyalar la cara sua*). The pair then allegedly paid two journeymen weavers to carry out their threat. Pasquala managed to protect her face from their daggers by raising her cape over it. Case inconclusive. The widow Romia allegedly threatened Peyrona, Pascual de Palacio's wife, with "'whore . . . I'll have your face marked'"—JC 40: M 4, 17r–v; M 5, 16r–18r (June 2, 1377).

57. Cohen, "Lay Liturgy of Affront," 864, sees the same thing in Italy.

58. ARV: JC 16: M 8, 14v (July 24, 1402). Carasquer responded to the Sanç' accusations with the *clam* that the latter, along with their slave woman, had climbed up to the windows of his house and thrown tiles at him and his wife inside (M 8, 14v, 16r). The justice then forbade both men to go beyond the thresholds of their own houses without his permission, on pain of a 200-morabatín fine (M 8, 16r–v).

59. ARV: JC 45: M 14, 5r–7v, 21r–v (July 19, 1380). This attack violated the *aseguramant* they had made to the Climents. On August 27, Barba appeared in the Criminal Justice's court and paid Johan Climent forty florins as compensation for the wounds inflicted.

60. ARV: JC 15: M 7, 28r bis (August 12, 1401).

61. A similar example is ARV: JC 15: M 4, 8v (April 6, 1401). The rope maker Berenguer Jusó informed the justice that his colleague Anthoni Simó had come to his house intending to kill him and had unsheathed his sword; this occurred, he claimed, only after he had found Simó in his house with his wife. In this case, Jusó's anxiety about Simó's attentions to his wife translated into the accusation that Simó intended to assault him and his house with his unsheathed (phallic) sword. The mental association that Jusó drew between Simó's possible violation of his wife's body and his possible violation of their shared domestic space is clear. Either way, Jusó and his household would have been dishonored.

62. Kelleher, *Measure of Woman*, 132, in her discussion of "home invasion narratives" involving attempted rape, suggests that "the violent invasion of the home might well be a stand-in for the violent invasion of the body." Sabaté, "Femmes et violence," 296–98, notes that in Catalonia, around half of the denunciations for rape were cases of attempted rape and that a fifth of these were attempted inside the house of the targeted woman. He asserts that in some of these cases the attempt was meant only to dishonor the victim. Herzfeld, "'As in Your Own House,'" 76, notes that in a Rhodian village "a man who had raped a young woman was said to have 'entered her father's house.'"

63. ARV: JC 41: M 1, 19r–v (July 19, 1395). Case inconclusive.

64. ARV: JC 16: M 5, 3r (April 4, 1402).

65. ARV: JC 42: M 1, 7r–v (March 6, 1396). Case inconclusive.

66. ARV: JC 42: M 1, 7r–v (March 6, 1396). Case inconclusive.

67. ARV: JC 42: M 1, 7r–v (March 6, 1396). Case inconclusive.

68. ARV: JC 42: M 1, 7r–v (March 6, 1396). Case inconclusive.

BIBLIOGRAPHY

Primary Sources

ARV. Archivo del Reino de Valencia

    JC. Justicia Criminal

    M. Manus

    Furs de València. Edited by Germà Colon and Arcadi Garcia. 9 vols. Barcelona: Editorial Barcino, 1970–2002.

Secondary Sources

Bahloul, Joelle. *The Architecture of Memory: A Jewish-Muslim Household in Colonial Algeria, 1937–1962*. Translated by Catherine du Peloux Ménagé. Cambridge: Cambridge University Press, 1996.

Baker, Cynthia M. "'Ordering the House': On the Domestication of Jewish Bodies." In *Parchments of Gender: Deciphering the Bodies of Antiquity*, edited by Maria Wyke, 221–42. Oxford: Clarendon Press, 1998.

Blok, Anton. "Rams and Billy-Goats: A Key to the Mediterranean Code of Honor." *Man* n.s. 16 (1981): 427–40.

Bourdieu, Pierre. "The Sentiment of Honour in Kabyle Society." In *Honour and Shame: The Values of Mediterranean Society*, edited by J. G. Peristiany, 193–241. London: Weidenfeld and Nicolson, 1966.

Bremmer Jr., Rolf H. "Insults Hurt: Verbal Injury in Late Medieval Frisia." In *Approaches to Old Frisian Philology*, edited by Rolf H. Bremmer Jr., Thomas Johnston, and Oebele Vries, 89–112. Amsterdam: Rodopi, 1998.

Bringa, Tone. *Being Muslim the Bosnian Way: Identity and Community in a Central Bosnian Village*. Princeton: Princeton University Press, 1995.

Burns, Robert I. *Islam under the Crusaders: Colonial Survival in the Thirteenth-Century Kingdom of Valencia*. Princeton: Princeton University Press, 1973.

Campbell, J. K. *Honour, Family and Patronage: A Study of Institutions and Moral Values in a Greek Mountain Community*. Oxford: Clarendon, 1964.

Cohen, Elizabeth S. "Honor and Gender in the Streets of Early Modern Rome." *Journal of Interdisciplinary History* 22 (1992): 597–625.

Cohen, Thomas V. "The Lay Liturgy of Affront in Sixteenth-Century Italy." *Journal of Social History* 25 (1992): 857–77.

Cohn Jr., Samuel K. *Women in the Streets: Essays on Sex and Power in Renaissance Italy*. Baltimore: Johns Hopkins University Press, 1996.

Corbin, John. "Insurrections in Spain: Casas Viejas 1933 and Madrid 1981." In *The Anthropology of Violence*, edited by David Riches, 28–49. Oxford: Basil Blackwell, 1986.

Córdoba de la Llave, Ricardo. "Violencia cotidiana en Castilla a fines de la Edad Media." In *Conflictos sociales, politicos e intelectuales en la España de los siglos XIV y XV*, 393–443. Logroño: Instituto de Estudios Riojanos, 2004.

Cruselles Gómez, Enrique. "La población de la ciudad de Valencia en los siglos XIV y XV." *Revista d'Història Medieval* 10 (1999): 45–84.

Das, Veena. *Life and Words: Violence and the Descent into the Ordinary*. Berkeley: University of California Press, 2007.

Davis, Natalie Zemon. *Fiction in the Archives: Pardon Tales and Their Tellers in Sixteenth Century France*. Stanford: Stanford University Press, 1987.

Dean, Trevor. "Gender and Insult in an Italian City: Bologna in the later Middle Ages." *Social History* 29 (2004): 217–31.

Delaney, Carol. *The Seed and the Soil*. Berkeley: University of California Press, 1991.

———. "Seeds of Honor, Field of Shame." In *Honor and Shame and the Unity of the Mediterranean*, edited by David Gilmore, 35–48. Washington DC: American Anthropological Association, 1987.

Dillard, Heath. *Daughters of the Reconquest: Women in Castilian Town Society, 1100–1300*. Cambridge: Cambridge University Press, 1984.

Dubisch, Jill. "Culture Enters through the Kitchen: Women, Food, and Social Boundaries in Rural Greece." In *Gender and Power in Rural Greece*, edited by Jill Dubisch, 195–214. Princeton: Princeton University Press, 1986.

Escriche Rivas, Benjamín. "Injurias, amenazas y agresiones. La violencia cotidiana en el mundo rural valenciano bajomedieval: Alcoi (1320–1335)." In *Condicions de vida al món rural. Cinquè Congrés sobre sistemes agraris, organització social i poder local*, edited by Jordi Bolòs, Antonieta Jarne, and Enric Vicedo, 115–30. Lleida: Diputació de Lleida, 2006.

Ewan, Elizabeth. "'Many Injurious Words': Defamation and Gender in Late Medieval Scotland." In *History, Literature, and Music in Scotland, 700–1560*, edited by Andrew R. McDonald, 163–86. Toronto: University of Toronto, Press, 2002.

Ferrero Micó, R. "Pau e Treua en Valencia." In *Estudios dedicados a Juan Peset Aleixandre*, Vol. 2, 1–15. Valencia: Universidad de Valencia, 1982.

Friedrich, Paul. "Sanity and the Myth of Honor: The Problem of Achilles." *Ethos* 5 (1977): 281–305.

Furió, Antoni. *Història del País Valencià*. Valencia: Edicions Alfons El Magnànim, 1995.

Garrioch, David. "Verbal Insults in Eighteenth-Century Paris." In *The Social History of Language*, edited by Peter Burke and Roy Porter, 104–19. Cambridge: Cambridge University Press, 1987.

Gilmore, David D. *Aggression and Community: Paradoxes of Andalusian Culture*. New Haven: Yale University Press, 1987.

———. "Why Sexual Segregation?" In *L'anthropologie de la Méditerranée*, edited by Dionigi Albera, Anton Blok, and Christian Bromberger, 111–31. Paris: Maisonneuve et Larose, 2001.

Giovannini, Maureen J. "Woman: A Dominant Symbol within the Cultural System of a Sicilian Town." *Man* n.s. 16 (1981): 408–26.

Glick, Thomas F. *From Muslim Fortress to Christian Castle: Social and Cultural Change in Medieval Spain*. Manchester: Manchester University Press, 1995.

Groebner, Valentin. *Defaced: The Visual Culture of Violence in the Late Middle Ages*. Translated by Pamela Selwyn. New York: Zone Books, 2004.

———. "Losing Face, Saving Face: Noses and Honour in the Late Medieval Town." *History Workshop Journal* 40 (1995): 1–15.

Guichard, Pierre. *Les musulmans de Valence et la Reconquête (XIe–XIIIe siècles)*. 2 Vols. Damascus: Institut Français de Damas, 1990–1991.

Herzfeld, Michael. "'As in Your Own House': Hospitality, Ethnography, and the Stereotype of Mediterranean Society." In *Honor and Shame and the Unity of the*

Mediterranean, edited by David Gilmore, 75–89. Washington DC: American Anthropological Association, 1987.

———. *The Poetics of Manhood: Contest and Identity in a Cretan Mountain Village.* Princeton: Princeton University Press, 1985.

———. "Within and Without: The Category of 'Female' in the Ethnography of Modern Greece." In *Gender and Power in Rural Greece,* edited by Jill Dubisch, 215–33. Princeton: Princeton University Press, 1986.

Iradiel, Paulino. "Familia y función de la mujer en actividades económicas no agrarias." In *La condición de la mujer en la Edad Media,* 223–59. Madrid: Universidad Complutense, 1986.

Joly, Barthélemy. "Voyage en Espagne." *Revue hispanique* 20 (1909): 460–614.

Kelleher, Marie A. *The Measure of Woman: Law and Female Identity in the Crown of Aragon.* Philadelphia: University of Pennsylvania Press, 2010.

Lesnick, Daniel R. "Insults and Threats in Medieval Todi." *Journal of Medieval History* 17 (1991): 71–89.

Madero, Marta. *Manos violentas, palabras vedadas: la injuria en Castilla y León, siglos XIII–XV.* Madrid: Taurus Humanidades, 1992.

Meyerson, Mark. "Clerical Violence in Late Medieval Valencia." In *La Corona catalanoaragonesa, l'Islam i el món mediterrani: estudis d'història medieval en homenatge a la doctora Maria Teresa Ferrer i Mallol,* edited by Josefina Mutge Vives, Roser Salicru i Lluch, and Carles Vela Aulesa, 467–74. Barcelona: CSIC, 2013.

Narbona Vizcaíno, Rafael. *Malhechores, violencia y justicia ciudadana en la Valencia bajomedieval (1360–1399).* Valencia: Ajuntament de València, 1987.

Navarro Espinach, Germán, David Igual Luis, and Joaquín Aparici Martí, "Los inmigrantes y sus formas de inserción social en el sistema urbano del Reino de Valencia (siglos XIV–XV)." *Revista d'Història Medieval* 10 (1999): 161–97.

Neu, Jerome. *Sticks and Stones: The Philosophy of Insults.* Oxford: Oxford University Press, 2008.

Ortner, Sherry B. "On Key Symbols." *American Anthropologist* 75 (1973): 1338–46.

Pérez García, Pablo. *La comparsa de los malhechores: Valencia, 1479–1518.* Valencia: Diputació de València, 1990.

Pitt-Rivers, Julian. *The Fate of Shechem or the Politics of Sex: Essays on the Anthropology of the Mediterranean.* Cambridge: Cambridge University Press, 1977.

———. "Honour and Social Status." In *Honour and Shame: The Values of Mediterranean Society,* edited by J. G. Peristiany, 19–77. London: Weidenfeld and Nicolson, 1966.

Riddy, Felicity. "Looking Closely: Authority and Intimacy in the Late Medieval Urban House." In *Gendering the Master Narrative: Women and Power in the Middle Ages,* edited by Mary C. Erler and Maryanne Kowaleski, 212–28. Ithaca: Cornell University Press, 2003.

Roca Traver, Francisco A. *El Justicia de Valencia, 1238–1321*. Valencia: Ayuntamiento de Valencia, 1970.

Sabaté, Flocel. "Femmes et violence dans la Catalogne du XIVe siècle." *Annales du Midi* 106 (1994): 277–316.

Simmel, Georg. *Conflict and the Web of Group Affiliations*. Translated by Kurt Wolff and Reinhard Bendix. Glencoe: The Free Press, 1955.

Skinner, Patricia. *Living with Disfigurement in Early Medieval Europe*. New York: Palgrave Macmillan, 2017.

Smail, Daniel Lord. *The Consumption of Justice: Emotions, Publicity, and Legal Culture in Marseille, 1264–1423*. Ithaca: Cornell University Press, 2003.

Spierenburg, Pieter. "Knife Fighting and Popular Codes of Honor in Early Modern Amsterdam." In *Men and Violence: Gender, Honor, and Rituals in Modern Europe and America*, edited by Pieter Spierenburg, 103–27. Columbus: Ohio State University Press, 1998.

Torró, Josep. *El naixement d'una colònia. Dominació i resistència a la frontera valenciana (1238–1276)*. Valencia: Universitat de València, 1999.

Viciano, Pau. "Violencia y sociedad en una villa medieval: Castellón de la Plana en el siglo XV." *Hispania. Revista Española de Historia* 66 (2006): 851–82.

Wessell Lightfoot, Dana. *Women, Dowries and Agency: Marriage in Fifteenth-Century Valencia*. Manchester: Manchester University Press, 2013.

Wilson, Stephen. *Feuding, Conflict and Banditry in Nineteenth-Century Corsica*. Cambridge: Cambridge University Press, 1988.

6

Mixed Marriages and Community
Identity in Fifteenth-Century Girona

ALEXANDRA GUERSON AND DANA WESSELL LIGHTFOOT

On December 3, 1420, Joan Vilar, inquisitor of heretical depravity, ordered a group of men from Girona to abandon their wives.[1] Not only were they to abandon their spouses but these men were not allowed to eat, spend time, drink, sleep, buy or sell with them; nor to speak with them in their houses. If they had children, those over the age of three were to be removed from their mothers and not permitted to live with them anymore; for those under the age of three, they were allowed to remain with their mothers until they were weaned. At issue was the fact that these men were Christians, recently converted from Judaism, while their wives remained Jewish. One of the men specifically mentioned in this document was Pere Joan Falcó who had married his first cousin Regina, the daughter of Bellshom Mossé Falcó, in 1409. Pere had converted to Christianity in 1417 but remained married to Regina, who chose not to convert. In the months after the inquisitor's warning to Pere in 1420, it seems Regina faced repeated pressures to become Christian, both from her husband and other ecclesiastical officials. On April 5, 1421, Pere promised the inquisitor that Regina would convert and if she did not, he would no longer live with her without license from the inquisitor.[2] By November of the same year, Regina and Pere's union was no more, and she successfully received the return of her 3300 sous dowry from her husband, stating the reason for the dowry restitution was because of his conversion to Christianity.[3]

This series of interactions between inquisitor and mixed couples was not the first time the ecclesiastical authorities in Girona had warned converso husbands about retaining their Jewish wives. Starting in 1418, numerous documents appear in the notarial records of Girona pressuring the Jewish wives of converso husbands to convert to Christianity or end their marital unions. Indeed, the topic was a controversial one that resulted in conflict between the ecclesiastical officials of the city and the king and queen, who issued numerous royal letters chastising the bishop in particular for the great "vexations and molestations" that these families were experiencing.[4] As Natalie Oeltjen's essay in this volume shows, such "vexations" did not end with conversion. Indeed, in Mallorca, conversas saw their dowries confiscated to pay debts previously owed by the Jewish community or as punishment when their husbands fled and were considered relapsed into Judaism.[5]

Much like for the Jews of Mallorca, the last decade of the fourteenth century and the first few decades of the fifteenth century were difficult times for the Jews of Girona. While in Girona Jews were not converted en masse as they were in Mallorca, the integrity of the community was threatened by emigration, individual conversions, and a financial crisis linked to both. On August 10, 1391, the wave of violence that had hit Jewish communities throughout Castile and the Crown of Aragon reached Girona. Letters from local officials to the king reported that forty Jews were killed, while most of the community was spared by taking refuge at a local fortified tower protected by royal and municipal officials. A number of Jews converted to Christianity at that time, while others converted in the years following the Disputation of Tortosa in 1413–1414. As a result of these events, mixed families of conversos and Jews were fairly common in Girona in the first few decades of the fifteenth century. In this article, we explore the effects of conversion on the institution of marriage and the family, considering in particular the role of Jewish wives in the maintenance or destruction of these unions.

As the foundational institution of both Christian and Jewish communities, marriage played a key role in developing and maintaining communal ties. From a legal, sociological point of view, conversion should sever these bonds, but when we look closely at the effects of conversion in Girona we see that the responses were more complex. Some Jewish wives sought to preserve their connection to the Jewish community while also protecting their marriages, yet others, like Regina Falcó, chose divorce over conversion. Marriage therefore served as both a site through which community bonds were created and maintained and a site that engendered communal conflict. Of particular interest here is how conversion impacted those alliances in the community created by marriage and how it created or exacerbated conflict within marriage. By focusing on women and marriage, we can consider how individuals negotiated their identities in the early years after conversion and how Jewish and converso communities gendered religious and familial roles—how did a Jewish wife, married to a converso, fit into these two communities? Why did the husbands convert and not the wives (at least initially)? Katherine Lynch discusses the use of familial and social kin networks as a means of support in an often-shifting society.[6] The Jewish community of the late fourteenth and early fifteenth-century Girona was one whose boundaries were constantly shifting due to conversions and fiscal crises and its resulting internal/external pressures. This essay considers the various ways that Jewish wives used family networks, often despite conversion of members of those networks, as a means of support in such times of crises. It also explores how conversion could break apart marital unions under the pressure of Christian authorities, Jewish and converso community members, and kin groups.

THE ROLE OF MARRIAGE, IDEOLOGICALLY AND SOCIOECONOMICALLY

Before turning to examine the impact that conversion had on marriage, and how the shift in religious beliefs impacted the conjugal union, it is important to consider the role that marriage played from a theological and socioeconomic perspective in medieval Christian and Jewish society. Medieval Judaism perceived marriage as the best state for a person to achieve. The later Midrash on Genesis Rabba states: "Whoever has no wife is in a situation of lacking in goodness, without help, without joy, without bless-ing, without atonement ... even without peace ... without life ... nor is he a complete person."[7] While this quotation highlights the importance of marriage for men, it was perceived as equally crucial for women who "first and foremost [were perceived] as belonging to the home and the family."[8] The perception of women as married or to be married was equally preva-lent in Christianity, despite the emphasis on virginity as the highest state a Christian could achieve. Much of Christian discussion around marriage for men and women focused on its alleviation of the sin of lust, highlighting the importance of the conjugal debt. Indeed, the Catalan writer Francesc Eiximenis emphasized this point in his didactic text, *Lo llibre de les dones*, "Thus the man in knowing his wife complies with the command of God; thus, the man in knowing his wife, or the lady in claiming the conjugal debt of the man, performs a virtuous and meritorious work."[9] For Christians, marriage therefore also bound the couple to God and aided them on the path to salvation.

Not only did marriage benefit men and women individually, it also served as a foundational relationship in medieval communities. Within both Christian and Jewish doctrine, the relationships formed by marriage extended beyond the conjugal bond, connecting the couple not only to God, but also to each other's kin groups and the broader community. As James Coughlin has remarked, "medieval theory understood marriage as ... one of the primary building blocks of the social order."[10] From a socioeconomic perspective, marriage worked to create alliances between families, expanding kin groups and creating new economic ties through the exchange of property and the development of a multitude of business relationships. The two marriages of Abraham Mossé del Portal provide examples of how such connections were developed. In February of 1402, Abraham Mossé del Portal married Tolrana, the daughter of Hasday and Astruga Taroç.[11] A few months later, Abraham acted as procurator for his mother-in-law, receiving payments for debts owed to her by various Christians.[12] He also engaged in a variety of credit transactions with his father-in-law, and even conducted business with his wife's grandmother, Gràcia Cerç, who was deeply involved in the credit market of Girona.[13]

Tolrana died sometime between 1416 and 1418, and Abraham married for a second time in October of 1419, to Astruga, the daughter of Astruch Vidal Lobell and Astruga, and granddaughter of Vidal Lobell and Regina. While retaining the economic ties created through his first marriage to Tolrana, Abraham now expanded connections he had already developed with the Lobell family, as he had served with Astruga's grandfather Vidal as a secretary of the aljama in 1400 and they were still officials of the aljama in 1410 and 1415.[14] Abraham Mossé del Portal's marriages to the daughters of two prominent Jewish families in Girona demonstrate the key role that marriage played in developing cross-familial bonds that created and cemented social, economic, and political networks within a Jewish community struggling with crises, due to conversion and fiscal pressure. For both men and women, these intrafamilial ties were crucial to surviving in such a context, and thus marriage worked to deepen connections within a community beset by crises.

THEOLOGICAL ATTITUDES TOWARD MIXED MARRIAGES

What impact, therefore, did conversion have on these unions that served as the bedrock of medieval communities? Both Jews and Christians pondered this question in the Middle Ages. The effect of conversion on marriage was a topic of debate among ecclesiastical authorities from the early days of the Christian community. Since it was understood that baptism did not abolish marriage, what to do in cases of mixed marriages was a matter that preoccupied Church Fathers and canonists. The issue was discussed by Paul in I Corinthians, in which he declared:

12 For to the rest I speak, not the Lord. If any brother hath a wife that believeth not, and she consent to dwell with him, let him not put her away.

13 And if any woman hath a husband that believeth not, and he consent to dwell with her, let her not put away her husband.

14 For the unbelieving husband is sanctified by the believing wife; and the unbelieving wife is sanctified by the believing husband: otherwise your children should be unclean; but now they are holy.

15 But if the unbeliever depart, let him depart. For a brother or sister is
   not under servitude in such cases. But God hath called us in peace.

16 For how knowest thou, O wife, whether thou shalt save thy husband?
   Or how knowest thou, O man, whether thou shalt save thy wife?[15]

While seeming to protect mixed marriages, Paul's passage was interpreted in two opposing ways in the Middle Ages: some, influenced by St
Augustine, argued that conversion entitled one party to separation but not
to remarry, while others argued that if the converted party was abandoned
by his or her spouse, the marriage was dissolved and the abandoned party
could remarry.[16] Gratian attempted to bridge the two by making a distinction
between cases in which the convert was abandoned by the spouse and cases
in which they continued to live together. If the convert was abandoned, the
convert could remarry but if they continued to live together, the Christian
should get a separation from his or her spouse.[17] Later commentaries on
this topic were gendered. Johannes Teutonicus, for example, argued that
female converts should not be treated the same as male converts. According
to Teutonicus, if the wife converted "she should leave her husband, lest he
recall her to her former error"; however, if the husband was the convert,
the couple should remain married "for women are more easily influenced
by a man than the other way around."[18] In 1199, Pope Innocent III clarified
that the papacy had no power to dissolve a legitimate marriage between
Christians, but it could dissolve marriages between non-Christians since
their marriages were not confirmed by the Church, suggesting that rather
than granting a divorce, the Church could dissolve marriages when one
spouse converted to Christianity.[19]

As Paola Tartakoff has shown in her study of conversion in the Crown
of Aragon, medieval Jews, before the forced conversions of 1391, saw apostasy from Judaism as a serious sin, particularly if the apostate converted to
Christianity.[20] She argues that converts were rejected by their communities,
perceived as traitors who often terrorized their former Jewish communities.
Rashba told Jewish wives of converts to "run away from their husbands 'as
one runs away from a snake.'"[21] Despite this communal rejection, from the
point of view of Jewish law, conversion did not erase marriage, and if the

Jewish wife of a converted husband failed to obtain a divorce, she could not remarry and could lose her children.[22] Tartakoff tells the story of a Catalan Jewish woman named Conort whose husband converted to Christianity early in the fourteenth century, taking the name Pere d'Avinyó.[23] Conort's case suggests she was unable to get a divorce from Pere because extant evidence indicates he abandoned her and their children. Conort's inability to receive a divorce, therefore, resulted in her inability to secure the return of her dowry, thus placing her and her children in a precarious financial position. With no divorce and no dowry, Conort was also unable to remarry, cutting off another avenue through which she could support herself and her children. Such concerns faced other spouses in mixed marriages after the violence of 1391, when husbands refused to return dotal goods to their wives, both wives that converted and those that remained Jewish.[24]

We know of Conort's story because of a letter, written by the Bishop of Barcelona in 1317, which highlights her concerns regarding the perception of the ecclesiastical authorities in terms of her relationship with her apostate husband. At some point after his conversion, Pere went to Tripoli, where he returned to Judaism and shortly thereafter, died. Conort wanted to return to Catalonia but was worried that the church officials would accuse her of having urged her husband to return to Judaism.[25] Indeed, Conort's anxiety around such accusations was not unfounded. We see in Girona inquisitorial concern about Jewish relatives of apostates bringing them back into Judaism. The concern was a long-standing one within the church. In his manual for inquisitors, Bernard Gui singled out "those connected [to apostates] by blood and marriage" as particularly dangerous, arguing that they were more likely to influence the new convert back to Judaism.[26] Much pressure, therefore, was put on the families of converts by either the convert himself or herself, or by ecclesiastical authorities. This pressure demonstrates the tension present within Christian thought and society regarding the continued existence of such mixed families.

Examples from Girona, however, show that despite ecclesiastical desires to extricate conversos from their Jewish families, some couples chose to remain together, acting as husband and wife.[27] Nevertheless, as we see below, conversion could prove destructive, creating an insurmountable wedge between husband and wife. In other words, the impacts of conversion on marriage and the family mirror its effect on the Jewish community—some Jews converted but continued to live in the same place and circulate in the same circles as if no conversion had taken place, while some families tried to carry on as before despite now living in mixed families. Yet other converts rejected their erstwhile communities, or were rejected by them in much the same way as spouses or family members rejected one another after conversion.

PRESERVATION OF MARRIAGE AND COMMUNITY

Despite ecclesiastical concern over mixed unions, marriages did survive the conversion of a spouse, and some Jewish wives remained Jewish for years after the husband's conversion. A notable case is that of Bellaire, wife of Guillem Bernat Desmaestre, a converso who was the son of one of the most prominent rabbis of the Jewish community of Girona: Bonastruch Desmaestre. Bonastruch was so well-known for his erudition and piety that King Ferran insisted that he attend the Disputation of Tortosa. Bellaire was a young heiress when she married Bonastruch Desmaestre's son, around 1412.[28] Her husband converted to Christianity sometime in May of 1418, taking the name of Guillem Bernat Desmaestre. Guillem Desmaestre's conversion did not estrange him from either his wife or his own family. He often appeared alongside his father conducting business, and Bonastruch Desmaestre continued to act as procurator for his Jewish daughter-in-law well into 1422.[29] Indeed, notarial evidence makes it difficult to tell if Guillem's conversion had any impact on his relationship with Bellaire or his Jewish parents because it appears they carried on their personal and business activities in the same ways they had before his conversion.

Other examples from Girona provide further evidence for the continuance of normal familial activities and actions after the conversion of a husband, demonstrating that the alliances created between families due to marriage could be retained, even across varying branches of a kin group. In 1413, Mossé Bellshom Falcó married Bonafilla, the daughter of Hasday Taroç and his wife Astruga.[30] Over the next few years, Mossé engaged in a variety of business activities, mostly related to credit, with Hasday,

Astruga, and even his wife's maternal grandmother, Gràcia Cerç. These transactions included the purchase of credit notes from Astruga in 1416, as well as the absolution of debts owed to Mossé by Hasday, Astruga, and Gràcia, in 1418, and a contract concluded after Mossé's conversion to Christianity and assumption of the name Asbert Falcó.[31] Mossé's mother Bonafilla, the widow of Bellshom Mossé Falcó also utilized the ties created by her son's marriage into the Taroç family to extend her economic activities, purchasing credit notes from Hasday Taroç on a number of occasions. She continued to employ her converso son to represent her in business dealings.[32] Even Mossé's convert brother-in-law Pere Joan Falcó, (whose marriage dissolution opened this article), engaged in business transactions with the Taroç family, selling fabric to Hasday and Astruga, in 1420. Indeed multiple members of various branches of the Falcó family converted to Christianity from 1417 to the early 1420s, yet evidence from the notarial archives indicates that they continued to engage in credit transactions with one another and with the various other Jewish families they had married into, despite repeated pressures from ecclesiastical and civil authorities not to.

While the mixed families of Girona did continue to retain both familial and communal ties, despite conversion, that does not mean pressure to convert from within disappeared. Although Jewish families did not necessarily disinherit their converso children, as often happened prior to 1391, converso parents did use inheritance as an enticement to conversion.[33] In 1428, another member of the Falcó family, the converso Bernat Falcó, dictated his will leaving property to all five of his children: four converso children—Pere, Antoni, Elienor, and Violant—and one Jewish son—David. He made a careful distinction among them—since Violant was married and had received her dowry, she was given a smaller gift. David was awarded twenty-five pounds, while his other siblings got equal parts as they were all named universal heirs of the rest of their father's inheritance. Interestingly, Bernat Falcó used his will to pressure his son David to convert—he offered an additional twenty-five pounds should David convert before the will was executed. The enticement was not sufficient since David was still listed as Jewish in his mother's will, nine years later, but the family had not broken apart, indicated by the fact that Blanca, his mother, left him an inheritance equal to that of her converso son Antoni.

Blanca had converted to Christianity alongside her husband Bernat, in 1417, but women who remained Jewish also chose to donate their assets to their convert children. On September 16, 1416, the Jewish widow Gràcia donated her dowry and other marital property to her converso son Joan des Vall.[34] The contract does not state why she was handing over these assets to Joan at this time, although legally he would have been entitled to them at the time of her death. It was not uncommon for widows to donate property, including their dowries, to their male children who were about to marry. In many cases, these donations contained stipulations regarding the dispersal of this property upon the death of the mother; however, Joan received the goods (thirty-three pieces of silver valued at 500 sous) at the time, perhaps to be used as the economic foundation for a new marital union.

Examples like these, of women and families who carried on interacting normally after a member converted, abound in the notarial records from Girona. It is no wonder that local religious authorities were concerned. Not all wives resisted conversion, of course, some did choose to convert. Johannes Teutonicus would have seen his gendered beliefs confirmed by the example of Dolça, the Jewish wife of the converso Pere de Bosc (Mossé Cabrit). While Pere and Dolça were still married in March of 1418, despite her Jewish status, by the end of the year she had converted and taken the name of Caterina.[35] Whether Dolça converted under the influence of her husband or because of legal problems at the vicar's court is unclear.[36]

CONFLICT WITHIN MARRIAGE AND COMMUNITY

Although some couples attempted to preserve their marital unions after the conversion of the husband—either through the conversion of the wife, as in the case of Dolça, or through ignoring the efforts of religious officials to prevent couples from continuing their conjugal relationships—such as Bellaire and Guillem Bernat Desmaestre—it is also evident that conversion could work to destroy marriage and shatter communal bonds. The dowry restitution contract between Regina and her convert husband Pere Joan Falcó, mentioned at the beginning of this article, is one example of such marital breakdowns. While it appears that the eventual dissolution of Regina and Pere's marriage was influenced by the intervention of the inquisition, the end of other mixed marriages may have been the result of personal differences, where conversion was potentially used as a method or excuse for ending a union already in trouble. Paola Tartakoff has explored how some Jews in the fourteenth-century Crown of Aragon chose baptism as a means of circumventing specific Jewish laws around marriage and divorce—including a Jewish woman who abandoned her husband in the 1380s, was baptized, and then married another convert.[37]

The case of Caravida Vidal, a prominent member of the Jewish community in Girona, and his wife Bonafilla, is suggestive of similar, although more complex, motivations behind conversion. Originally from Peratallada, Caravida Vidal had moved to Girona with Bonafilla, by 1402.[38] Soon after their move, the couple began to engage in credit transactions of various kinds, both together and separately. Twelve years later, however, in December of 1414, Caravida asked King Ferran for permission to take a second wife, alleging that Bonafilla was incapable of having children.[39] Bonafilla disputed her husband's claim and approached Queen Violant, emphasizing that she was not too old to bear children in the future.[40] On January 8, 1415, King Ferran ordered the local judge in Girona to determine whether or not, according to Hebrew law, Caravida and Bonafilla's situation merited his marriage to a second wife.

Setting aside the surprising fact that the king had ordered a Christian official to adjudicate a case involving two Jews using solely Jewish law, Caravida's request to take a second wife was not necessarily an unusual one in late medieval Catalonia. Polygamy has long been a topic of much controversy in Jewish communities. By the fourteenth century several bans against the practice existed among Ashkenazi Jews, but it is unclear to what extent such prohibitions had an effect on Jewish communities of the Iberian peninsula.[41] What we do know is that Christian rulers prohibited such practice under the penalty of death, unless a license was issued by the king.[42] Yom Tov Assis found at least fifty cases of bigamy in sources from the royal archives and responsa from fourteenth-century Catalonia and Aragon, including a number of licenses granted to Jews allowing them to take a second wife.[43] Although some Jews found the legal means to marry a second wife, Jewish sources from the Crown of Aragon characterized such polygamous families in negative terms as full of "arguments, resentment, and divorce."[44] Such texts emphasize the disharmony that bringing a second wife into an already established household could create, noting "there is no one who brings dispute into his home like one who takes another wife into his home."[45] While we have no way of knowing the internal workings of Caravida and Bonafilla's marriage, the fact that Bonafilla attempted to prevent Caravida from being granted a license to marry for a second time indicates she was unhappy with his decision to do so. Conflict of some kind was present in the marriage at the time Caravida made his request because an arbitration settlement had been determined between the couple in October of 1414. Unfortunately the notarial contract related to this case only states that the settlement was related to "various questions, reasons, and causes," while mandating that if the settlement was not followed, the parties would each be fined 200 pounds.[46] A later document in the same register, however, indicates that Caravida had accused his wife of stealing a quantity of money from a chest he owned. He eventually found the funds in a different chest, and thus recognized in this document the error of his accusation.[47] Caravida's accusation against Bonafilla seems to suggest that their relationship was already somewhat fractured at the time he petitioned the King to take a second wife.

The tensions between Caravida and Bonafilla only increased after he was given permission to marry again, in May of 1415.[48] One month later, Caravida concluded a dowry contract with Regina, the daughter of Bonsenyor Samuel.[49] Regina brought with her a large dowry of 5000 sous and connections to a very prominent family in Girona. Her father Bonsenyor, then deceased, served as a counsellor in the aljama from 1398, until his death in 1415.[50] Her mother Bonafilla was deeply engaged in the credit market, as were her two brothers Rovén and Vidal Bonsenyor. Bonafilla Vidal attempted to get Caravida's second marriage to Regina annulled, but King Ferran confirmed his permission in December of 1415, presumably after conferring with the local judge who had investigated the case earlier in the year.[51] Evidence from Girona is frustratingly silent on conditions within the Vidal family following Caravida's marriage to Regina. Jewish law required that he provide separate living spaces for the two women and any children they had, and thus Caravida's ability to set up two households attests to his economic power within Girona. While we have dozens of notarial records relating to his involvement in various financial transactions in the years after his second marriage, so far we have uncovered little evidence of the day to day experiences of this polygamous family.

Did Bonafilla's resentment of her husband and his new wife continue to grow or did she eventually come to terms with the situation? We have no way of knowing. What we can ascertain, however, is that the situation changed with Caravida's conversion to Christianity in 1417, and his assumption of the name Bernat Vidal. The local inquisitor and vicar general, Pere Ermengol, had attempted to arrest Caravida in January of 1416, claiming that he had promised to convert to Christianity.[52] That promise, if actually given, was not fulfilled until a year later, but Bernat's problems with the inquisition would only grow in the coming years. In July of 1419, Bernat promised the inquisitor he would not enter, stay, eat, or drink in Jewish households, nor would he engage in such activities in the households of conversos who had Jewish wives—an interesting promise to make when he himself was a converso who had a Jewish wife. He was also ordered to ensure he attend church services for all important feast days and every Sunday.[53] Less than a year later, in May of 1420, he was formally accused by the inquisition of continuing to practice Judaism and ignoring the inquisitor's previous requests to refrain from interacting with Jews or entering the call, or Jewish quarter, of Girona.[54] In October of the same year, Bernat was condemned by the inquisition, fined 100 florins, reminded of the inquisitor's mandate to avoid all contact with Jews and the call, and ordered to reaffirm his Catholic faith before the bishop.[55]

None of the notarial documents involving Bernat Vidal and various inquisitors mention his two wives. Given the prohibition against bigamy within Catholicism, this fact seems surprising; however, it appears that by the time his troubles with the inquisition increased in 1419, Bernat had divested himself of one wife, and soon after, the other would convert to Christianity. Starting in February of 1418, Bonafilla began to be referred to as the "former wife of Bernat Vidal" in notarial records.[56] At some point, therefore, she and Caravida/Bernat were divorced. Whether their divorce took place after his conversion in 1417, or in the months leading up to it, we do not know, but it seems likely that conversion played a large role in the end of their marriage for, as a Christian, Bernat could not have two wives. It also seems that Bonafilla had no interest in converting, since notarial documents into the late 1420s identify her as the Jewish former wife of the converso Bernat Vidal.[57] Conversely, Bernat's second wife, Regina, did convert, taking the name Elionor.

Although present from as far back as 1414, the fractures within the marriage of Caravida/Bernat and Bonafilla were blown apart by his conversion to Christianity. Within a year of his conversion, he had divorced his first wife. Of course, as a Jew, he could have divorced her at any time, and why he did not do so earlier is unclear. It is possible that he did not want to have to return her dowry to her so instead chose the bigamy route, allowed in Jewish law, to get himself a new wife.[58] His conversion, however, forced him to choose between his two wives, or perhaps provided Bonafilla with the opportunity to escape from a familial structure she had resisted from the beginning. With her dowry returned, she had the ability to support herself, and indeed, continued to engage in the credit market into the 1420s.

CONCLUSION

The family became a site in which community could be remolded, preserved, or destroyed. The tensions affecting the Jewish and converso communities of Girona in the generation after 1391 can be seen at its most dramatic in the control of minor children. When the Jew Nacim Rovén died in 1415, he left his wife and daughter in seemingly good hands by appointing three Jewish guardians for his young daughter. One of the tutors, Caravida Mercadell, eventually married Nacim's widow Bonadona and converted to Christianity, taking the name Ramon Mercader, prompting the other guardians to remove him from the guardianship of Nacim Rovén's daughter, by December of 1416.[59] They were clearly concerned that the infant girl would be converted to Christianity as well, so much so that the remaining Jewish guardians decided to kidnap the daughter (Bonafilla) and remove her altogether from the possession of the mother and stepfather. By then, their efforts to preserve the girl's Jewish identity were perhaps too late as she was already described as Elionor, a conversa. Had she still been Jewish, the authorities might not have concerned themselves with her being under the control of her Jewish guardians, although it is likely they would have preferred she remain with her conversa mother, as a means of ensuring her own eventual conversion. As a conversa, however, the possibility of her relapse into Judaism prompted them to act at the request of her stepfather, Ramon Mercader. In March of 1420, the case appears before the *jurats* of the city, and by August, little Elionor seems to have been returned home, and Ramon was made sole guardian of the young girl by the city's iudex ordinarius.[60]

Much like conversion could serve as a means of fracturing marital unions, in the case of the Mercader/Rovén family, tensions present within the Jewish and converso communities worked to split apart a family, as Christian officials and, presumably, Jewish officials negotiated the various legal, social, and economic minefields created by changing religious identities. That the mixed families of Girona were under increasing scrutiny as the 1420s rolled on is clear in the inquisitorial investigation into these kin groups that continued during that decade. Yet, that some couples continued to coexist and live together as family despite conversion, is equally clear. Resisting increasing pressure to convert from Christian ecclesiastical and civil officials, as well as converso family members, some Jews continued their relationships with converso spouses, children, siblings, or parents. The impact of conversion on Jewish family life was therefore complex and manifold, highlighting a range of communal responses and reflecting how communities could act as both sites of conflict and cooperation, often at the same time.

NOTES

1. AHG, Protocols Notarials, Berenguer Ferrer Sasala, G4: 81 (December 3, 1420), n/f.
2. AHG, Protocols Notarials, Berenguer Ferrer Sasala, G4: 79 (April 5, 1421), n/f.
3. AHG, Protocols Notarials, Berenguer Ferrer Sasala, G4: 79 (November 21, 1421), n/f.
4. AHG, Protocols Notarials, Berenguer Ferrer Sasala, G4: 74 (June 16, 1419), n/f; AHG, Protocols Notarials, Berenguer Ferrer Sasala G4: 75 (October 13, 1419), n/f.
5. See Oeltjen, "Challenges Facing Mallorcan Conversas," chapter 2 in this volume.
6. Lynch, *Individuals, Families and Communities*, 2.

7. Quote from Midrash Bereshit Rabbah in Grossman, *Pious and Rebellious*, 9.

8. Goldin, *Jewish Women in Europe*, 18.

9. Quoted in Silleras-Fernández, *Chariots of Ladies*, 91. See also Eiximenis, *Lo llibre*, 104.

10. Coughlin, *Law, Person, and Community*, 166.

11. AHG, Protocols Notarials, Bernat Pintor, G7: 75 (February 16, 1402), n/f.

12. AHG, Protocols Notarials, Francesc Vidal, G6: 95 (April 17, 1402), n/f and (May 24, 1402), n/f.

13. AHG, Protocols Notarials, Francesc Vidal, G6: 122 (May 6, 1410), n/f.

14. See for example AHG, Protocols Notarials, Francesc Vidal, G6: 121 (April 12, 1410), n/f; Riera, *Els jueus de Girona*, 168–70; 295–96.

15. 1 Cor. 7:12–16. Discussion in Brundage, *Law, Sex, and Christian Society*, 61, 244.

16. Brundage, *Law, Sex, and Christian Society*, 61; "Intermarriage," 28.

17. Brundage, *Law, Sex, and Christian Society*, 244.

18. Quoted in Brundage, "Intermarriage," 29. Ironically, research shows the opposite to be true: the conversion of women tends to be much more indicative of family conversion than the conversion of men. See for example Blanca de Banyoles (Astruga) and her husband Pere (Jucef Falcó) who both converted in August of 1391; Elionor (Estellina) and her husband Dalmau Dala (Jafuda Alfaquim) who converted along with their adult son Lluís Joan Dala (Bonanasch Alfaquim) in 1416. AHG Protocols Notarials, Bernat Capella G2: 59 (September 8, 1391); AHG Protocols Notarials, Berenguer Vidal G10: 68 (September 10, 1426).

19. Brundage, "Intermarriage," 29; Tartakoff, "Jewish Women and Apostasy," 15.

20. Tartakoff, *Between Christian and Jew*, chapter 5.

21. Tartakoff, *Between Christian and Jew*, 113.

22. Tartakoff, *Between Christian and Jew*, 113; "Jewish Women and Apostasy," 12.

23. Tartakoff, *Between Christian and Jew*, 111–13; "Jewish Women and Apostasy," 14.

24. For example, see the case of a conversa, Constança, whose Jewish husband Issac Rovén refused to return her dowry, despite his willingness to get an annulment. AHG, Protocols Notarials, Cast. 480, Pere Pellicer, (November 28, 1391), n/f. Also see Guerson and Wessell Lightfoot, "Crisis and Community."

25. Tartakoff, *Between Christian and Jew*, 111–12. For the text of the letter written by the bishop to Conort, see Tartakoff, "Jewish Women and Apostasy," 20.

26. *Practica inquisitionis*, 288, quoted in Tartakoff, *Between Christian and Jew*, 118.

27. Nirenberg, *Communities of Violence*, 144.

28. The first mention of the couple appears in AHG, Protocols Notarials, Bernat Soler, G3: 45 (March 28, 1412), n/f.

29. AHG, Protocols Notarials, Antoni-Bernat Ferran, G7: 83 (September 20, 1418), n/f; AHG, Protocols Notarials, Berenguer Ferrer Sasala, G4: 73 (December 2, 1418), n/f; AHG Protocols Notarials, Berenguer Vidal G10: 69 (October 5, 1422).

30. AHG, Protocols Notarials, Berenguer Ferrer Sasala, G 4: 62 (August 3, 1413), n/f.

31. AHG, Protocols Notarials, Berenguer Ferrer Sasala, G 4: 70 (July 24, 1416), n/f and AHG, Protocols Notarials, Berenguer Ferrer Sasala, G 4: 71 (May 6, 1418), n/f.

32. AHG, Protocols Notarials, Berenguer Ferrer Sasala, G 4: 71 (March 18, 1418), n/f.

33. For the disinheritance of conversos see Tartakoff, *Between Christian and Jew*, 110; Guerson, "Seeking Remission," 42.

34. AHG, Protocols Notarials, Berenguer Ferrer Sasala, G 4: 70 (September 16, 1416), n/f.

35. AHG, Protocols Notarials, Berenguer Ferrer Sasala, G 4: 71 (March 3, 1418), n/f; AHG, Protocols Notarials, Berenguer Ferrer Sasala, G 4: 73 (December 16, 1418), n/f.

36. AHG, Protocols Notarials, Berenguer Ferrer Sasala, G 4: 73 (November 21, 1418), n/f.

37. Tartakoff, *Between Christian and Jew*, 70–71.

38. See AHG, Protocols Notarials, Bernat Pintor, G 7: 75 (February 1402), n/f.

39. ACA, Reial Cancelleria, Registres, 2393: 194r–v (December 5, 1414).

40. ACA, Reial Cancelleria, Registres, 2034: 28r (January 8, 1415).

41. Grossman, *Pious and Rebellious*, 68–78.

42. Grossman, *Pious and Rebellious*, 84.

43. See a discussion of Assis's conclusions in Grossman, *Pious and Rebellious*, 84–87. See also Guerson de Oliveira, "Coping with Crises," 135–40.

44. Grossman, *Pious and Rebellious*, 90.

45. Grossman, *Pious and Rebellious*, 90.

46. AHG, Protocols Notarials, Antoni-Bernat Ferran, G 7: 80 (October 9, 1414), n/f. Two later documents in this same notarial register indicate that Bonafilla has absolved her husband of all debts owed to her because he has fulfilled them (October 24, 1414).

47. AHG, Protocols Notarials, Antoni Bernat Ferran, G 7: 80 (October 24, 1414).

48. ACA, Reial Cancelleria, Registres, 2034: 35v–36r (May 23, 1415).

49. AHG, Protocols Notarials, Berenguer Ferrer Sasala, G 4: 68 (June 26, 1415), n/f.

50. Riera, *Els jueus de Girona*, 156–57.

51. See Gemma Escribà, *Tortosa Disputation*, 132.

52. Escribà, *Documents dels jueus de Girona*, 236. Why he promised to convert is unclear. Jews did sometimes offer to convert to get out of legal problems. See Guerson, "Seeking Remission."

53. AHG, Protocols Notarials, Berenguer Ferrer Sasala, G 4: 75 (July 30, 1419), n/f.

54. AHG, Protocols Notarials, Berenguer Ferrer Sasala, G 4: 77 (May 9, 1420), n/f.

55. AHG, Protocols Notarials, Berenguer Ferrer Sasala, G 4: 81 (October 10, 1420), n/f.

56. See AHG, Protocols Notarials, Berenguer Ferrer Sasala, G 4: 71 (February 7, 1418), n/f.

57. See AHG, Protocols Notarials, Berenguer Ferrer Sasala, G 4: 88–90 (1425–1426).

58. While in the early fourteenth century Catalan Jews were able to get licenses to have more than one wife by simply mentioning that Jewish law allowed it, by the

late fourteenth century the Crown seems to only issue those licenses in cases of infertility. See discussion in Guerson de Oliveira, "Coping with Crises," 135–40.

59. AHG, Protocols Notarials, Berenguer Ferrer Sasala, G4: 71 (September 24, 1417), n/f.

60. AHCG, Ordinacions dels Jurats, RE 028 UI 9179–1418–1420 (March 21, 1420); AHG, Protocols Notarials, Berenguer Ferrer Sasala, G4: 77 (August 20, 1420).

BIBLIOGRAPHY

Primary Sources

AHCG. Arxiu Històric de la Ciutat de Girona
    Ordinacions dels Jurats

AHG. Arxiu Històric de Girona
    Protocols Notarials, Girona 1–10
    Protocols Notarials, Castellón d'Empúries

Arxiu de la Corona d'Aragò
    Reial Cancelleria, Registres

Eiximenis, Francesc. Lo llibre de les dones. Vols. 1–2. Barcelona: Biblioteca Torres Amat, 1981.

Escribà, Gemma, and Raquel Ibáñez-Sperber, eds. The Tortosa Disputation: Regesta of Documents from the Archivo de La Corona de Aragón, Fernando I, 1412–1416. Sources for the History of the Jews in Spain 6. Jerusalem: Hebrew University of Jerusalem, 1998.

Escribà i Bonastre, Gemma, and M. Pilar Frago Pérez. Documents dels jueus de Girona (1124–1595): Arxiu Històric de la Ciutat, Arxiu Diocesà de Girona. Girona: Ajuntament de Girona, 1992.

Secondary Sources

Brundage, James A. "Intermarriage between Christians and Jews in Medieval Canon Law." Jewish History 3, no. 1 (1993): 25–40.

———. Law, Sex, and Christian Society in Medieval Europe. Chicago: University of Chicago Press, 1987.

Coughlin, John J. Law, Person, and Community: Philosophical, Theological, and Comparative Perspectives on Canon Law. New York: Oxford University Press, 2012.

Goldin, Simha. Jewish Women in Europe in the Middle Ages: A Quiet Revolution. Manchester: Manchester University Press, 2011.

Grossman, Avraham. Pious and Rebellious: Jewish Women in Medieval Europe. Hanover: Brandeis University Press, 2004.

Guerson, Alexandra. "Seeking Remission: Jewish Conversion in the Crown of Aragon, c.1378–1391." Jewish History 24, no. 1 (2010): 33–52.

Guerson, Alexandra, and Dana Wessell Lightfoot. "Crisis and Community: Catalan Jewish Women and Conversas in Girona, 1391–1420." Tamid: Revista Catalana Anual d'Estudis Hebraic 14 (2019): 91–130.

Guerson de Oliveira, Alexandra E. P. "Coping with Crises: Christian-Jewish Relations in Catalonia and Aragon, 1380–1391." University of Toronto, 2012.

Lynch, Katherine A. *Individuals, Families and Communities in Europe, 1200–1800: The Urban Foundations of Western Society.* Cambridge: Cambridge University Press, 2003.

Nirenberg, David. *Communities of Violence: Persecution of Minorities in the Middle Ages.* Princeton: Princeton University Press, 1996.

Riera i Sans, Jaume. *Els jueus de Girona i la seva organització. Segles XII–XIV.* Girona: Patronat Call de Girona, 2011.

Silleras-Fernández, Núria. *Chariots of Ladies: Francesc Eiximenis and the Court Culture of Medieval and Early Modern Iberia.* Ithaca NY: Cornell University Press, 2015.

Tartakoff, Paola. *Between Christian and Jew: Conversion and Inquisition in the Crown of Aragon, 1250–1391.* Philadelphia: University of Pennsylvania Press, 2012.

———. "Jewish Women and Apostasy in the Medieval Crown of Aragon, ca. 1300–1391." *Jewish History* 24, no. 1 (January 19, 2010): 7–32.

7

In Defense of Community

Morisca Women in Sixteenth-Century Valladolid

STEPHANIE M. CAVANAUGH

In the sixteenth century, a small neighborhood in the Castilian city of Valladolid became a battleground in a fight for the souls and allegiances of converts. The Barrio de Santa María was formerly a Muslim quarter, or *morería*; its residents continued to live there after their mass conversion from Islam to Catholicism in 1502 and remained—despite repeated plans for their removal—until their expulsion from Spain in 1611.[1] In the long century between these forced acts of baptism and exile, the problem of how to transform Moriscos into sincere Catholics preoccupied the Spanish monarchy, Inquisition, and clergy throughout the Spanish kingdoms. Moriscos were baptized nominal Catholics widely suspected of retaining Muslim beliefs and practices. Crown and Church deemed social and residential integration to be necessary for their genuine religious conversion. Consequently, Morisco tenancy and property became controversial matters. A succession of plans aimed to disperse the Moriscos in order to promote their assimilation into Catholic society, and the Spanish Inquisition routinely confiscated the property of Morisco penitents. In response, the Moriscos regularly took legal action.[2] This article illustrates how Morisca women, notably widows and property owners, participated in the collective legal defense of their community, properties, and shared neighborhood in Valladolid.

Scholars have established how Morisca women were guardians of pre-conversion faith and customs.[3] The case of Valladolid's Barrio de Santa María demonstrates how Morisca women also took on legal and economic responsibilities to support their families, and the community at large. In Valladolid, Morisca women who signed new leases in 1538 were litigants in a community-wide and decades-long fight to remain in the barrio. In 1557, Morisca women and Morisco men collectively petitioned the Inquisition for relief from the regular religious prosecution of their community and the confiscation of their property; as owners of houses and land, and as heads of households, Morisca women contributed to the resulting fiscal agreement reached between their community and the Valladolid tribunal of the Spanish Inquisition. The centrality of Morisca women to the survival of their community is evident in both their active legal engagement and their considerable economic activities. These public roles must be examined in conjunction with their domestic labor and responsibilities to better understand the experiences of both women and Moriscos in early modern Iberia.

The meaning of *Morisco* was manifold; across time and place, this category contained a multitude of experiences, beliefs, and modes of surviving restrictive royal policies and religious prosecution.[4] Moriscos who retained elements of their former faith had to do so in secret because Catholic baptism meant the loss of the ability to worship and live publicly as Muslims. The Spanish Inquisition prosecuted Moriscos for practicing Muslim ceremonies (*ceremonias de moros*) or observing the sect of Muhammad (*secta de mahoma*), charges that encompassed a range of everyday actions related to diet, dress, and work, as well as assertions of Islamic beliefs. Neglecting to observe the precepts of the Catholic Church was, of course, not the sole jurisdiction of New Christians; Old Christians, too, were commonly found guilty of skipping mass, working on Sundays, blasphemy, and a litany of commonplace sins.[5] However, for Moriscos to eat meat or dress in clean clothes on a Friday would signal a specifically Muslim nonconformity to Catholic teachings. Spanish inquisitors paid close attention to Moriscos for signs of their adherence to Islam, often focusing on "Morisco bodies as the site of their cultural practices" that included bathing for ritual purposes and abstaining from eating pork or drinking wine.[6] The slaughter of meat, the preparation and consumption of food, and fasting could all be associated with Islamic worship, so too could the ways in which Moriscos celebrated weddings, attended to births, and prepared dead bodies for burial.[7]

These largely domestic practices continued under the command of Morisca women. Both Muslim and Christian social, cultural, and religious ideals placed the bulk of household labor and organization in the purview of women. Moreover, the framework for the private observance of Islam—overseen by women in the home, with the informal education of girls—predated and survived the Catholic conversion of Spanish Muslims. With the loss of formal Islamic leadership and public places of worship at the time of that conversion, this domestic sphere became the sole mechanism for observing Islam and teaching it to younger generations.[8] Vincent, Perry, and others have convincingly argued that, as such, "Morisca women played a fundamental role in the survival of Islam in Spain."[9] In fact, in her assessment of the "similarities between the two worlds of crypto-observance," Levine Melammed finds striking parallels between Judeoconversa and Morisca women who observed and preserved Jewish or Islamic customs regarding food and fasting, bathing and clothes, weddings and the naming of children, birth and death.[10]

Of course, domestic spaces were not necessarily private. The presence of servants, apprentices, customers, neighbors, and others meant that early modern households of all socioeconomic levels were not secluded. Domestic labor could be witnessed by many onlookers. In the town of Deza, for example, inquisitors received the testimonies of Old Christian domestic servants accusing their Morisca employers of feeding their families meat and eggs during Lent or refusing to feed their families meat not slaughtered according to Islamic law; others were denounced for allegedly reburying their dead according to Islamic rites or fasting in observance of Ramadan.[11] Throughout Iberia, New Christian women were investigated for how they prepared food, how and when they arranged their families' celebrations, and when they did and did not work.[12] In her analysis of this "dangerous domesticity," Perry asserts that "the great majority of those [cases] in which accused Moriscos identified the person from whom they had learned Islam named their mothers, grandmothers, and mothers-in-law."[13] This dynamic spanned the sixteenth century across the Spanish empire.[14] Generations after the mass baptism of Castilian Muslims, for example, a parish priest in Valladolid wrote that local Moriscos were still "like their grandparents" ("como sus abuelos"), to describe what he perceived to be their failed conversion.[15]

Religious authorities believed that in addition to the work of Morisca women, the relative seclusion afforded by segregated Morisco neighborhoods was crucial to the maintenance of Muslim traditions.[16] Fear of crypto-Islam persisting in Morisco households engendered proposals to dismantle Morisco communities through dispersal and demolition. In Valladolid, priests and inquisitors insisted that the Moriscos "living together is damaging their souls."[17] This opinion led to attempts to disband the Barrio de Santa María throughout the sixteenth century, attempts led in turn by the quarter's landlord, municipal authorities, parish priests, the Inquisition, and the monarchy. The Moriscos' collective residency in the barrio first came under attack soon after their baptism. The morería had been established nearly one century earlier in compliance with a 1412 royal edict ordering the physical segregation of Jews and Muslims.[18] In 1502, the Moriscos' communal lease (dated 1414) was declared void by their landlord, the church chapter of the Iglesia de Santa María La Mayor, on the grounds that they had lost their legal status as Muslims (their "condición de moros") upon baptism and thus were no longer represented by the contract. The resulting lawsuit took place in turns from 1505 to 1537.[19] One hundred and ninety-four Morisco heads of household, including Morisca widows, litigated collectively with the aim of remaining in the barrio.[20]

This move to annul their lease was an attempt to separate the neophyte New Christians from one another. By 1506, the church chapter had confiscated the *almaxi y casa de bodas*; *almaxi* derives from *al-masjid* (Arabic for mosque) and *casa de bodas* means "wedding house" in Castilian. It was soon demolished (exactly when is unclear) along with several unidentified residential properties.[21] The Moriscos pursued a claim to the property on which the mosque had stood and later sought the return of the wood from the demolished building. Its location seems to have remained a landmark in the barrio; in a 1565 registry of Morisco property, one house was described as adjacent to the "lane that leads to the mosque."[22] Both the close-knit quarters of the walled neighborhood and the mosque were tangible and symbolic ties to the shared Islamic past of the Moriscos, so recently severed. In the eyes of local religious authorities, these were dangerous impediments to their full assimilation. To Morisco men and women, this fight was even bigger than the matter of losing their homes. Living together in the old morería was a way to safeguard their community, kinship, and traditions in the aftermath of their coerced conversion.

Judges at the Royal Chancery Court of Valladolid eventually ruled in favor of the Moriscos and ordered that each head of household sign a lease as an individual tenant. Many of the leases, which are preserved in a collection of notarial protocols at the Provincial Historical Archive of Valladolid, describe the stated purpose of the new contracts as the resolution of the legal dispute.[23] Notably, a number of women were recorded among the leaseholders.[24] For example, one lease reads:

> That all who see this letter of obligation and long-term lease contract know that I, Ana la Serrana, widow of Luis Castaño, deceased potter, citizen of this noble town of Valladolid in the Barrio de Santa María of this town of Valladolid, say: that as there is a lawsuit between the most reverend sirs of the priory and church chapter of the collegiate church of *Nuestra Señora Santa María la Mayor* of this town of Valladolid as masters of the property [with] direct dominion over the said Barrio de Santa María, on the one hand, and on the other the citizens and masters of the houses and possessions of the said neighbourhood who reside in the said town, sentences were pronounced on appeal and an executive order to the effect that among other things they ordered that all of the citizens of the Barrio de Santa María and persons who have houses, lots, and possessions in the said Barrio de Santa María make and authorize contracts of long-term leases [...] and it falls to them to pay the rent of forty florins that the church and chapter have every

year forever more, on the said neighborhood [. . .] it is necessary to refer to these because I, the said Ana la Serrana, possess in the said Barrio de Santa María a house on the *calle de la Carpinteria* with its exit and door on the *calle Mercado*, bordered on one side by the house of Ana la Seguina, widow of Antonio Padel, and on the other the house of Gonçalo del Trigo, a potter, with the *calle del Mercado* behind the house and the *calle de la Carpinteria* in front of the house.[25]

These leases applied to Morisco men and women as individual "citizens and masters" holding long-term contracts for the distinct "houses, lots, and possessions" they each owned. The leases also reflect bonds of community in the account of the Moriscos' joint litigation, in the statements of their shared fiscal obligation to pay rent, and in descriptions of the placements of their homes and how they bordered with those of their Morisco neighbors.

The Morisca widows Ana la Serrana and her neighbor Ana la Seguina were not exceptional as proprietors of their own homes. It was, in fact, common for women to own property in early modern Castile. Through partible inheritance, estates were bequeathed in equal parts to legitimate descendants both male and female.[26] Women's property rights were guaranteed and reaffirmed in a long tradition of Iberian law codes: the seventh-century Visigothic *Liber iudicum*, translated into Castilian in the thirteenth century as the *Fuero Juzgo*; Alfonso X's *Siete Partidas*; and the 1505 *Leyes de Toro*.[27] Women had a range of legal and economic rights and options that allowed them to administer their properties, make wills, arrange marriages and provide dowries for their children, litigate in court, and fulfill other public roles.[28] For Morisca women, these traditions predated their baptism to Catholicism in 1502. Muslim women had been legal and economic actors in societies throughout medieval Iberia. Catlos describes their labor in business, agriculture, production, arts, medicine, and midwifery, as well as their property and inheritance rights, and their activities in courts of law.[29] Miller presents evidence of the literacy, commercial activities, and legal action of Muslim women in late medieval Aragon.[30]

A variety of factors intersected to determine a woman's control over her finances, properties, and children, as well as the legal actions she could take. Those factors included her socioeconomic status, where she lived, and the nature of her relationships with her relatives through both birth and marriage.[31] While noble women could wield enormous political and economic power, most women did not have the same legal and financial independence as adult men. If she could afford it, a woman could hire notaries, lawyers, or commercial agents; some conducted business or took legal action with the permission of a husband or with the intercession of a male relative or representative.[32] A woman's marital status also dictated the extent of her control over her legal and economic rights. Married women had legal ownership of their dowries (*dotes*) and bride gifts (*arras*) "as well as one-half of any community property (*gananciales*) acquired during the marriage. But," as Vassberg explains, "she could not freely dispose of this property, or administer it, until she became a widow."[33] This emancipated status makes widows especially "visible to the historian."[34] Archived legal records—including lawsuits, leases, petitions, wills, and notarized contracts pertaining to sales, loans, guardianship, and power of attorney—reveal the legal and economic transactions of women of all marital statuses.

Such documents demonstrate the gap between prescriptive patriarchal ideals and the daily reality of women's legal and financial autonomy. Identifying this divergence is an ongoing and critical turn in scholarship on the early modern era undertaken largely by social historians of women and gender.[35] As Poska emphasizes, through many means "the public spaces of early modern Spain were filled with women. . . . The fact that women, even married women, could own property, transact business, work in a wide variety of occupations, and take legal action meant that they were constant presences in nearly all public forums."[36] In the case of Valladolid, the lease contracts written in 1538 are significant (along with other records of property and petitioning discussed below) because they reveal Morisca women who, as lease holders, property owners, and co-litigants, used their legal and economic prerogatives to protect their property and sustain their community.

The conclusion of the trial did not halt attempts to separate the Moriscos of Valladolid from one another. In fact, plans to disperse Morisco communities took many forms throughout the Spanish kingdoms over the course of the sixteenth century. In 1529, Charles V (r. 1516–1556) ordered the chief magistrates of royal towns to meet with Morisco leaders to discuss how to relocate the inhabitants of former morerías. Inquisitor-General Manrique wrote to all local tribunals with similar instructions. This initiative yielded few results, though consultations and reports continued through the mid-sixteenth century.[37] In 1531, the Inquisition of Valladolid ordered that Moriscos in its jurisdiction live among Old Christians.[38] Likewise, a 1543 Edict of Grace issued by that same tribunal required as a condition of pardon that Moriscos live apart from one another and reside among Old Christians.[39] In Valladolid, the demolition of the walls surrounding the Barrio de Santa María was discussed and attempted on multiple occasions between 1541 and 1573; this project faced a series of practical delays, financial setbacks, and opposition from the Morisco inhabitants of the barrio.[40] Yet the Moriscos remained, and there is no evidence that the walls were torn down before their expulsion in the early seventeenth century.[41] Attempts to "open" (*abrir*) the barrio were about more than urban planning. Like the legal challenge to the Moriscos' tenancy in their barrio, this project can be interpreted as an attempt to undo the closed physical space of the Moriscos' community.

In defense of that community, Morisca women again entered into collective legal action on September 14, 1557. One hundred and fourteen Morisco citizens from the Barrio de Santa María initiated negotiations with the Spanish Inquisition on that day, and a scribe noted "among them a number of Morisca widows."[42] This Morisco delegation represented itself, and acted on behalf of twenty-six Moriscos who were in jail or had fled the jurisdiction, as well as eight Moriscos from neighboring towns who were in similar straights. They authorized a writ that "requested His Majesty and the Council of the Inquisition to give mercy to all of the newly converted Muslims and their descendants of the cities and towns and places in the district of the said Inquisition of Valladolid and to concede to them certain conditions."[43] In return for an annual payment called the *situado*, the Moriscos requested an Edict of Grace to protect their community from the regular religious prosecution it endured. The Moriscos of Valladolid took this action together with Morisco communities from within the same inquisitorial district, including Arévalo, Ávila, Medina del Campo, and Palencia. They agreed to pay 400,000 *maravedís* collectively to the Valladolid tribunal each year.[44] In exchange, the Inquisition would stop confiscating their property and would extend mercy to Morisco prisoners and fugitives. Among other conditions, the Moriscos requested permission to remain in their places of residence, "ask[ing] for license to have their own houses to live in and in the neighborhood where they are, even though they have been ordered to leave it." The Inquisition agreed to this request; it was not uncommon for minority groups to pay tributes or special taxes to governing bodies in exchange for protection or accommodation, and the cash-strapped Valladolid tribunal would use the situado to pay inquisitors' salaries.[45]

Morisca women played multiple roles in these negotiations. First, they were petitioners. As heads of their households, widowed Moriscas appeared as citizens alongside Morisco men in settling the conditions of the situado. Women were obliged to pay the annual tribute, too. Their names emerge in a registry created by the Spanish Inquisition for the purposes of administering situado payments. The first part of this registry lists one hundred and forty-three Morisco citizens of Valladolid, along with four from Tordesillas and three from Toro. Included in the Valladolid contingent were thirty Morisca women from the Barrio de Santa María.[46] Some of these women were described as wives and were perhaps "virtual" widows, that is, acting heads of household in the name of absent husbands.[47] Finally, Morisca women appear as property owners in two censuses of Morisco-owned property tied to the situado tribute: one was a list of houses in the Barrio de Santa María, while the other itemized agricultural lands, mostly vineyards, in the environs of Valladolid. Some women were named among citizens obliged to pay the tribute and as property owners, including the widows Isabel del Castillo, Luisa de la Serna, Leonor Carretona, and Ana la Enamorada. Leonor de Cuellar, the Morisca widow of Lope Zapatero, was obliged to pay the situado; she was also named in the first census as the owner of two houses and in the second as proprietor of two vineyards.[48]

While the Morisca women included in these censuses were predominantly widows recorded as sole titleholders, some were listed as co-owners of property alongside their husbands, including Juan de Ulloa and his wife

Casilda la Garzona, Martin Guisado and his unnamed wife, and Alexo Ramirez and his unnamed wife.[49] Despite the missing names of these women, such cases illustrate the common sharing of economic and administrative power within marriages—an experience emphasized by social historians of women and gender in early modern Europe.[50] There are also examples of Morisca mothers, daughters, and sisters listed among the property owners. Alonso de Montemayor owned houses in the Barrio de Santa María with his mother, who would likely have been his legal guardian if he was under the age of twenty-five and his father was deceased.[51] Together, the unnamed daughters of Gaspar Moreno owned a house and four rural plots of land (one section of riverbank and three sections of vineyard). Isabel Andada, sister of Hernando Andado, owned a vineyard that bordered her brother's property.[52] Finally, the census records include many unnamed Morisca women identified only as the widows of their deceased husbands as well as a few women with no given relationships. The marital statuses of the latter are not described, and it is possible that some were single women, given that the estimated average of Spanish women who never married was 10 percent during this era.[53]

Widows formed 15 to 19 percent of the citizen population of Valladolid in the mid- to late-sixteenth century and up to 21 percent in nearby towns.[54] Military conflict and immigration to the Americas caused high rates of widowhood, absentee husbands, and women heads of household in early modern Castile. It was generally less common for widows to remarry than it was for widowers.[55] In fact, the legal autonomy granted to widows may have motivated women not to remarry after the death of a husband.[56] The death, absence, and incarceration of Morisco men targeted by the Spanish Inquisition left many Morisca wives and widows as the heads of their households. A register of ninety-four Morisco households in the Barrio de Santa María in 1610 includes twenty-eight headed by widowed Moriscas. Some were all-female households: Isabel de Robles lived with her two daughters and one orphaned niece; Isabel de la Rua lived with her three orphaned granddaughters; Leonor de Ulloa lived with her three daughters.[57]

Censuses, registers of property, and other legal records reveal how Morisca heads of household played a range of public and legal roles, with responsibilities that could include the legal guardianship of children and the administration of family properties and business. While many would have had to work to earn an income, few records name the paid work of Morisca women in Valladolid. In one lucky exception, a 1594 census lists the occupations of three Morisca widows in the city: the seamstress María Hernández was fifty-five years old and the mother of three sons, aged seventeen to twenty-four; the midwife Isabel Garcia was sixty years old with no known relatives; and the innkeeper Beatriz Ortiz was forty-four years old and mother to one daughter, aged twenty.[58] Officially, widows did not have the political rights of citizens (*vecinos*) and so could not, for example, participate in municipal government. Vassberg draws attention to their "partial rights of citizenship" due to their "ambiguous position in the socio/administrative life of the Spanish municipalities of the day: although they had no political rights, they were recognized as the heads of households; they controlled property, operated productive enterprises, participated in communal activities and paid taxes."[59] Working-class widows did not challenge men's political power. Yet their authority over their households, property, and dependents put them in a position to defend and maintain their communities. The involvement of Morisca women in the fight for the barrio and in the situado settlement are important examples of the legal and economic roles they played in their community.

The negotiation of the situado did not quell objections to the Moriscos' collective residency or accusations of Islamic religiosity. While the majority of the trial records from the Valladolid Inquisition are lost, extant visitation records and correspondences permit a partial reconstruction of the tribunal's surveillance and prosecution of Moriscos. In 1561, for example, parish priests charged the Moriscos of the Barrio de Santa María with a litany of infractions. Fathers Martínez and Calbo complained to inquisitors that the Moriscos were absent from church, unable to recite Catholic prayers, and did not interact with or marry their children to local Old Christians.[60] The two priests suspected the Moriscos of avoiding pork and wine and of adhering to Islamic burial rites. They asserted that many Morisco "husbands, wives, their children and the servants of their households" did not fulfill the obligations of their baptism or attend to their souls as Christians.

Martínez recommended their removal from the Barrio de Santa María based on these accusations, writing: "If they are dispersed throughout the town as I have said, they would communicate with Old Christians, and when the Old Christian and his wife go to mass, so too would the New Christians, from shame or from fear, because they would know [that they were being held accountable]. And the sons would converse with the sons of their neighbours, and daughters would do the same, and [little by little over time] they would make friends and would join in marriage."[61] These recommendations did not become reality, and religious authorities continued to identify closed and communal Morisco spaces as decisive factors in the Moriscos' "poor conversion" generations after the baptism of their Muslim predecessors.[62]

Valladolid inquisitors recorded their opinions (called *parescers*) of this situation in 1566. Inquisitor Ramírez asserted that in their own confessions, the Moriscos admitted to having "dogmatized their sons and daughters in their ceremonies and damned sect."[63] Letters sent during this era between Valladolid inquisitors and the General Council of the Inquisition in Madrid name many Morisco men and Morisca women accused of and punished for observing Islam. In one example from October 1575, a Morisca named Leonor Hernández was in prison on charges of celebrating her wedding day according to what were perceived as Muslim rituals. She had been observed "on the day of her wedding, being sat above the other women, and having her face covered, and not speaking nor eating," but there was no *alfaquí*, or expert in Islamic law, in the town to confirm to the inquisitors whether or not these were Muslim ceremonies.[64] It is not made clear in the letters whether Leonor Hernández was a Morisca from the Barrio de Santa María or a newcomer, perhaps one of many deportees from the kingdom of Granada resettled in Valladolid after 1570. In any case, the discovery of a number of women found celebrating a wedding in this fashion clearly disconcerted the inquisitors. A secretary of the Valladolid tribunal read a public edict warning against performing Islamic ceremonies at weddings and betrothals.[65]

The relationship between cultural practices and religious identities was a continual subject of debate. The matter had come to a breaking point in 1567 when Philip II (r. 1556–1598) enforced a royal edict that banned the Arabic language and Morisco dress and customs in the kingdom of Granada. A Granadan Morisco elder named Francisco Nuñez Muley responded to the edict in his *Memorandum*, in which he famously argued that Morisco cultural practices did not necessarily correspond to Islamic faith.[66] The king issued the edict despite such protests, ultimately provoking a Morisco rebellion and the Second Granadan War (1568–1570). The eventual royal victory resulted in the deportation of an estimated eighty thousand Granadan Moriscos and their forced resettlement throughout the rest of the Crown of Castile, beginning in 1570.[67] Arguments justifying the expulsion focused on the need to assimilate Moriscos into Old Christian society in order to bring about their full conversion as well as on the impossibility of trusting the residential seclusion of Moriscos. "To avoid the inconveniences that have and could occur from their being together," the king proclaimed, "and so that they might be better indoctrinated and be Christians, we are resettling them in cities and towns and places in our kingdoms, separated and divided."[68] Royal orders prohibited Granadan deportees from living among Castilian "Old Moriscos" (*antiguos moriscos*) such as those in Valladolid's Barrio de Santa María.[69] Although *antiguos moriscos* and the exiled Granadans had different statuses and were sometimes subject to different policies, religious and lay authorities viewed residential proximity between any and all Moriscos with suspicion and disdain.

Morisco homes and neighborhoods were spaces that could conceal clandestine adherence to Islamic customs, the teaching of those traditions to Morisco children, and the preservation of bonds of kinship and community between Moriscos; this binding was practical and conceptual, serving the Muslim concept of the Islamic community of believers, or *umma*.[70] The domestic labor and traditional knowledge of Morisca women was vital to the survival of Morisco culture and communities. Formal petitioning and negotiating to defend those spaces and bonds were tactics for surviving in an inquisitorial society. The example of Valladolid's Barrio de Santa María demonstrates how widowed Morisca heads of household participated in the legal defense of their community alongside male Morisco citizens, first in the lawsuit over leases and later in the situado settlement. Morisca women also appear in the legal records generated by the administration of the property they owned, records that includes leases, census enrollment, and the payment of taxes and tributes associated with that property. The stories these documents tell exemplify wider scholarship that reveals how early modern women were public and legal actors with a range of abilities and experiences, helping to "repopulate the streets of early modern Spain with women."[71] These particular records do not, however, provide a full view of their lived experiences and gendered identities; further research is required to better understand the status of Morisca women within their communities, especially how the legal and economic endeavors they undertook jointly with Morisco men may have been internally characterized by cooperation or conflict.

Understanding the many roles Morisca women played in defending and maintaining the bonds of their communities is critical in challenging long-held assumptions about both New Christians and women as silent minorities. Morisca women did experience marginalization based on their gendered, religious, and socioeconomic statuses. Yet that marginalization did not mean complete exclusion. It is more fruitful to acknowledge the intersection of various forms of marginalization, using the concept to consider a "spectrum of social experience instead of a binary of inclusion and exclusion," and recognizing, as Cohen urges, "disadvantage and its consequences but also agency."[72] The women of the Barrio de Santa María did not hold elected offices, noble titles, or great riches; they experienced religious prosecution at the hands of the Spanish Inquisition as well as the assimilationist policies of local and royal governments. Contemporary Catholic Castilian ideals prescribed their silence, obedience, and subordination, yet Morisca women were not silent or passive, nor were they confined to a domestic sphere. While most Morisco households were headed by men, many Morisca women had considerable control over their own finances, families, dependents, and properties. Both Morisco men and Morisca women acted to protect their properties, families, and communities. The public legal and economic roles of Morisca women were central to those endeavors, just as their domestic labor and organization was fundamental to the subsistence and survival of Morisco families and communities.

1. In 1502, Muslims living in the Crown of Castile were ordered to leave the Spanish kingdoms or convert to Catholicism because the Muslim rebellion in Granada (1499–1501) was considered a violation of the 1492 capitulation treaties that had permitted Muslims to practice Islam in post-conquest Granada; see "Provisión de los Reyes Católicos ordenando la expulsion de los musulmanes del reino (1502, febrero, 12.)" in Carrasco Manchado, *De la convivencia a la exclusión*, 233–40. The forced conversion of Muslims in the Crown of Aragon in 1526 took place in the aftermath of the Germanías revolt; see Ehlers, *Between Christians and Moriscos*, 14–17. The final expulsion of Moriscos from the Spanish Kingdoms took place between 1609 and 1614; see García-Arenal and Wiegers, *Expulsion of the Moriscos*.

2. My doctoral dissertation (under revision for my book manuscript) is a broader study of Morisco legal action. See Cavanaugh, "The Morisco problem."

3. See Vincent, "Mujeres moriscas"; Levine Melammed, "Judeo-Conversas and Moriscas"; Perry, *Handless Maiden*; and Fuente, "Christian, Muslim and Jewish Women."

4. Here I agree with Perry, who writes, "Examples of Moriscos in various parts of Spain reveal the diversity of minority strategies for accommodation, resistance, and developing power." (*Handless Maiden*, 5)

5. Converts and their descendants from both Judaism and Islam were known as New Christians (*cristianos nuevos*); this category distinguished Judeoconversos and Moriscos from Old Christians (*cristianos viejos*), who had no known Muslim or Jewish ancestry and therefore claimed to have purity of blood (*limpieza de sangre*). For more on blood purity, see Martínez, *Genealogical Fictions*.

6. Perry, "Between Muslim and Christian," 187.

7. AHN, Inq., libro 1229, folios 172–76 (16th c.). The General Council of the Inquisition (the *Suprema*) issued this list of Islamic practices. It was likely intended to be read publicly to instruct people how to identify different forms of heresy.

8. Perry, "Moriscas and the Limits," 276. Levine Melammed discusses how "Jewish women adapted and created their own informal system of education" in "Crypto-Jewish," 198–99. In *Frontiers of Heresy*, Monter writes that Aragonese Morisca women "filled part of the institutional gap caused by the absence of mosques and the rarity of trained clergy," 227.

9. Vincent, "Las mujeres moriscas," 625 (my translation).

10. Levine Melammed, "Judeo-Conversas and Morisca," 158. On *conversas*, see also Levine Melammed, *Heretics or Daughters?*

11. O'Banion, *This Happened*, especially pages 16–20, 34–35, 48–49, 102–4.

12. Levine Melammed points out that abstinence from work could also prompt suspicion, such as when conversa women finished their work of cooking the evening meal before sundown on the Sabbath. See "Castilian Conversas at Work," 82–83.

13. Perry, *Handless Maiden*, 79.

14. See, for example, the testimonies of Morisca women cited in Cook, *Forbidden Passages*, 20–24. Monter notes a similar dynamic in Aragon, where Morisca women were routinely punished by the Spanish Inquisition for teaching Islamic traditions to their families, *Frontiers of Heresy*, 227.

15. AHN, Inq., legajo 2136, expediente 3 (May 6, 1561).

16. For the similar case of Ávila, see Tapia Sánchez, *La comunidad morisca*, 224–25. For southern Aragon, see Monter's description (in *Frontiers of Heresy*, 227) of how Morisco dwellings were often physically connected to one another but quite separate from Old Christian residences, allowing Morisca women a great deal of seclusion in which to preserve Islamic traditions.

17. AHN, Inq., legajo 2136, expediente 3, (May 6, 1561).

18. Moratinos García and Villanueva Zubizarreta, "Consecuencias," 118–20. See also Perry, "Moriscas and the Limits," 275.

19. It appears the case was primarily active between 1505–1507 and 1526–1537.

20. For more on this lawsuit, see Moratinos García and Villanueva Zubizarreta, "Consecuencias."

21. Moratinos García and Villanueva Zubizarreta call the appropriation and demolition of these buildings a "real insult" to the Moriscos of Valladolid. They locate the mosque and *casa de bodas* between the calle de la Carnicería and the calle de la Ronda, between houses on one side and a lane called "del almají" on the other. See "Consecuencias," 131–33.

22. AHN, Inq., legajo 2110, expediente 2, "Apeo de las casas."

23. AHPV, PN 13. I remain grateful to Doña Guadalupe Ramos de Castro (Professor Emerita of Art History, University of Valladolid) for pointing me to this file while working at the *Archivo Histórico Provincial de Valladolid* in October of 2011. I later encountered the detailed article that deals with this case by Moratinos García and Villanueva Zubizarreta, "Consecuencias," 117–39.

24. AHPV, PN 13. These women include: Ana la Seguina; Ana la Serrana; Ana, wife of Antonio de Malpartido; Ana de Ulloa; Ana de Castellanos; Angelina de Cuellar; Catalina de Torquemada; Ynes de Biras; Leonor de Medina; Leonor de Benavides; María la Gallarda, widow of Francisco Gallardo; María de Medina, widow of Gaspar Andado; María Velez; María del Trigo; Mayor de Torquemada; María la Guissada; and María de la Rua.

25. AHPV, PN 13, folio 143. I translate "Censo perpetuo enfitéutico" as a long-term lease contract. I translate "señores" as masters in regard to the ownership of space

and property in the contract. See Poska, *Women and Authority*, 175, for more on widows and lease contracts in the case of Galicia.

26. Poska, *Women and Authority*, 44. For more on inheritance and guardianship, see Grace E. Coolidge, *Guardianship, Gender, and the Nobility* and "Neither Dumb, Deaf, nor Destitute."

27. See Poska, *Women and Authority*, 43, n12, and Coolidge, "Neither Dumb, Deaf, nor Destitute," 676–78.

28. For the case of Seville, see Perry, *Gender and Disorder*, 14–18. Kagan discusses widowed litigants at the Royal Chancery Court of Valladolid in *Lawsuits and Litigants*, 85. Lehfeldt examines religious women as litigants in early modern Valladolid in "Convents as Litigants" and *Religious Women*.

29. Catlos, *Muslims of Medieval Latin Christendom*, 498–504.

30. Miller, *Guardians of Islam*, 76–77; 98–99.

31. See *Women, Dowries and Agency*, in which Wessell Lightfoot examines how marriage, class, and other factors impacted the legal and economic agency of women in late medieval Valencia. In *Muslims of Medieval Latin Christendom*, Catlos acknowledges that "social class, kinship networks, religious knowledge, and prestige, were all factors that contributed to individual women's status and power," 501.

32. Perry, *Gender and Disorder*, 15–16.

33. Vassberg, "Status of Widows," 181.

34. Cavallo and Warner, *Widowhood*, 3.

35. In "How Women's History Transformed," Poska explains it as largely having been uncovered by the work of social historians researching the lives of women, stating, "The prescriptive literature of the period has been relegated to merely that—prescriptions for—not descriptions of—early modern realities." See Poska, *Women and Authority*, 1–9 for a discussion of this in relation to early modern Galicia. In her article "Women on the Margins," Cohen considers how "situational negotiation" deviated from "black-and-white language of general prescriptions," 315; Coolidge ("Neither Dumb, Deaf, nor Destitute," 674) describes the "tension in early modern Spanish society between the traditional expectations that a good woman be virtuous, secluded, and chaste, and the reality of a harsh world that demanded active participation from both men and women to maintain the power and prestige of the nobility." See also Nader, *Power and Gender*, 3, and Vassberg, "Status of Widows," 180–81.

36. Poska, "How Women's History Transformed."

37. Lea, *Moriscos of Spain*, 152.

38. Tapia Sánchez, *La comunidad morisca*, 224–25.

39. Tapia Sánchez, *La comunidad morisca*, 232.

40. Once work was finally set to begin in 1549 (after years of negotiating funding for the project) a physical confrontation broke out between Morisco residents and the workmen hired to tear down the walls. After this fight, the project was delayed and never recommenced; see Lea, *Moriscos of Spain*, 153–54. Valladolid's town council quarreled over the plan as late as November 1572 and the project gathered some momentum throughout the following year. See AHN, Inq., legajo 3191; the fight in council ("pelotero") is reported in expediente 101.

41. During the final expulsion, the last Moriscos families to leave the Barrio de Santa María departed in July of 1611. (AGS, Consejo y Junta de Hacienda, legajo 496, 4.18.)

42. AHN, Inq., legajo 2109, expediente 1 and AGS, Consejo y Junta de Hacienda, legajo 496, #4, folio 13, both copies made May 13, 1611.

43. AHN, Inq., legajo 2109, expediente 1 and AGS, Consejo y Junta de Hacienda, legajo 496, #4, folio 13, both copies made May 13, 1611.

44. Kagan explains that "Castile's money of account in the sixteenth and seventeenth centuries was the *maravedí*. Coins in general usage included the *real*, officially pegged at 34 mrs., the ducat, which was equal to 375 mrs., and the *escudo* which was worth 400 mrs. after a revaluation in 1566." See "Note on Currency," in *Lawsuits and Litigants*.

45. AHN, Inq., libro 1254, folios 270–73, "Lo que pidieron los nuevamente convertidos de Ávila, Arévalo, Valladolid y lo demas, para lo situado" (1557). Miller (*Guardians of Islam*, 4) discusses the taxes paid by religious minorities living in Islamic and Christian medieval Spanish kingdoms. In the sixteenth century, Moriscos in Granada owed a tribute called the *farda*, which paid for coastal defense in that kingdom.

46. AHN, Inq., legajo 2110, expediente 2 (1565): "Apeos de las haziendas de Moriscos de Valladolid, Medina del Campo, Arévalo, y Ávila." The women were: Elena la Roja , wife of Pedro Andado; Ynes Alvarez, wife of Alonso de Montemayor, deceased; María la Pinonera, wife of Gaspar Moreno; María la Serrana; Isabel del Castillo, wife of Lope de Ulloa; Leonor de Cuellar, wife of Lope Capatero; Mari Velez, wife of Beltran de Abanades; Francisca de Sepulveda, wife of Luis de Madrid; Mayor Clavijo, wife of Alonso de Torquemada, deceased; Luisa de la Serna, wife of Alonso Catalan; María de Buenaño, wife of Garcia Alcalde, deceased; María de Alcalde, wife of Gonzalo de Trigo, deceased; María la Morena, wife of Gaspar de Buenaño, deceased; Mayor de Ávila, wife of Luis Castañon, deceased; María la Guisada, wife of Diego Ramirez, deceased; Ana la Castañona, wife of Gabriel de Viras; Ana de Torquemada, wife of Alexandre Carretona; Ana la Enamorada, wife of Joan Calderon, deceased; Leonor la Carretona, wife of Alonso Lopez Enamorado, deceased; Ana la Enamorada, formerly the wife of Alonso (alias Baltasar) de Torquemada; Isabel de Tobar, wife of Francisco de

Malpartido, deceased; Ana (alias María) la Mejorada, wife of Alonso de Cuellar; Catalina la Serrana, widow; Ana de Benavides, wife of Lope Hurtado, deceased; Ana la Caballera, wife of Francisco Caballero, deceased; Ynes Palomades, wife of Juan Palomades; Elena Ruiz, wife of Francisco Retaco; Isabel de Viras; Isabel de Cuellar; Graçia la Castillera.

47. On abandoned wives as virtual widows, see: Bennassar, *Valladolid en el Siglo*, 180, n48; Cavallo and Warner, *Widowhood*, 6.

48. AHN, Inq., legajo 2110, expediente 2.

49. AHN, Inq., legajo 2110, expediente 2.

50. Poska, "Upending Patriarchy," 201 and *Women and Authority*, 163. Nader discusses the joint responsibilities of husbands and wives for the "economic prosperity of the family"; see *Power and Gender*, 4.

51. Coolidge, "Neither Dumb, Deaf, nor Destitute," 678; Poska, *Women and Authority*, 179–83. For more on legal minority in the early modern Spanish empire, see Premo, *Children of the Father King*.

52. AHN, Inq., legajo 2110, expediente 2. Hernando Andado was also listed as the owner of a vineyard that was part of his wife's dowry.

53. Poska, *Women and Authority*, 42. In "Upending Patriarchy," Poska writes that more in-depth research on the lives of early modern women of all socio-economic levels has revealed that incidences of single women were generally higher than assumed by earlier generations of scholars, 199.

54. Bennassar (*Valladolid en el Siglo de Oro*, 180) gives the following figures for 1561: 19 percent in Segovia; 20 percent in Burgos; 21 percent in Medina del Campo. Further northwest, widows headed 12 percent of Galician households, though figures varied by parish; Poska, *Women and Authority*, 164.

55. Poska, *Women and Authority*, 164.

56. Vassberg, "Status of Widows," 181–82. Furthermore, as Coolidge explains, "women were not legally allowed to remarry while they held a guardianship." See "Neither Dumb, Deaf, nor Destitute," 681.

57. AHN, Estado, legajo 227, #7. Widowed *antiguas* Moriscas (of Castilian and not of Granadan descent) in Valladolid (1610): María de Duenas, widowed mother-in-law of Luis de Ulloa; Ana de Valladolid, widowed mother of Luis de Cuellar; Catalina de Porras, widowed mother with two sons and one daughter; Isabel de Valladolid, widow; Isabel de Robles, widowed mother with two daughters and an orphaned niece; María de Valladolid, widow; Francisca de Morejon, widow with one orphaned girl; Isabel de Clavijo, widow with two sons; Francisca de Clavijo, widow; Angelina de Madrid, widow; Ana de Montoya, widow with two sons; Isabel de Piedrahita, widow; María de Molina, aka Isabel Guisada, widow; Isabel de San Juan, widow; María de Castañon, widow with two sons; Angelina

de Morejon, widow with one son and sister to María de Morejon, also a widow; María de Cuellar, widow with one daughter; Isabel de la Rua, widow with three orphaned granddaughters; Ana del Rincon, widowed mother of Diego del Rincon; Leonor de Ulloa, widow with three daughters; Luisa de Jinete, widow; María de la Serna, widow with two sons; María de Valbuena, widow; Ana Palomera, widow with one son; Isabel Ortiz, widow; Luisa Catalan, widow; Yfabiana Copete, widow with two sons.

58. AHN, Inq., legajo 2109, expediente 1, "Lista de los moriscos vezinos y habitantes en el distrito y partido de la Inquisición de Valladolid," entries 234, 280, and 1025.

59. Vassberg, "Status of Widows," 182; see Vassberg for more on poor and rural widows. Poska deals with peasant widows in early modern Galicia in *Women and Authority*, 163–92. See Nader on the role of social status in determining women's "autonomy and agency" (*Power and Gender*, 18–21); see, too, Jodi Bilinkoff, "Elite Widows and Religious Expression," 181–92 in Cavallo and Warner, *Widowhood*.

60. AHN, Inq., legajo 2136, expediente 3.

61. AHN, Inq., legajo 2136, expediente 3.

62. AHN, Inq., legajo 2136, expediente 3, and legajo 2108, expediente 16 e.

63. AHN, Inq., legajo 2108, expediente 16 e.

64. AHN, Inq., legajo 2108, expediente 16 e. For more on *alfaquís* in the late medieval Spanish kingdoms, see Miller, *Guardians of Islam.*

65. AHN, Inq., legajo 3192, expediente 170. The general edict was read in Valladolid on October 8, 1575. See also AHN, Inq., libro 578, folio 335r (October 1, 1575) for the letter from the General Council of the Inquisition to the Valladolid tribunal.

66. Núñez Muley, *A Memorandum.*

67. Vincent, "L'expulsion des Morisques."

68. AGS, Consejo de Castilla, legajo 2159, folio 7 (Philip II from Madrid on December 11, 1570).

69. Philip II, "Pragmatica" (October 6, 1572), 27–38.

70. Perry, *Handless Maiden*, 66–67.

71. Poska, "How Women's History Transformed."

72. Cohen, "Women on the Margins," 312.

BIBLIOGRAPHY

Primary Sources

AGS. Archivo General de Simancas

    CC. Cámara de Castilla, Legajo 2159 (folios s.n.).

    CJH. Consejo y Junta de Hacienda, Legajo 496, #4, folios 13 and 18.

    Sección Estado, Legajo 227 (n7).

AHN. Archivo Histórico Nacional

    Sección Inquisición (Inq.), legajo 2108 (expediente 16 e), legajo 2109 (expediente 1),

    legajo 2110 (expediente 2), legajo 2136 (expediente 3), legajo 3191 (expediente 101), legajo 3192 (expediente 170).

    Sección Inquisición, Libros 578 (folio 335r), libro 1229 (folios 172–76), libro 1254 (folios 270–73).

AHPV. Archivo Histórico Provincial de Valladolid

    PN. Protocolos Notariales, 13 (Cristobal de Montesinos, Año 1538).

Núñez Muley, Francisco. *A Memorandum for the President of the Royal Audiencia and Chancery Court of the City and Kingdom of Granada* (1567). Edited by Vincent Barletta. Chicago: University of Chicago Press, 2007.

Philip II, "Pragmática y declaración sobre los moriscos del reyno de Granada, y la orden que con ellos se ha de tener" (October 6, 1572, Madrid). In Francisco Izquierdo, *La Expulsión de los Moriscos del reino de Granada: (pragmáticas, provisiones y órdenes reales)*, 27–38. Madrid: Azur, 1983.

Secondary Sources

Bennassar, Bartolomé. *Valladolid en el Siglo de Oro: una ciudad de Castilla y su entorno agrario en el siglo XVI*. Valladolid: Ayuntamiento de Valladolid, 1989.

Carrasco Manchado, Ana Isabel, ed. *De la convivencia a la exclusión. Imágenes legislativas de mudéjares y moriscos. Siglos XIII–XVII*. Madrid: Sílex, 2012.

Catlos, Brian A. *Muslims of Medieval Latin Christendom, c.1050–1614*. Cambridge: Cambridge University Press, 2014.

Cavallo, Sandra, and Lyndan Warner. *Widowhood in Medieval and Early Modern Europe*. Harlow: Pearson Education, 1999.

Cavanaugh, Stephanie M. "The Morisco Problem and the Politics of Belonging in Sixteenth-Century Valladolid." PhD dissertation, University of Toronto, 2016.

Cohen, Elizabeth S. "Women on the Margins." In *The Ashgate Research Companion to Women and Gender in Early Modern Europe*, edited by Jane Couchman, Allyson M. Poska, and Katherine A. McIver, 312–34. Burlington: Ashgate, 2013.

Cook, Karoline. *Forbidden Passages: Muslims and Moriscos in Colonial Spanish America*. Philadelphia: University of Pennsylvania Press, 2016.

Coolidge, Grace E. *Guardianship, Gender, and the Nobility in Early Modern Spain*. Surrey: Ashgate, 2011.

———. "'Neither Dumb, Deaf, nor Destitute of Understanding': Women as Guardians in Early Modern Spain." *The Sixteenth Century Journal* 36, no. 3 (2005): 673–93.

Ehlers, Benjamin. *Between Christians and Moriscos: Juan de Ribera and Religious Reform in Valencia, 1568–1614*. Baltimore: Johns Hopkins University Press, 2006.

Fuente, María Jesús. "Christian, Muslim and Jewish Women in Late Medieval Iberia." *Medieval Encounters* 15, nos. 2–4 (2009): 319–33.

García-Arenal, Mercedes, and Gerard Wiegers. *The Expulsion of the Moriscos from Spain: a Mediterranean Diaspora*. Leiden: Brill, 2014.

Kagan, Richard L. *Lawsuits and Litigants in Castile, 1500–1700*. University of North Carolina Press, 1981.

Lea, Henry Charles. *The Moriscos of Spain: Their Conversion and Expulsion*. Westport CT: Greenwood Press, 1968 (1901).

Lehfeldt, Elizabeth A. "Convents as Litigants: Dowry and Inheritance Disputes in Early-Modern Spain." *Journal of Social History* 33, no. 3 (2000): 645–64.

———. *Religious women in Golden Age Spain: The Permeable Cloister*. Burlington: Ashgate, 2005.

Levine Melammed, Renée. "Castilian Conversas at Work." In *Women at Work in Spain: from the Middle Ages to Early Modern Times*, edited by Carmen Benito-Vessels and Marilyn Stone, 81–100. New York: Peter Lang, 1998.

———. "Crypto-Jewish Women Facing the Spanish Inquisition: Transmitting Religious Practices, Beliefs, and Attitudes." In *Christians, Muslims, and Jews in Medieval and Early Modern Spain: Interaction and Cultural Change*, edited by Edward D. English and Mark D. Meyerson, 197–219. Notre Dame: University of Notre Dame Press, 1999a.

———. *Heretics or Daughters of Israel? The Crypto-Jewish Women of Castile*. New York: Oxford University Press, 1999b.

———. "Judeo-Conversas and Moriscas in Sixteenth-Century Spain: A Study of Parallels." *Jewish History* 24, no. 2 (2010): 155–68.

Martínez, María Elena. *Genealogical Fictions: Limpieza de Sangre, Religion, and Gender in Colonial Mexico*. California: Stanford University Press, 2008.

Miller, Kathryn A. *Guardians of Islam: Religious Authority and Muslim Communities of Late Medieval Spain*. New York: Columbia Press, 2008.

Monter, William E. *Frontiers of Heresy: The Spanish Inquisition from the Basque Lands to Sicily*. Cambridge: Cambridge University Press, 1990.

Moratinos García, Manuel, and Olatz Villanueva Zubizarreta. "Consecuencias del decreto de conversión al cristianismo de 1502 en la aljama mora de Valladolid." *Sharq Al-andalus* 16–17 (1999–2002): 117–39.

Nader, Helen. *Power and Gender in Renaissance Spain: Eight Women of the Mendoza Family, 1450–1650*. Urbana: University of Illinois Press, 2004.

O'Banion, Patrick J. *This Happened in My Presence: Moriscos, Old Christians, and the Spanish Inquisition in the Town of Deza, 1569–1611*. Toronto: University of Toronto Press, 2017.

Perry, Mary Elizabeth. "Between Muslim and Christian Worlds: Moriscas and Identity in Early Modern Spain." *The Muslim World* 95, no. 2 (2005a): 177–98.

———. *Gender and Disorder in Early Modern Seville*. Princeton: Princeton University Press, 1990.

———. "Moriscas and the Limits of Assimilation." In *Christians, Muslims, and Jews in Medieval and Early Modern Spain: Interaction and Cultural Change*, edited by Edward D. English and Mark D. Meyerson, 274–89. Notre Dame: University of Notre Dame Press, 1999.

———. *The Handless Maiden: Moriscos and the Politics of Religion in Early Modern Spain*. Princeton: Princeton University Press, 2005b.

Poska, Allyson M. "How Women's History Transformed the Study of Early Modern Spain." *Bulletin of the Society for Spanish and Portuguese Historical Studies* 23, no. 1 (2008): 5–19, https://www.ucmo.edu/asphs/2008/women.html (site discontinued).

———. "Upending Patriarchy: Rethinking Marriage and Family in Early Modern Europe." In *The Ashgate research companion to women and gender in early modern Europe, edited by* Jane Couchman, Allyson M. Poska, and Katherine A. McIver, 198–214. Burlington: Ashgate, 2013.

———. *Women and Authority in Early Modern Spain: The Peasants of Galicia*. Oxford: Oxford University Press, 2005.

Premo, Bianca. *Children of the Father King: Youth, Authority, and Legal Minority in Colonial Lima*. Chapel Hill: University of North Carolina Press, 2005.

Tapia Sánchez, Serafín de. *La comunidad morisca de Ávila*. Salamanca: Universidad de Salamanca, 1991.

Vassberg, David E. "The Status of Widows in Sixteenth-Century Rural Castile." In *Poor Women and Children in the European Past*, edited by John Henderson and Richard Wall, 180–95. London: Routledge, 1994.

Vincent, Bernard. "Las mujeres moriscas." In *Historia de las mujeres en Occidente, v.3: Del Renacimiento a la Edad Moderna*, edited by George Duby and Michelle Parot, 614–25. Madrid: Taurus, 2000 (1992).

_____. "L'expulsion des Morisques du Royaume de Grenade et leur répartition en Castille (1570–1571)." *Mélanges de la Casa de Velázquez* 6, no. 1 (1970): 211–46.

Wessell Lightfoot, Dana. *Women, Dowries and Agency: Marriage in Fifteenth-Century Valencia*. Manchester: Manchester University Press, 2013.

Part 3

Institutional Relationships and Creating Communities

8

Looking for a Way to Survive

Community and Institutional Assistance to Widows in Medieval Barcelona

MIREIA COMAS-VIA

For many medieval married women, the death of their husbands brought hardships and often a substantial change in social status.[1] In late medieval Barcelona, widows, from all social backgrounds, often did not have the means to maintain their social and economic positions. Sometimes they were not successful in recovering their dowry; even when they were able to secure it, it was often insufficient as subsistence for widows. On occasion, they were forced to cope with their late husbands' problems and debts, and they could have small children to take care of or be too old to work.[2] Impoverishment was common, and for some, even destitution. Although documentation is limited, it does suggest both informal strategies and official resources to which needy widows could turn for support.[3]

Considering that the return of their dowry and their own work were sometimes not enough to make a living, many widows had to look for alternatives to complement the meagre incomes they had.[4] Less fortunate women did not have any kind of regular income, and thus, in order to be able to provide for themselves, they had to seek the support of official charitable institutions as well as that of other forms of unorganized welfare, such as the help provided by relatives, friends, and neighbors. The assistance widows received from the community as a whole took different forms, including alms in the event of specific financial difficulties, support in cases of illness, and protection and companionship in circumstances of helplessness and loneliness. Widows from all social backgrounds appear in the extant documents of charitable institutions asking for financial support, either occasionally, or on a regular basis. In other words, the urban community provided a number of forms of assistance for widows, which were not only available to the poorest women of the city but also to those who had enjoyed a comfortable social position close to the court while their husbands were alive. Thus, the aim of this study is to analyze the different forms of formal and informal solidarity that widows could call upon, especially when family ties were weak or nonexistent.[5] The city was certainly a favorable environment for the creation of solidarity networks among women, especially those who lived alone, such as widows. In fact, according to the tax records of late fourteenth-century Barcelona, most of the women living on their own were widows, 24 percent of whom claiming to be too poor to pay taxes. However, some of the other widows documented in hearth tax records (*fogatjaments*), who belonged to the so-called "middle hand," were also close to the poverty line.[6] Given this situation, it is not surprising that the widows of Barcelona sought the protection of the community in order to survive as full members of society.

It thus stands to reason that, in order to analyze their reality, it is essential to take into account all forms of assistance, both institutionalized and unregistered, although the latter are much more difficult to trace, for they were often not explicitly recorded. In the following pages we will first focus on the social networks formed by various communities of women, and then we will turn to the charitable institutions that were available to widows in the event of economic need or sickness—such as the royal almsgiver, the parochial "collection plates" for the deserving poor, and the Hospital de la Santa Creu—to show how the urban community assisted destitute widows through family, friendship, and neighborhood ties.

The city enabled the confluence of women who were going through the same difficulties and shared the same needs. These women wove solidarity networks in order to overcome their circumstances. It should be noted that these women were not only widows, but also freedwomen, servants, and foreigners; in sum, women without men, without families, who obtained the support they needed from other women in the same situation. On average, they belonged to the poorest groups of the city, but these networks can also be documented among women of the upper classes, who also helped each other in cases of need.[7] The extant documents show how these often unnoticed links between women were articulated.[8] In some cases, these were women who already knew each other when they were married, and created closer ties after being widowed. In other instances, they were immigrants from the same place of origin who, finding themselves alone in a strange city, ended up together. In other circumstances, the relationship was the result of neighborhood, or was established through ties related to work. In these latter cases, their employers, with whom they often lived, were the sources of help if times became difficult.

Aware of the opportunities they could find in the city, some widows chose to move, often encouraged by the support they received from family and friends. This kind of situation can be seen in sources dealing with citizenship that are preserved in the Historical Archive of the City of Barcelona. Thus, for example, the merchants Joan Bertran and Guillem Alegret advised Violant, probably after the death of her husband, the merchant Arnau Grissó, to live in the city of Barcelona; and so she moved, along with her three daughters and two sons, and settled in a house that was owned by Joan Bertran.[9] Avinent Cugullada, a resident of Cagliari, turned to her brother-in-law Gabriel Cugullada in order to return from Sardinia with her daughters. In all likelihood, her expectations of maintaining her living conditions on the island were not fulfilled, and thus, given the uncertainty inherent in being a woman alone, away from home, she wanted to return to Barcelona to rebuild her life.[10] As these two cases show, the city offered all sorts of advantages for women who, following the death of their husbands, had no ties whatsoever in their place of residence. Moving to a place where a family member or friend lived was probably the best option, given that they could turn to them for support in case of need. At any rate, they could build new connections there because, given the presence of other migrants with similar needs, the city was doubtlessly a favorable environment for the creation of solidarity networks.[11]

Thus, in addition to the help that widows might find in urban settings, migration was also seen as a strategy to improve their economic and social situations, for they hoped to find better opportunities in a city like Barcelona. It is worth looking into the relationships that women (especially widows) who shared no family ties established with each other, because they often had no close relatives to turn to. A common background could be one of the reasons for the creation of such ties, in particular among women who probably had no access to any other means of support. This is the case in a group of widows of craftsmen who had first lived in Sardinia, where they had established strong friendship ties. After the death of their husbands and probably in view of the lack of future prospects, they migrated to Barcelona, where they shared a house. Thus, they faced the difficulties they encountered together, such as helping the daughter of Clara, the widow of Guillem Comes.[12] The girl, named Blanca, had been raped by the weaver Guillem Rifà, who also got her pregnant while she lived in his house as a servant, helping his wife after childbirth. Clara, who had children and lived on alms, claimed to be poor, and pleaded with the judge that Guillem Rifà should be imprisoned. She asked this as a reward for the many services that Blanca's father had rendered in Sardinia.[13] In the same court proceedings, Margarida, the widow of Bartomeu Artigues, a tailor from Sassari, claimed that the women had once gone to Tortosa, where Queen Eleanor of Sicily was, hoping to improve their hopeless situation, because they had heard that the king had promised favors to all those who had been in Sardinia. Although the circumstances were unfavorable to them, either the terrible ordeal of Blanca's rape, or failing to secure any alms from the Queen, prompted them to weave a solidarity network on the basis of their shared bond, that is, the fact that they had first met in Sassari and then returned to

Barcelona. Indeed, these women managed to leave behind the loneliness often inherent to widowhood by creating links with others who were in the same situation, thus replacing the lack of family relationships both at home and in their new destination. It is thanks to solidarity networks, such as the one mentioned above, that the urban community could reach the people in greatest need. The links among them were strengthened precisely through contact, shared experiences, or a common origin, and as a result, the networks established by women who lived in this sort of community multiplied all over the city.

FORMS OF INSTITUTIONALIZED CHARITY

While the parish church played the most preeminent role within the medieval charity system, the institutions that made up this charity system were quite diverse. For instance, the Pia Almoina—the cathedral's charity—hospitals, monasteries and convents, religious confraternities, guilds, and even the king himself were also part of this assistance network.[14] The beneficiaries of these charities were mainly people whose economic situation had suffered a serious setback, as was the case of some widows who, after the death of their husbands, could find themselves without the means to survive. Almsgiving was the means to alleviate the situation of the so-called *pobres vergonyants* (deserving poor) that is, those who were ashamed of their situation and who, unlike beggars—at least in the eyes of medieval society—deserved to be helped.[15]

In regard to the charitable endeavors of the monarchy it is necessary to mention, above all, the officer expressly appointed by the king for the distribution of alms, the almoner. Several widows are documented among the beneficiaries of the aid that the monarch distributed through this royal institution. However, according to the data provided by the extant account books of the tenure of Guillem Deudé as almoner—a monk of the Cistercian monastery of Poblet—widows were not in the majority.[16] A few among these women were favored with *violaris*, and therefore received a lifelong monthly pension of thirty *sous*.[17] This regular payment was usually granted to people of a certain standing that had fallen into destitution, such as the widows of noble servants or friends of the king. In the period between 1378 and 1382, some of the women who most benefitted from these alms were Sibil·la de Togores, the widow of Oliver de Togores, Gueralda de Puigverd, Auger de Malleho's widow, and Antònia, the widow of Masèn Dardo. All of them were linked to the court in one way or another, which made it possible for these widows to receive a considerable annual pension that helped them maintain their social status despite the death of their husbands.[18]

A number of non-elite widows were granted more exceptional donations. In most cases these women, who are described as *"fembra viuda pobra"* (female, widow, and poor) or *"fembra viuda i miserable"* (female, widow, and destitute), were specifically provided funds by the king's almoner for their sustenance. The sums ranged from eleven to 200 *sous*, and the average donation amounted to 48.5 *sous*. However, on other occasions, alms had a more concrete purpose and consisted of a donation to marry a daughter or a sister of the widow. In these cases the sums were higher, ranging from fifty to 120 *sous*, and amounting to 85 *sous*, on average.[19] It is interesting to note how, in view of the families' lack of ability to provide their daughters with a proper dowry, this royal allowance contributed to the endowment of girls from underprivileged classes who had turned to the king to improve their condition. Thus, the material assistance that the sovereign could provide was a plausible option for widows in need, both from the wealthier and the lower classes of Barcelona. Although the sources are not explicit in this regard, these were women who had suffered an economic setback that made them eligible for the help of charitable institutions, in this case, the king. Therefore, in practice, the loss of their husband led many women to join the ranks of the deserving poor.

Besides the royal almoner, the main charitable institution within the assistance network was undoubtedly the Bací dels Pobres, an institution whose name could be roughly translated as the "collection plate for the poor," which depended on the parishes of the city.[20] Its purpose was to distribute the donations of some parishioners among the neediest people of their parish. The community of parishioners provided material assistance to their neighbors by means of different types of donations that were channeled through this institution. Part of the contributions came from the sums of money that the testators of the city bequeathed in their wills.

It was frequent to find widows among the donors, especially widows of honored citizens, merchants, and wealthy craftsmen.[21] For example, in the 1421 record book of the Bací dels Pobres of the Church of Santa Maria del Mar, nineteen out of the eighty-three documented contributors were widows.[22] In addition to testamentary legacies, the *baciners*, who were also called *prohoms* (good men) of the Bací dels Pobres, carried out a collection around the church every Sunday morning and every holiday. In the case of the parish of Santa Maria del Pi, a remarkable crowd gathered to contribute their donations to the collection, which usually took place around the landmarks of the neighborhood: the Carmelite convent, the convent of Santa Anna, the convent of the Fratres Saccati, the church of Santa Maria del Pi, the plaça Nova, the old city gate of La Boqueria, and the cathedral.[23] The *baciners* were responsible for the monthly distribution of alms among the poorest members of the parish. The beneficiaries of the Bací dels Pobres were both men and women that came from a wide variety of backgrounds and conditions and needed to resort to the parish to cover their basic needs. However, there were also those who had more specific problems, such as settling a debt, dowering a daughter, or paying for the shroud in which a loved one was to be buried.[24] The usual amounts that were distributed among the deserving poor of the parish of Santa Maria del Pi in the early fifteenth century ranged between one and a half and two *sous* a month, which were actually very low sums.[25]

Let us now turn to two examples from the parish of Santa Maria del Pi where the beneficiaries of the alms were widows who received money from another widow's testamentary executor. These were Mateua, widow of Galceran Pinós, and Clara, widow of Humbert de Vilafranca, and they were granted twenty and 110 *sous*, respectively, in the testament of Maria, widow of Bernat Vidal.[26] The aforementioned Clara was ill, and appeared several times in the books of the Bací of Santa Maria del Pi. In fact, despite belonging to the upper bourgeoisie, she was the "deserving poor" of the parish who received the most generous alms between 1423 and 1428.[27] It should be noted that the criterion governing the distribution of alms was often based on being able to contribute to the maintenance of the lost social and economic status of a person, at least to the extent that this was possible.

At any rate, thanks to the *bacins*, parishes clearly played an important role in providing assistance to medieval widows within the urban community. Certainly, these contributions were of little significance when considered individually, but in many cases they helped widows to solve their economic needs, both on specific occasions and on a more regular basis.

Medieval widows could also resort to another type of charitable institution—hospitals—which in some parts of Europe were founded with the distinct goal of sheltering widows in need. This phenomenon led P. J. P. Goldberg to consider the creation of exclusively female hospitals, specifically toward the end of the Middle Ages, as one of the most clear indications of the feminization of poverty.[28] The hospitals of Saint Avoye and the Haudriettes in Paris and the hospital of Orbatello in Florence exemplify this situation. The first one, Saint Avoye, was established in 1283, by a rich Parisian widow, with the intention of giving shelter to forty poor and elderly widows. A few years later, in the same city, the Haudry marriage founded a house to accommodate thirty-two widows. Over time, this institution came to be known as the hospital of the Haudriettes.[29] As for Florence, widows could find asylum in the hospital of Orbatello, founded in 1372 by the rich merchant Niccolò degli Alberti. This institution could accommodate up to two hundred women, most of them elderly, but it also housed widows with children.[30]

In spite of the existence of hospitals created for widows in several European cities, and even though Barcelona boasted a large number of hospitals during the Middle Ages,[31] no exclusively female hospital can be documented in the city,[32] and neither can we find an institution that only assisted widows. The analysis of the patient registers of the Hospital de la Santa Creu,[33] the general hospital of Barcelona, founded in 1401, evinces that the number of women admitted to this institution was much smaller than the number of men, which, according to James Brodman's analysis of the extant sources related to different medieval hospitals, also happened in other European cities.[34] The percentage decreases even more if we focus our attention on widows. One of the possible causes we consider for the low percentage of women attended in this institution is that, as I will show later on, they would mostly opt for other types of support within the community in case of difficulties or illnesses. Nevertheless, we must also take into account that women's lives were more stable and sedentary, and therefore, unlike men, they were less likely to suffer certain accidents or diseases. Furthermore, the medical knowledge that women possessed allowed them to solve certain health problems at home, with the aid of homemade remedies.[35] In the earliest extant patient register of the aforementioned hospital, dated in 1457, only nineteen of the 365 entries correspond to women and, of these, only two can be identified as widows.[36] However, it is hard to believe that these two women, who were explicitly described as being widowed, were the only actual widows admitted to the hospital; actually, given that the entries in the registers were not always complete regarding women and their marital statuses, some elements suggest that their number was indeed higher. For instance, the fact that some of them appear under a feminized male name with an advanced age, points in this direction. However, the administrators' lack of zeal in this matter does not allow us to make more accurate assertions. The women admitted to the Santa Creu hospital were sick, belonged to the lower social sectors, and arrived with the hope of healing. They came not only from Barcelona, but also from rural areas of inland and coastal Catalonia (Orcau, Llagostera, Olot, and Rupit, among others). The presence of several foreigners is also documented, but widows came mostly from Catalonia.[37] Thus, we cannot claim that female patients were, in general, women without any kind of roots in the city, or that the hospital was the only way out for their ills. We cannot know whether the widows born outside of Barcelona had moved to the city or were just passing through. Although their number was considerable, we cannot overlook the fact that it was nonetheless similar to the number of those that came from the city itself. Therefore, their origin and the consequent lack of family ties in the city cannot account for the small number of foreign widows in the register, for the widows from Barcelona were also few. As for their social standing, the women admitted to the hospital were the widows of farmers, fishermen, shoemakers, farmhands, and bakers, but also of notaries and merchants. As the description of the clothes they wore reveals, they were clearly poor, and moreover, most did not carry money on them. In all likelihood, some had lost their status due to widowhood and sought to be cured of their illnesses, although some of them died only a few days after entering the hospital. All this leads us to believe that it was precisely the lack of resources that led them to the hospital, probably in addition to the absence of family members and friends who could help them.

ASSISTANCE BEYOND HOSPITALS

Admission to the hospital was a plausible option for the widows who lived in Barcelona who wanted to avoid ending their days sick and on the streets. However, I am inclined to think that women mainly opted for informal charity, that is, they used family or neighborhood solidarity networks, with the aim of being assisted by other women.[38] The books of the Bací of the deserving poor of the parish of Santa Maria del Pi of Barcelona for 1441 and 1447, studied by Jordina Camarasa, also strongly suggest that sick women were welcomed in the houses of other women.[39] In fact, according to the record, alm ost half of the women who lived in other women's homes were ill. Only two of the women in this situation were widows, but it must be noted that in most cases we actually do not know who these women were because they are generically described as "dona malalta" (sick woman) or "dona pobra" (poor woman). For instance, two women were registered at the home of Sança Ximenis de Cabrera, lady of Novalles. In 1441, "una dona pobra" (a poor woman) received 2.5 sous in Sança's house, and, in 1447, a woman named Rosa, who lived in a shop owned by Sança Ximenis, received 1.5 sous as alms.[40] Since the information recorded in the books of the Bací of the deserving poor is very sparse, we know little about these women who were assisted in the house of other women. We do not know whether they were servants or benefitted from the charity of the owners because they were relatives, friends, neighbors, or acquaintances. In any case, it is likely that some of these women were taken in because they were sick. This circumstance highlights the community's role in caring for widows who could not afford to care for themselves. The links woven over the years, especially with other women, became more tangible during the most difficult times. However, I would also like to point out the other side of the solidarity coin, which was largely extrafamilial, namely the people who selflessly offered their help. Although these were generally women with a favorable social situation that allowed them to receive widows in need, the examples below show that they did not belong to the upper class either.

These relationships among women with no family ties, which can be glimpsed in the records of the Bací of Santa Maria del Pi, are clearly evident in the letters exchanged by a group of wealthy women from Barcelona—which are preserved in the Archive of the Cathedral. The correspondence between these women reveals how they took care of each other. For instance, following the high death toll of 1374, Guillemoneta, widow of Francesc Togores, steward of Queen Eleanor of Sicily, fell ill. Although she was reluctant to leave the palace of the Queen, where she resided, Guillemoneta was welcomed by Sereneta de Tous, the wife of Ramon de Tous, a merchant from Barcelona and the administrator of the Countess of Luna. Sereneta took care of Widow Togores; and Queen Eleanor, who remained concerned about her health, sent the physicians that the sick woman needed. Once cured, she returned to the royal palace, but in a letter from Francesca—the widow of Guillem Morey, lord of La Roca, in Roussillon—addressed to Ramon de Tous, we learn that Guillemona de Togores had relapsed into sickness. Thus, she returned to Sereneta's house. Guillemoneta overcame this epidemic episode, but finally died in early 1399.[41]

Finally, with regard to sick widows who were cared for by other women, I would like to mention an example in which the two women were related. These cases are certainly more difficult to document, as they leave almost no trace; in this instance, however, the two widows agreed to the terms of their relationship before a notary. On February 12, 1369, Margarida, widow of the sword maker Nadal Parellada, promised to take care of Romia, widow of Galceran Vilella, from the parish of Sant Julià de Palol, in case of illness, after agreeing that from that moment onward they would live together. Romia moved to Margarida's house in Barcelona and carried with her twenty-seven *lliures*, between money and personal possessions. In addition, she had to serve Margarida and assist her in everything she needed. For her part, Margarida undertook meeting Romia's needs, thus recognizing the many services rendered by Romia, and the family bond between them, (for their mothers were first cousins).[42] The examples presented above show how, in cases of illness, the widows of late medieval

Barcelona could turn to their relatives, friends, and neighbors. Thus, it becomes evident that hospital institutions were not the only solution to dealing with health problems. Moreover, this circumstance can account for the low percentage of women, and particularly, widows, in the patient registers of the Hospital de la Santa Creu.

CONCLUSION

The charity that many widows benefitted from was an essential aid to their subsistence. Parish assistance, the mutual fraternity of the guilds, testamentary legacies, family help, individual acts of charity, and the support they could receive from friends and neighbors complimented each other in the day to day life of those widows who were most in need. Therefore, there were multiple sources they could resort to in order to deal with the hardships they endured. However, the help provided was not always in the form of an economic contribution, for often what some widows really needed was simply companionship and someone to take care of them.

The solidarity networks that widows created within their surroundings were indispensable for their survival. Theirs was a social framework of relationships, which was often established outside the family and the work environment, and to which they turned in case of difficulties. The existence of these ties between widows was due to social and economic reasons, but, undoubtedly, in all cases they were created by seeking in other women a similar life experience and shared realities and feelings. In fact, the significant ties of friendship established between women were the basis of their relationships and solidarity networks. Without a doubt, in addition to charitable institutions, women's communities made up for the lack of roots in the city and replaced family ties with solidarity bonds that were strong enough to help the poorest among them.

Finally, it should be noted that there are always two sides to assistance: the person who receives it, on the one hand, and the person who lends it, on the other. In this sense, it is also important to recall that many widows, in turn, acted as benefactors of charitable institutions and left important testamentary legacies for those women that needed them the most.

NOTES

1. This work has been developed within the framework of the project "El notariado en Cataluña, siglos XIII–XIV: práctica y actividad (NOTCAT) (HAR 2015–65146-P)," funded by the Spanish Ministry of Economy and Competitiveness, and the Consolidated Research Group (MAHPA). "Grup de Recerca en Estudis Medievals d'Art, Història, Paleografia i Arqueologia" (2014 SGR 794) of the Commissioner for Universities and Research of the Generalitat de Catalunya. Translated by Delfi Nieto.

2. Comas-Via, "Widowhood and Economic."

3. The documents on which this study is based come mainly from the charitable institutions presented below, such as the Hospital de la Santa Creu and the *bací* of the deserving poor of the parish of Santa María del Pi in Barcelona. We have also used municipal and juridical documentation, as well as notarial sources from the Historical Archive of Protocols of Barcelona (hereinafter, AHPB).

4. The dowry was to be returned to the widow after her husband's death. However, this restitution was not always immediate or complete, which made the economic situation of many widows falter. On the difficulties in the return of the dowry, see Comas-Via, *Entre la solitud*, 106–16.

5. In this sense, we share the definition of Katherine A. Lynch, see Lynch, *Individuals, Families and Communities*, 1.

6. The "middle hand" included merchants, notaries and other liberal professions. Comas-Via, *Entre la solitud*, 147–48.

7. See, for instance, the relationship networks established among women from the aristocracy in the biography of Estefania Carròs i de Mur. Comas-Via and Vinyoles i Vidal, *Estefania Carròs*, 37–46.

8. Literature also provides examples of these support structures created by women, as I have explained in Comas-Via, *Entre la solitud*, 70.

9. Arxiu Històric de la Ciutat de Barcelona (AHCB), 1C.Consellers, V. Miscel·lània, 5 (1451 April 2).

10. Martorell, *Epistolari del segle XV*, 70–72.

11. On the city as a favorable space for the formation of communities, see Lynch, *Individuals, Families and Communities*, 2.

12. Arxiu de la Corona d'Aragó (ACA), Processos de la Reial Audiència, any 1374.

13. "Per tal que els amics de la filla, que són molts, no es vengessin, ho van tenir en secret. Però, com que ara ja es sap, la dita dona, que és pobra i viu d'almoines, per esguard dels serveis que el pare de la dita fadrina ha fet a Cerdenya, demana que facin prendre el teixidor." [They kept it secret so that the friends of the daughter, who are many, did not take revenge. But, as it is now known, this woman, who is poor and lives on alms, in view of the services that the father of said maiden

rendered in Sardinia, asks that they take the weaver into custody]. ACA, Processos de la Reial Audiència, any 1374.

14. The assistance that guilds provided for their members and their families will be discussed in depth elsewhere, but it is worth questioning here the effect of the charity of confraternities and guilds both on the widows of deceased members, and on those widows that were members in their own right. The first consideration we have to make in this regard is that the majority of women carried out their work outside the protection of guilds, so that this form of assistance was limited to only a small group among them. In particular, in the case of Barcelona, it must be borne in mind that the guilds that had well-organized mutual aid systems in place were related to the most physically demanding trades, such as that of boatman and courier, which were evidently not performed by women. Furthermore, according to Ben McRee, the effectiveness of the charity offered by guilds also needs to be questioned. In this sense, this author puts forward certain discrepancies between the promise and the practice of the distribution of aid among the members in need, given that the sums that were handed out represented a very small contribution to the improvement of the life conditions of these poor people (McRee, "Charity and Gild," 197). In fact, Pierre Bonnassie considers that only in exceptional cases did the associations of Barcelona actually give out money and that, generally, mutual aid consisted of taking care of the sick or defraying the burial expenses of the members whose families could not afford them (Bonnassie, *La organización*, 133).

15. On medieval poverty and the differences between the poor, see Brodman, *Charity and Welfare*, 5–6. On gender and poverty, see also, Farmer, *Surviving Poverty*, especially, 136–64.

16. Altisent, *L'Almoina reial*.

17. The *violaris* were contracts whereby the right to receive a monetary pension during the lifetime of one or two persons was granted in exchange for payment of a sum secured through a mortgage. In this case, money was invested to buy a *violari* that would guarantee the pensions of these widows favored by royal charity.

18. Altisent, *L'Almoina reial*, 25–26.

19. Altisent, *L'Almoina reial*.

20. The parishes of Barcelona that had established a Bací—also called *collecta* or *plat*—for the deserving poor were Santa Maria del Mar, Santa Maria del Pi, Sant Pere de las Puelles, Sant Jaume, Sants Just i Pastor, Sant Miquel, and Sant Cugat del Rec. This charitable institution was not exclusive to the city of Barcelona but could be found throughout Catalonia, for example in Reus or Elna.

21. To name but a few, I will only mention here three widows who donated various amounts to the Bací dels pobres of the Church of Santa Maria del Pi by means of testamentary legacies. The widow of Pere Aleu, a skipper who traded with Rhodes, Cyprus, and Beirut in the early fifteenth century, left one lliura; Beatriu, the widow of the banker Pere Pascual, who went bankrupt in 1382, established a bequest of five lliures; finally, the widow of Gaspar Andreu, a skipper from Sant Feliu de Guíxols, bequeathed the same amount. Claramunt, "Los ingresos," 379.

22. Aramayona, "El cuaderno de 1421," 179.

23. Claramunt, "Los ingresos," 380.

24. On this issue, see the study by Jordina Camarasa devoted to analyzing the reasons for which women received alms from the Bací of Santa Maria del Pi. Camarasa, "Les dones."

25. Claramunt, "L'ajut mutu," 48.

26. AHPB, Nicolau de Mediona, 163/1 (1437–1438); these documents are quoted in Ferrer, "Després de la mort," 322–23.

27. Claramunt, "L'ajut mutu," 49.

28. Goldberg, *Women in England*, 23.

29. Farmer, "Down and Out," 359.

30. Roberts, "Helpful Widows," 35.

31. On hospitals in medieval Catalonia, see Conejo, "Assistència i hospitalitat" and Brodman, *Charity and Welfare*.

32. In Barcelona, at the end of the Middle Ages, there were other institutions whose purpose was housing women without men, such as the convent of the *repenedides* (literally, repentant women). Even so, their mission was not exactly the same as in the case of the hospitals and hospices for women that could be found across Europe. The goal of these institutions was instead to confine women so that they could repent of their "dissipated" life through the practice of penance. Thus, in no case were these establishments meant to shelter women who lacked resources, for their function was not to alleviate economic circumstances but to redress moral shortcomings.

33. The present study includes the analysis of the earliest five registers, which correspond to the medieval period. Biblioteca de Catalunya (BC), Arxiu de l'Hospital, 1–5.

34. Brodman, "Unequal in Charity?" 29–30.

35. Vinyoles, "El rastre dels més desvalguts," 83.

36. BC, Arxiu de l'Hospital, 1.

37. One of the few foreigners documented is a French widow listed in the register of 1497–1501. BC, Arxiu de l'Hospital, 5.

38. Sharon Farmer reaches the same conclusion after studying poverty in the city of Paris in the late Middle Ages, *Surviving Poverty*, especially, 163–64.

39. Camarasa, "Les dones," 43–45.

40. Camarasa, "Les dones," 44.

41. Vinyoles, "L'amor i la mort."

42. Comas-Via, *Entre la solitud*, 146. Similarly, Carles Vela recounts how a widow from Tortosa was welcomed at the house of her cousin, the apothecary Gaspar Canalda. Vela, *Especiers i candelers*, 413. In the *catasto* of Florence of 1427, studied by Isabelle Chabot, some widows who claimed to be too poor to pay taxes stated that they lived on alms or that they were provided accommodation by either friends or other widows. Chabot, "Widowhood and Poverty," 304.

BIBLIOGRAPHY

Primary Sources

ACA. Arxiu de la Corona d'Aragó
    Processos de la Reial Audiencia, any 1374

AHCB. Arxiu Històric de la Ciutat de Barcelona
    1C. Consellers, V. Miscel·lània

AHPB. Arxiu Històric de Protocols de Barcelona
    Nicolau de Mediona 163/1 (1437–38)

BC. Biblioteca de Catalunya
    Arxiu de l'Hospital

Secondary Sources

Altisent, Agustí. *L'Almoina reial a la cort de Pere el Cerimoniós: estudi i edició dels manuscrits de l'almoiner fra Guillem Deudé, monjo de Poblet (1378–1385)*. [Poblet]: Abadia de Poblet, 1969.

Aramayona Alonso, Guillermo. "El cuaderno de 1421 de 'el bací dels pobres vergonyants,' de la parroquia de Santa Maria del Mar, de Barcelona." In *La pobreza y la asistencia a los pobres en la Cataluña medieval. Volumen misceláneo de estudios y documentos*, edited by M. Riu i Riu, 2, 173–89. Barcelona: Consejo Superior de Investigaciones Científicas, 1981–1982.

Bonnassie, Pierre. *La organización del trabajo en Barcelona a fines del siglo XV*. Barcelona: Consejo Superior de Investigaciones Científicas, 1975.

Brodman, James. *Charity and Welfare: Hospitals and the Poor in Medieval Catalonia*. Philadelphia: University of Pennsylvania Press, 1998.

———. "Unequal in Charity? Women and Hospitals in Medieval Catalonia." *Medieval Encounters* 12, no. 1 (2006): 26–36.

Camarasa, Jordina. "Les dones en la documentació del Bací dels Pobres Vergonyants de la Parròquia de Santa Maria del Pi de Barcelona. Estudi i edició dels llibres dels anys 1441 i 1447." Masters dissertation, University of Barcelona, 2016.

Chabot, Isabelle. "Widowhood and Poverty in Late Medieval Florence." *Continuity and Change* 3 (1988): 291–311.

Claramunt, Salvador. "Los ingresos del 'bací o plat dels pobres' de la parroquia de Santa Maria del Pi de Barcelona." In *La pobreza y la asistencia a los pobres en la Cataluña medieval. Volumen misceláneo de estudios y documentos*, edited by M. Riu i Riu, 1, 374–90. Barcelona: Consejo Superior de Investigaciones Científicas, 1981–1982.

——— . "L'ajut mutu. L'assistència a la Barcelona del segle xv." *Revista d'etnologia de Catalunya* 11 (1997): 44–51. http://www.raco.cat/index.php/revistaetnologia/article/viewFile/48863/57060.

Comas-Via, Mireia. *Entre la solitud i la llibertat: Vídues barcelonines a finals de l'Edat Mitjana*. Roma: Viella, 2015.

——— . "Widowhood and Economic Difficulties in Medieval Barcelona." *Historical Reflections/Réflexions Historiques* 43, no. 1 (2017): 93–103. doi:http://dx.doi.org/10.3167/hrrh.2017.430108.

——— ."La asistencia a las viudas en el Hospital de la Santa Creu de Barcelona en el siglo XV y el Hospital de los pobres de San Juan de Perpiñán." In *Abriles del Hospital*, Zaragoza: Institución Fernando el Católico, in press.

Conejo da Pena, Antoni. "Assistència i hospitalitat a l'Edat Mitjana. L'arquitectura dels hospitals catalans: Del gòtic al primer renaixement." PhD dissertation, University of Barcelona, 2002. https://www.tdx.cat/handle/10803/2006.

Farmer, Sharon. "Down and Out and Female in Thirteenth-Century Paris." *The American Historical Review* 103, no. 2 (1998): 345–72.

——— . *Surviving Poverty in Medieval Paris. Gender, Ideology and the Daily Lives of the Poor*. Ithaca NY: Cornell University Press, 2005.

Ferrer Mallol, M. Teresa. "Després de la mort. L'actuació d'algunes marmessories a través d'un manual del notari barceloní Nicolau de Mediona (1437–1438)." *Analecta Sacra Tarraconensia* 71 (1998): 281–325. http://hdl.handle.net/10261/24075.

Goldberg, P. J. P. *Women in England c. 1275–1525. Documentary Sources*. Manchester: Manchester University Press, 1995.

Lynch, Katherine A. *Individuals, Families and Communities in Europe, 1200–1800: The Urban Foundations of Western Society*. Cambridge: Cambridge University Press, 2003.

Martorell Trabal, Francesc. *Epistolari del segle XV. Recull de cartes privades*. Barcelona: Atenes, 1926.

McRee, Ben R. "Charity and Gild." *The Journal of British Studies* 32, no. 3 (1993): 195–225.

Roberts, Anna. "Helpful Widows, Virgins in Distress: Women's Friendship in French Romance of the Thirteenth and Fourteenth Centuries." In *Constructions of Widowhood and Virginity in the Middle Ages*, edited by C. L. Carlson, A. J. Weisl, 26–47. New York: St. Martin's, 1999.

Vela i Aulesa, Carles. *Especiers i candelers a Barcelona a la baixa edat mitjana. Testaments, família i sociabilitat*, Barcelona: Fundació Noguera, 2007.

Vinyoles Vidal, Teresa. "L'amor i la mort al segle XIV. Cartes de dones." *Miscel·lània de Textos Medievals* 8 (1996): 111–98.

———. "El rastre dels més desvalguts entre els papers de l'Hospital de Barcelona." *Summa* 2 (2013): 77–101. doi: 10.1344/Svmma2013.2.6.

Vinyoles Vidal, Teresa; Comas Via, Mireia. *Estefanía Carrós y de Mur (ca. 1455-1511)*, Madrid: Ediciones del Orto, 2004.

9

Founders, Sisters, and Neighbors in the Thirteenth Century

Women and Community at Santa Maria de Celas, Coimbra

MIRIAM SHADIS

From its foundation in the early thirteenth century, until its dissolution in the nineteenth, the Cistercian women's community of Santa Maria de Celas in Coimbra was small, but relatively rich and powerful, able to draw upon the elites of Portuguese society as patrons, and for its sisterhood. Its special status was epitomized in 1525, when the reforming Abbess Leonor de Vasconcelos commissioned a paneled altarpiece depicting the life of the Virgin Mary, and the king of Portugal, João III, paid to have the artwork transported from the Low Countries and installed in the convent church. The extravagance of these actions was matched by the deluxe nature of the altarpiece itself, part of which today remains in the convent church, and most of which is housed at the Museu Nacional Machado de Castro in the city of Coimbra. This level of prestige and availability of resources marked Celas from its foundation—although it was not always smooth sailing for the community—which was one of the earliest for Cistercian women in Portugal.[1] Founded in a politically contentious moment by royal women who insisted on their status as queens, the first decades of the community's existence were characterized by civil war and regime change in Portugal at large, and contextualized by a rich, diverse, and fractious religious landscape in Coimbra itself.

Almost reflexively, the use of the word *community* when associated with medieval monastics implies a hermetic social environment, sealed off both materially and spiritually from the world. The community—mentioned so often as such in medieval documentation—refers to the body of cloistered or vowed monks or nuns under the rule of an abbot or abbess. Even without strict claustration, then, community has a discrete, specific meaning. I argue that this traditional framing of community, which serves a purpose to be sure, is insufficient to understand the lives and identities of the earliest women at Santa Maria de Celas in Coimbra. Like Michelle Herder, I argue that the "community" was in fact porous, "embedded in a local social environment," and made up of donors, family members (male and female, clerical and lay), and neighbors.[2] In particular, I consider the variety of women who engaged in the economic foundation of Celas as part of its community. The personal relationships that existed between donors, patrons, and business partners, framed by their physical environment (in this case the city of Coimbra), and the convent, are key features of this community.[3]

Charters, primarily recording property transactions, but also wills and narrative sources, show how the circumstances of the foundation of Celas, its environmental and social context, including connections to other abbeys, clergy, and inhabitants of Coimbra, and permit a revision of the concept of community. Santa Maria de Celas was founded in the early thirteenth century by the royal daughter Sancha (d. 1229) and, to a lesser extent, her sister Teresa (d. 1250). Teresa and Sancha, daughters of King Sancho I of Portugal and his wife Queen Dulce of Aragon, were extraordinarily wealthy and politically powerful women, endowed with vast estates and wealth in their father's will.[4] As Sancha and Teresa were founding Celas, they were also working to resolve a bitter conflict over inheritance with their brother king Afonso II and his son Sancho II.[5] Teresa had already proven disruptive on the monastic scene when, in around 1210 she evicted the Benedictine monks from the ancient community of Lorvão and replaced them with the first Cistercian community of women in Portugal.[6] Although Sancha is rightly considered the primary founder of Celas, her relationship with Teresa and Teresa's influence as a Cistercian reformer are important to Celas's story.

Most importantly, the circumstances of the foundation set the community, from the beginning, in communication with a multitude of religious foundations in the city of Coimbra, and with the very particular communities of Lorvão and Celas of Alenquer. It is unclear whether the first women at Celas were strictly cloistered. In the days before Urban IV's *Periculoso* enforced women's cloistering in 1298, it seems they were not—certainly, Sancha and Teresa were not.[7] Despite the fact that at some point in the thirteenth century religious women in Coimbra (including at Celas) became known as "inclusas" (those enclosed), in the beginning at least, the boundaries of their community were porous. The royal founders came and went; surely the clerics of the community came and went, perhaps donors did as well. Celas was part of a religious landscape in Coimbra, along with a number of other institutions: it overlapped with them in its identity and purpose. The specific religious community (the object of building, of accumulation, and donation) may have been made up of elite women, but the larger community (of donors, of petitioners, of retirees, and the sick who sought refuge at Celas) were much more diverse.[8]

Finally, therefore, I propose that a full consideration of the Celas community prompts a more liberal definition of the word: who were the women who entered the convent (and relatively new order) in the thirteenth century? Who were the women (and men) outside of the convent, who nonetheless engaged with it through donation, purchases and sales, and the arrangement of corrodies?[9] Despite the dominant presence of Teresa and Sancha, or perhaps because of it, we in fact know very little about the individual women who first entered the monastery and the order. We can know more, however, about the women who through the economic activities mentioned above in some way participated in the foundation of the monastery. Such women, I argue, must be considered part of the early community of Celas. In the case of the new foundation of Santa Maria de Celas in Coimbra, the economic and legal landscape, as well as the religious and institutional frame, contextualize the activity of a larger community of women of which Celas was a part. This landscape further potentially reveals more women associated with the monastery than might readily be apparent at first glance.

Now tucked in at the end of a little street in an urban residential neighborhood of Coimbra, Celas was described in medieval charters as being "beyond the Porta do Sol"—a reference to one of the castle gates. The area was also known as Guimarães, and thus, often Celas appears in the charters as "Celas de Guimarães," to distinguish it from Celas da Ponte, discussed below. At its founding, the convent was located outside of the city walls, about a half hour's walk from the Old Sé Cathedral of Coimbra, as well as the royal residence, over and down a steep hill and then up again. Early sources discuss the choice of location based on the "abundance of water, the fertility of the land, and the temperate air."[10] This practical approach to the abbey's location may have been a consideration for the founders. It is also not surprising that the convent was situated outside the walls of the town, where land was likely cheaper, more plentiful, and in need of development—all fitting within a Cistercian ideal, had that been in mind.[11] The choice for Celas proved to be a good one: other female communities in Coimbra were plagued by the constant flooding of the Mondego River, along which they were located. The church, discussed in more detail below, retains traces of its original layout and chapter house, along with the fourteenth-century cloister. The physical plant was likely small; in its earliest years, probably no more than three dozen women lived there, and by 1532, no more than forty-eight.[12] Account books describe a very active and wealthy organization throughout the seventeenth and eighteenth centuries.[13] In 1834, the community was subject to the *Decreto de 30 de maio* "extinguishing" all monasteries. From that point on the community would not grow, only diminish with the death of each sister, until Sister Maria Felismina de Nossa Senhora de Ó do Figueiredo Negrão died in April of 1883.[14]

In the early thirteenth century, however, Celas was new. The royal daughter Sancha (always referred to as a queen) held the lordship of the castle and district of Alenquer, located to the south and east of Coimbra. A small community of religious women seems to have already been established there by the time she came to control the castle in 1211. It may have been the imminent defeat of her claims to the castle of

Alenquer that inspired Sancha to establish a community in Coimbra. After settling with her brother and nephew over the terms of Sancho I's will, Sancha focused on supporting the community at Alenquer, and on founding a convent near Coimbra. Many historians have thought that the first women to enter Celas in Coimbra came from Alenquer, and they well could have, but Morujão has convincingly argued that the two communities remained separate, at least while Sancha lived, and speculates that the first nuns at Celas came from Teresa's foundation of Lorvão.[15] She bases this assertion on the fact that Sancha continued to acquire property and donate it to Alenquer. Sancha certainly kept the two communities linked through her purchasing activity and donations in both locales. For example, she purchased a valuable mill in Alenquer, which she subsequently donated to Celas in Coimbra.[16] In May of 1224, Pope Honorius III issued a bull permitting the sisters of "Sancte Marie Rotunde de Alankier" to celebrate mass despite an interdict, testifying to continued activity there.[17] Later, in around 1234, Teresa moved the bodies of some of the women (apparently deceased) from Alenquer to Lorvão, because of their special holiness, signaling the decline of the community at Alenquer after Sancha's death.[18]

That the two communities remained interconnected is demonstrated by Alenquer's unusual origin story, preserved in the *Livro Indice do Mosteiro de Santa Mara de Celas 1219–1662, Memorias*. The *Livro* is a compilation of histories of the convent, a descriptive list of the abbesses, and an index of charters associated with the monastery. Buried within its index of the first *maço* (folder) of charters is the following story:

> It is thought that this monastery of Santa Maria de Celas could be said to have its origin in that of the town of Alenquer. Queen Dona Sancha, the daughter of King Don Sancho, the first of the name and the second king of Portugal, was the patron of that town. As there were first in that town religious women (. . . not more than seven, for the site did not have the capacity for more people), in which site is still today her chapel in the structure of the convent, and is called Santa Maria Redonda where Our Lady performed many miracles in particular for women

lacking milk, and they offered pans of milk and thus they recovered what they had lost.[19]

This story is uniquely related in this manuscript book, which otherwise reproduces or accounts for the document record of Celas with surprising accuracy. The idea of a shrine at which women having difficulty nursing petitioned the Virgin was fitting for a community of women, although the Virgin's "many" miracles should have warranted greater traces in the literary or hagiographic record. I have not discovered any donation material to either institution that articulates the purpose of the donation, at least in terms of gratitude—for example, for help with nursing or childbearing—although, in fact, very few records of donation from Celas's first century survive. However, there may be a sensible echo of this original purpose in the very name and architectural plan of both the original shrine (Santa Maria la Rotunde) in Alenquer and the "new" foundation in Coimbra—Celas retains a circular plan and vaulted, dome-like crossing, suggestive of a large, lactating breast.[20]

Over the course of the 1220s, Sancha dedicated herself to building the religious community and physical environment of Celas in Coimbra. Beginning in 1221, forty-seven charters attest to Sancha's avid acquisition of property, in Alenquer, but also in Aveiro, Lisbon, Coimbra, and Torres Vedras. Charters exist in the original, in a partial cartulary, and in copies. Some copies replace "Regina Sancha" with the *inclusas et priorissa* of the abbey. Why this is the case is not completely understood, but it is clear that Sancha was the original purchaser. She bought houses, olive groves, vineyards, mills, and so on. Sancha's aggressive purchasing activity continued until her death in 1229. She spent well over 5700 morabitinos, which may represent money of account, or, it may represent real gold pieces. Her father, in his will, had indicated that her money was stored at Santa Cruz, suggesting it was real coin. In any event, Sancha spent an enormous sum.[21] As she worked to gather wealth in the form of real estate for her foundation, the community itself emerged. In early January 1223, Bishop Pedro of Coimbra authorized clergy to celebrate mass at the church of Santa Maria de Celas, as long as they were not under interdict or bound by the chains of excommunication.[22] In March, Santa Maria de Celas reached another milestone, when Bishop Pedro authorized Sancha to turn the convent over to whatever order she preferred, and conferred on her as well the right to represent the monastery.[23] Celas was not yet explicitly associated with the Cistercian Order, although historians have accepted that the reference to the intended construction of the "daughter of the king of Portugal" in the 1227 Cistercian statutes in fact refers to Sancha's project of Celas.[24]

In March 1226, the young king of Portugal, Sancho II, received both institutions, Celas of Alenquer and Celas of Guimarães (Coimbra), under his protection. This charter exists only in cartulary copies from the late thirteenth century. Sancho acted "at the request of my 'amite' the most illustrious queen lady Sancha [who] built and loved those places."[25] In December of 1227, the community at Celas had its first explicit contact with the Cistercian order, when it purchased a fourth part of Vila Nova with all its belongings, vineyards, and palaces. The seller in this instance was Abbess Vierna of Lorvão, acting with her community.[26] There is no evidence to indicate that Sancha herself joined the Cistercian Order. In fact, she may have been inclined toward the new mendicants, suggested by her association with the martyrs of Morocco and the eventual flourishing of the mendicant orders under female royal patronage. Sancha's sister Branca, half-sister Constança Sanches, and the early fourteenth-century "santa-rainha" Isabel of Aragon were all active patrons of Franciscan women.[27]

Finally, in March of 1228, archbishop Estevão of Braga authorized the sacralization of the church at Celas.[28] One year later, in March 1229, Sancha died, and Teresa assumed the protection of the convent in Coimbra. This protection has the character of a foral charter: Teresa claimed the monastery as her own, as well as lands in Montemor, Alenquer, and Torres Vedras, and declared anyone who caused any sort of trouble there to be her enemy and owing her and the convent a major fine.[29] From 1229 forward, Teresa actively represented the monastery, and continued her sister's purchasing program, and, I argue, finally affiliated the convent with the Cistercian Order. She herself joined the Order in 1231.[30]

It is worth it, in order to imagine the larger social community that Celas was part of, to describe medieval Coimbra. In the early 1200s, the town was one of the largest in Portugal, and the center of royal administration. During the reign of Afonso Henriques (1128–1185), Coimbra became the royal capital, and a building boom that would last into the thirteenth century began. The population was characterized by a substantial Mozarab community, and the city was a bustling trade center on the Mondego River with access to the sea. Afonso Henriques's conquest of Lisbon in 1147 set the stage for that city to become the new capital, but in the early thirteenth century Coimbra was still the center of gravity for the realm.

Coimbra already had several female monasteries when Celas was begun there, with Lorvão relatively nearby, the better part of a day's walk. São João das Donas was a women's community associated with the Augustinian Santa Cruz; it had been established by 1180 at the latest, and possibly much earlier. Santa Cruz itself was founded in 1130, and in 1166 King Afonso Henriques mentioned a "countess Elvira Peres, who had been a sister at Santa Cruz," in a royal charter.[31] Santa Cruz was also connected to the hospital of São Nicolás, also for Augustinian women. Yet another Augustinian foundation for women was nearby—just "beyond the bridge": Celas alem da Ponte. In a difficult-to-date charter from the long fourteenth century, the prioress Maria Bermudes identified the convent as belonging to "Santa Ana," and in the later Middle Ages, this institution became known as Santa Ana.[32] In short order, Santa Maria de Celas (de Guimaraes) would become much wealthier than these convents, if not much bigger; initially however it seemed that Celas da Ponte flourished at the expense of Celas de Guimarães. Why Sancha chose to found Celas in Coimbra when there were already a number of institutions for women in or near the city, and she already had a viable patronage project in Celas de Alenquer, may be related to her sister's influence and the promotion of the Cistercian order. Probably the flourishing of religious culture at Coimbra and its antiquity as a center of royal religious patronage made it an obvious choice for her.

Records of sales, but also records of donations, reveal women associated with Celas as nuns and as secular women, members of Celas's larger community. Charters from the first decades of the foundation are dominated by purchases made by Sancha and Teresa (or, conversely, sales by individuals to them). Ecclesiastical charters from that period establish the religious organization of the community and the sacralization of the church. Toward the end of the thirteenth century, surviving documentation is dominated by records of conflict (and resolution) over jurisdictions and privileges, indicating the solid presence of the institution in Coimbra. Around 150 charters have been collected in relation to Celas's first century. Very few of them are donations, and most of those donations come from either Sancha herself ("for the work of Celas"), or later, from King Dinis (d. 1325), although even his "donations" were in actuality usually some sort of property exchange.[33] This pattern corresponds to that of Santa Ana; most charters associated with the monastery in the thirteenth century are records of purchases or sales.[34] The fact that the nuns were able to purchase property does not mean selling to them was not a pious activity, however. Purchasing was essential for strategic accumulation (even when, surely, all sorts of gifts were welcome), especially in the monastery's earliest years, as Sancha sought to build up a viable estate for Celas's support.[35]

In 1223, however, Maria Pais, identified as the sister of Martim Pais, a cantor at Coimbra, gave the earliest "outsider" donation to Sancha directly, "for the work of the queen in the district of Coimbra, in the place called Guimarães."[36] Later that year Maria Pais made a separate sale to Sancha as well, in which she actually mentioned the monastery at Celas.[37] Unlike Lorvão, which had a complete physical plant in which a female Cistercian community was imposed, the community at Celas was founded *de novo*. The patterns of patronage to the monastery reflect its shifting identity from a completely new place to a well-established entity with a developed physical plant, all in the control of its founder, Sancha. Her relationship to the monastery tends to obscure the presence or role of the other women associated with Celas. Although an abbess or a prioress were both referred to in later documents, from the beginning it was Sancha, along with her sister Teresa, to whom ecclesiastical documents and more prosaic documents of practice were directed. It was Sancha, along with Teresa, who aggressively bought up the real estate that eventually became the monastery's domain.

Apart from the royal sisters Sancha and Teresa, it is difficult to identify the individuals who first entered Celas. For whatever reasons, no abbess is identified in the Celas charters until 1235, when Mendo Mendes and his wife Maria Soares entered into an agreement with "Lady F., abbess."[38] Abbess F. continued in her role through 1240.[39] By 1242, Elvira Lopes had taken over the abbatial chair.[40] She last appears in charters in 1274; according to Morujão, she served as abbess until 1279, and died in 1285.[41] The first mention of individual women who were nuns at Celas comes from the testament of the archbishop of Compostela (and former bishop of Coimbra) Egas Fafes, who in 1268 named Maria and Elvira Fernandes as nuns there.[42] Not until 1279, when a gift was made to Alda Lourenço by the Hospitaller Pedro Fernandes, does a document originating from Celas name a nun at the convent. Alda is believed to have been the natural daughter of the nobleman Lourenço Martins de Berredo and Teresa Pires de Bragança; before her profession she had been married to Martim Peres de Barbosa. Alda's elite status suggests that most of her professed sisters were also elite women. In the same year, Justa and Marinha Martins were also named.

Women at Celas were also connected to the clerical elite of Coimbra. This network is epitomized by the 1279 will of Maria, which reveals that her four children were all members of the ecclesiastical community: her two sons, Pedro Martins and Paio Martins, were priors at San Salvador in Coimbra and San Miguel at Montemor-o-Velho, respectively, and her two daughters, Justa Martins and Marinha Martins, nuns at Celas. The family's connection to Celas may have reached back a generation, for the testament describes Maria's (unnamed) mother-in-law as the "friend" or "companion" (*amite*) of the "lady queen Teresa."[43] Maria left a detailed will naming a number of beneficiaries and accounting for various contingencies of survival among them, but in the end, most of her property was to be divided between Celas and a few Franciscan and Dominican monasteries.

A number of churchmen in the later thirteenth century remembered both the larger community of Celas as well as individuals in their testaments. Individual nuns were remembered as "my niece," or "daughter of my sister . . . ,"and sometimes by name. More often, the community was endowed as a whole. Preferences for the older institutions of São João das Donas and Santa Ana suggest a sort of institutional hierarchy in Coimbra. More useful to historians, testators sometimes named individual women who were nuns at Celas. In 1230, João Eanes, a cantor at the Sé in Coimbra, remembered his niece who was a nun at Lorvão (he did not give her name), but also left Celas ten morabitinos.[44] In 1264, Martim Pais (possibly the brother of the above mentioned Maria?), a canon of Coimbra, left the abbess of Celas of Guimarães eleven and a half pounds.[45] But in a codicil he left a small sum for a mass there, to be taken from the profits of an olive orchard he had next to (or near) Celas, the lifetime use of which was to go to Marina Fernandes. She was, furthermore, to divide a vineyard and olive orchard with the said "monastery of ladies," and that estate was to be used "pro infirmas." Overall, in his will, Martim Pais favored Santa Ana, but the document gives a sense not only of Celas's integration into the environment, but also perhaps some of the work that went on there—care for the sick.[46]

In 1268, the above-mentioned Egas Fafes made his will. This massive document provides details about a number of institutions: Arouca was to receive fifty pounds for pittances; Lorvão, Celas and Santa Ana received thirty pounds apiece. More significantly, Archbishop Egas remembered individuals: Maria Mendes and Teresa Mendes, nuns at Arouca, who he described as "consobrinis;" the prioress and subprioress at Celas of Guimarães, "consanguineis nostris," forty pounds each; Maria Fernandes and Elvira Fernandes, nuns at Celas, thirty pounds each. Other nuns at Arouca and a friar all described as relatives of Egas suggests that Maria and Elvira were relatives as well. Overall, Egas heavily favored the nuns at Arouca, even leaving them some of his canon law books.[47]

Celas was remembered by others: in 1284, by canon João Gonçalves Chancinho; by João Peres, a schoolmaster, in 1301; and by Domingo Martins, a "raçoeiro" (prebendary), in 1297.[48] Domingo left one pound each to the women at Santa Ana, São Jorgi, and Celas as pittances, so he would be remembered in their prayers; for the same reason, the newly founded Santa Clara received ten *soldos*. To his "criada," Catalina, he left a vineyard (in this case probably an olive grove) near Celas, on the condition that enough oil annually would be given to the See of Coimbra to light a lamp in front of the altar of Santa Maria. He even left his share in a nearby press (a "lagar") to make sure this would happen.[49] In 1322, Pedro Martins, a cantor in Coimbra, left a bequest to a relative, Aldonza Benedicti, for her (and her mother's) service; this was a house that she should hold for life, then turn over to Celas for an obituary mass, for which he dictated the prayers and their responses. Another *oliveto* was left to relatives Lourenço Domingues and João Lourenço as a usufruct; after their deaths the property was to go to Celas, along with fifty pounds, as a pittance: twenty-five to go to the unnamed abbess, and twenty-five to the community. The abbess was Constança Lourenço, and possibly also a relative.[50] A nun at Celas named Aldonza Domingues, who received three pounds, may have been Lourenço's sister, and thus also a relative of Pedro's.

Similarly, Sancha's half-sister Constança Sanches demonstrates the complexity of Coimbra's religious landscape and the integration of community members, as well as the interests of the royal family. Historically, she has been associated with the Augustinian São João das Donas; in her will of 1269, Constança revealed herself to be extraordinarily wealthy, connected to her extended family, and deeply interested in the wider religious landscape. She was devoted to the male foundation of Santa Cruz, where her grandfather Afonso Henriques and father, Sancho, were buried, and where she herself elected burial. In her will, Constança remembered no fewer than twenty churches and monasteries, including her sisters' foundations of Lorvão, Arouca, and Celas. To Lorvão she left three houses in the district of Alenquer; the rest of her estate in Alenquer she left to Celas, on the condition that the nuns would hear a mass annually for her soul.[51] It is significant that Constança also used her wealth in her lifetime to acquire property in the region of Alenquer, property that she then turned over to her sisters' foundations—much in the same way Sancha had done. Constança favored men's houses, Santa Cruz above all, but she remembered the women, and among them, Celas of Guimarães took pride of place.[52]

These testaments point to a key feature of religious life and community in Coimbra, of which Celas was so much a part. These intersections were personal, and institutional. In 1229, Teresa confirmed a donation made by

Sancha to Celas da Ponte (Santa Ana), of a daily donation of food to come from Celas de Guimarães (three portions plus some of the daily leftovers). This act of charity suggests not only a relationship between the nuns but also, perhaps, the relative poverty of Santa Ana. Moving the food would have furthermore occasioned daily communication between the women at the two institutions.[53]

A COMMUNITY OUTSIDE THE WALLS

The word *community* has a very particular resonance when discussing medieval monasticism. To understand more fully the life and experience of the women at Celas, the notion of community needs to include those who, although on the outside, contributed in the most fundamental way to its operation: the donors, patrons, and business partners who gave or sold property to Sancha's foundation. Such patronage was a way for lay people to benefit from, and/or participate in, the good works and prayers to which monks and nuns devoted themselves; it was also a way for them to participate in the community itself.[54] This approach forces us to expand our notion of community, beyond those who were bound to the convent by their profession, to include those who interacted with it in a variety of ways. Sancha's many purchases served more than the purpose of building up the physical plant and patrimony of her new foundation. As Barbara Rosenwein argued in regard to Cluny's real estate transactions, there was "nothing intrinsically impersonal about a sale;"[55] the occasions of sales were social events, and depending on the purposes served, might address social needs as much as economic ones. All transactions, she says, have a social element to them, and the associations of people and land did not end when donations or sales were made.[56] The fact that so very often charters of sale appear in monastic archives which seemingly have nothing to do with the institution underscores the continued association of people and property.

If we take this approach, we can know a great deal more about the earliest women associated with Celas, and thus about the first women who were associated with the Cistercian order in some way in Portugal. In Iberia, Christian women inherited equally with male siblings, held property, and participated in a society of acquisitions with their husbands. This system meant that any time a piece of property was alienated, charters recorded the names of all the invested parties—husbands, wives, siblings, in-laws, and children. Sometimes charters also recorded the names of the people from whom a piece of property was previously inherited or bought. Furthermore, Iberian naming practices, particularly the use of patronymics, meant that when couples acted together in documents, which they did most of the time, and their full names were included, it becomes much easier to identify their repeated activity. When there are generations involved in the same activity, concerning the same property, even more information can be learned. There are other qualities of Portuguese charters that help identify women, such as the tidy habit of describing in detail any property by indicating the physical boundaries of that property, such as a road or a river, or who holds the adjoining plot.

These features allow us to identify more than one hundred individual women who had some contact with the new foundation of Celas in its first century of existence. This number does not include the royal sisters Teresa and Sancha, nor Abbesses F. and Elvira Lopes. Rather, it includes women who bought, sold, or gave property to the convent, or who owned property adjacent to the convent. In some cases, it involved women like Gontina Eanes who entered into an agreement, along with her husband Mendo Peres, to be cared for by the convent and to "obey the abbess."[57] Were these women lay sisters? Obviously, as married women, they did not take vows and were not nuns. But, some other women were widows. Others certainly must have become widows. About a dozen women can be identified as independent property holders with lands adjacent to Celas's property.[58] Others may have been associated with Sancha's court. For example, before 1229 Sancha's "man," Pedro Eanes, received a mortgage on Sancha's behalf; later, in 1234, Pedro Eanes, together with his wife Elvira Gonçalves, sold a different piece of property to Celas.[59] These active propertied women, who engaged repeatedly with the new foundation, may be able to give us a clue in searching for the first women who entered Celas, and who comprised its wider community.

Founded and sustained by elites, the Cistercian community of Celas de Guimarães was part of a larger religious and secular (but pious) community of Coimbra. Clerics' wills, for example, show not only that the nuns at Celas were members of elite families, but also that the convent was expected to serve the poor and remember the dead alongside other Coimbran foundations. These wills have revealed earlier nuns at the convent by name (Maria and Elvira Fernandes), shifting the initial profile of the community from being simply elite, or noble, to being part of the religious family life of Coimbra. Probing charters even further and thinking more liberally about people who conducted business with the convent as part of the wider community, has revealed even more women who could be said to be part of Celas. Donors, dealers in real estate, adjacent property owners, and family members—especially women—all participated in the communal activities that characterized the building and work of this foundation. The story of the first century of Celas de Guimarães allows another view of the role of community and religious life in a small medieval city in Iberia.

NOTES

1. Celas's wealth can be indexed by the tithes/taxes levied on all religious institutions in Portugal in 1321. Celas was assessed a tax of around 1000 pounds; other female Cistercian convents of Lorvão paid 5000 pounds and Arouca a staggering 9000 pounds, Bernardo De Vasconcelos e Sousa, et al., *Ordens Religiosos*, 120. Other institutions in Coimbra, such as the Augustinian convent for women known as Celas da Ponte or Santa Ana were taxed at much lower rates—Santa Ana paid 250 pounds, *Ordens*, 211.

2. See Michelle Herder, "Scandal and Social Networks," in this volume.

3. That religious women were well integrated into their local environments and especially interacted with secular women is demonstrated by the essays covering Catalonia, France, Flanders, and Germany, published in the 2008 special issue "Secular Women in the Documents" of *Church History and Religious Culture*; see especially Mecham, "Cooperative Piety," 581–611.

4. Azevedo, *Documentos Sancho I*, Doc. 194.

5. In a forthcoming essay I examine the emergence of Celas as a Cistercian institution in the context of the Cistercian reforms of the monasteries of Lorvão and Arouca, led by Sancha's sisters, Teresa and Mafalda respectively. I argue that Celas was not necessarily intended to be Cistercian, but the influence of her sisters, especially Teresa, destined Sancha's foundation for that order.

6. Explained in Marques, "Inocêncio III e a passagem," throughout the text.

7. Makowski, *Canon Law and Cloistered Women*, 11, 22, 44, 127.

8. Tiffany A. Ziegler demonstrates how women from "across the social spectrum" conceived of themselves and their social spaces as they formed networks of donors to the Hospital in Brussels, suggesting another perspective on the integration between religious communities and urban women. Ziegler, "Just Another Day in the Neighborhood," 157–76. Kurpiewski demonstrates the integration of religious women in the wider urban political and religious life in thirteenth- and fourteenth-century Speyer in "Power in Pursuit of Religion:" 199–223. These important essays, like the ones appearing in *Church History and Religious Culture*, cited above, make great strides against an outmoded vision of the separated public and private, religious and secular characterization of the medieval world.

9. Corrodies were arrangements for support, such as food, clothing and shelter, generally made as a sort of social security for the old or the sick.

10. *Livro Indice*. AUC Celas-35; Alenquer, maço 1, folio 1.

11. By comparison, see Freeman, "Cistercian Nuns," 26–39. For new assessments of Cistercian women and their environmental and economic contexts, see Berman, *White Nuns*, especially chapter 3. Possibly, the site in Coimbra was historically significant to the royal women, as the legendary location of the appearance of S. Tiago (Saint James) to Fernando I, enabling his victory over the Muslims at Coimbra in 1064. Morujão, *Celas*, 23 n. 3, 32.

12. Morujão, *Celas*, 32–33.

13. For example, *Livro de prazos*, AUC Celas-20.

14. Inventário de extinção PT/TT/MF-DGFP/E/002/00030.

15. Morujão, *Celas*, 27.

16. Morujão, *Celas*, Docs. 10, 12, 13, 16, 27, 30, 32–34, 36–38, 66 all show Sancha collecting, and then donating, shares in the mill associated with Gonçalvo David in Alenquer.

17. Morujão, *Celas*, Doc. 50.

18. Morujão, *Celas*, 26–27.

19. *Livro Indice*. AUC Celas-35; Folio 1, Alenquer, maço 1.

20. The circular church plan is also obviously reminiscent of Templar plans.

21. Azevedo, *Documentos Sancho I*, Doc. 194.

22. Morujão, *Celas*, Doc. 40.

23. Morujão, *Celas*, Doc. 42.

24. Morujão, *Celas*, 28, citing Canivez, *Statuta Capitulorum Generalium*, v. II, 62.

25. Morujão, *Celas*, Doc. 56.

26. Morujão, *Celas*, Doc. 64.

27. Gomes, "As Ordens Mendicantes," Ivars, "Los mártires de Marruecos," and Ryan, "Missionary Saints," throughout the text.

28. Morujão, *Celas*, Doc. 68.

29. Morujão, *Celas*, Doc. 71.

30. Flórez, *Espana Sagrada*, v. 16, 50. On the Leonese succession, see Shadis, *Beren-guela of Castile*, 113–15.

31. Azevedo, *Documentos Sancho I*, Doc. 290.

32. Ordem dos Eremitas, PT/TT/CSACMB/M01/59. Although thirteenth-century charters refer to this institution only as "Celas da ponte," from this point in the essay I will refer to Celas da Ponte as Santa Ana, which it later became, in order to help distinguish it from Santa Maria/Celas de Guimarães (in Coimbra) and Celas de Alenquer.

33. For example, Morujão, *Celas*, Doc. 38 (Sancha) and Doc. 140 (Dinis).

34. Convento de Santa Ana, PT/TT/CSACMB/ maços 1 and 2.

35. Berman, *White Nuns*, 38–39, offers a comparative case of the community at Rifreddo, in Italy.

36. Morujão, *Celas*, Doc. 44.

37. Morujão, *Celas*, Doc. 48.

38. Morujão, *Celas*, Doc. 91.

39. Morujão, *Celas*, Docs. 100, 101, 102, 103.

40. First noted in Morujão, *Celas*, Doc. 106.

41. Morujão, *Celas*, 41; Doc. 133.

42. *Testamenti*, Doc. 2.28.

43. Morujão, *Celas*, Doc. 135.

44. *Testamenti*, Doc. 2.41.

45. In 1264, the abbess would have been Elvira Lopes.

46. *Testamenti*, Doc. 2.27.

47. *Testamenti*, Doc. 2.28.

48. *Testamenti*, Doc. 2.32 (João Gonçalves); 2.42 (João Peres); 2.39 (Domingo Martins).

49. *Testamenti*, Doc. 2.39.

50. *Testamenti*, Doc. 2.53. Morujão, *Celas*, 41.

51. *Provas*, 21–25.

52. Vivas, "Constança Sanches," 69–104, provides a good overview of Constança's economic activity.

53. Morujão, *Celas*, Doc. 72.

54. Mecham, "Cooperative Piety," 598–601, for examples.

55. Rosenwein, *To Be the Neighbor*, 98–99, 130–34.

56. Rosenwein, *To Be the Neighbor*, 98–99, 130–34.

57. Morujão, *Celas*, Doc. 101.

58. Morujão, *Celas*, Docs. 39, 53, 92.

59. Morujão, *Celas*, Docs. 70, 85.

Primary Sources

Archivo Nacional de Portugal

 Torre do Tombo: Inventário de extinção do Convento de Santa Maria de Celas de Coimbra PT/TT/MF-DGFP/E/002/00030.

AUC. Archivo da Universidade de Coimbra

 Livro de prazos, sentenças, e outras escrituras . . . 1272–1806; AUC Santa Maria de Celas-20.

 Livro Indice do Mosteiro de Santa Maria de Celas 1219–1662, Memorias; AUC Santa Maria de Celas-35; Folio 1 Alenquer, maço 1.

Azevedo, Rui de; Costa, P. Avelino de Jesus da; Pereira, Marcelino Rodrigues. *Documentos de D. Sancho I (1174–1211)* Coimbra: University of Coimbra, 1979.

Caetano de Sousa, Antonio, ed. *Provas da História Genealogia de Casa Real Portuguesa,* t. 1. Coimbra: Atlantide, 1846.

Flórez, Enrique. *España sagrada: Theatro geographico-historico de la Iglesia de España: tomo XVI, De la santa Iglesia de Astorga.* Madrid: Imp. de d. Gabriel Ramirez, 1762.

Joseph-Marie Canivez. *Statuta capitulorum generalium ordinis Cisterciensis ab anno 1116 ad annum 1786.* Louvain: Bureaux de la Revue d'histoire ecclésiastique, 1933, 5.2.

Morujão, Maria do Rosário Barbosa. *Um Mosteiro Cisterciense Feminino: Santa Maria de Celas (Século XIII–XV).* Coimbra: University of Coimbra, 2001.

Morujão, Maria do Rosário Barbosa et alia., eds. *Testamenti Ecclesiae Portugaliae (1071–1325).* Lisbon, 2010.

Ordem dos Eremitas de Santo Agostinho

 Convento de Santa Ana de Coimbra PT/TT/CSACMB/M01/59.

Secondary Sources

Berman, Constance H. *The White Nuns: Cistercian Abbeys for Women in Medieval France.* Philadelphia: University of Pennsylvania Press, 2018.

Berman, Constance H., ed. "Secular Women in the Documents for Late Medieval Religious Women," Special issue, *Church History and Religious Culture* 88, no. 4 (2008).

De Vasconcelos e Sousa, Bernardo, et alia. *Ordens religiosas em Portugal das origens a Trento—Guia Histórico.* Lisbon: Livros Horizonte, 2006.

Freeman, Elizabeth. "Cistercian Nuns in Medieval England: the Gendering of Geographic Marginalization." *Medieval Feminist Forum* 43, no. 2 (2007): 26–39.

Gomes, Saul António. "As ordens Mendicantes na Coimbra Medieval: Notas e documentos." *Lusitania Sacra* (2nd ser.) 10 (1998): 149–215.

Ivars, Andrés. "Los mártires de Marruecos de 1220 en la literatura hispano-lusitana," *Archivo Ibero-Americano,* 14 (1920): 344–81.

Kurpiewski, Christopher M. "Power in Pursuit of Religion: The Penitent Sisters of Speyer and their Choice of Affiliation." In *Medieval and Elite Women and the Exercise of Power 1100–1400: Moving beyond the Exceptionalist Debate*, edited by Heather J. Tanner, 199–223. Cham, Switzerland: Palgrave Macmillan, 2019.

Makowski, Elizabeth. *Canon Law and Cloistered Women: Periculoso and Its Commentators, 1298–1545*. Washington DC: CUPA, 1997.

Marques, Maria Alegria Fernandes. "Inocêncio III e a passagem do mosteiro de Lorvão para a ordem de Cister." *Revista portuguesa de Lusitania* 28 (1980): 229–81.

Mecham, June. "Cooperative Piety among Monastic and Secular Women in Late Medieval Germany." *Church History and Religious Culture* 88, no. 4 (2008): 581–611.

Rosenwein, Barbara. *To Be the Neighbor of Saint Peter: The Social Meaning of Cluny's Property, 909–1049*. Ithaca NY: Cornell University Press, 1989.

Ryan, James D. "Missionary Saints of the High Middle Ages: Martyrdom, Popular Veneration, and Canonization." *The Catholic Historical Review* 90 (2004): 1–28.

Shadis, Miriam. *Berenguela of Castile (1180–1246) and Political Women in the High Middle Ages*. New York: Palgrave MacMillan, 2009.

Vivas, Diogo. "Constança Sanches: Algumas observações em torno de uma bastarda régia." *Clio. Revista do Centro de História da Universidade de Lisboa*. Nova série no. 16/17 (2008): 69–104.

Ziegler, Tiffany A. "Just Another Day in the Neighborhood: Collective Female Donation Practices at the Hospital of Saint John in Brussels." In *Medieval and Elite Women and the Exercise of Power 1100–1400: Moving beyond the Exceptionalist Debate*, edited by Heather J. Tanner, 157–76. Cham, Switzerland: Palgrave Macmillan, 2019.

10

Scandal and the Social Networks
of Religious Women

MICHELLE M. HERDER

In 1367, Bishop Ennec de Vallterra of Girona, a city in Catalonia, discovered that one of the Benedictine nuns in his city had recently given birth to a child. The nun in question, Constancia de Palol, was no bored or innocent novice; she had been a sister at the venerable nunnery of Sant Daniel de Girona for at least sixteen years, and had held the post of subprioress since 1360.[1] The bishop discovered Constancia's transgression in the course of a routine visitation to Sant Daniel. There, too, he discovered that Constancia, together with the community's abbess and prioress, had endeavored to conceal the potentially scandalous pregnancy—from the bishop's notice, at least. Their efforts, manifestly, failed. Once the bishop began inquiring directly about Constancia's pregnancy, he found an ample supply of witnesses who willingly named the father of Constancia's child (one of Girona's cathedral canons, Felip de Palau) and revealed the details of the nuns' attempted cover-up. In fact, one gets the impression that the bishop was the last to know what everyone in the area was already talking about.

The story of Constancia's pregnancy is preserved in a single source, now conserved in Girona's diocesan archive in the Processos Medievals series.[2] The document consists of a grouping of paper folios sewn together, the ink much faded on several leaves, with evidence of dirt and moisture deterioration. Heavily abbreviated and emended, the pages are likely the original notes of the bishop's scribes; Nicolau Figuera began the record, though other scribes may have continued it, as the bishop's inquiry lasted several weeks. The presence of marginal notes about admonitions to be made furthers the conclusion that what we see is a rough transcript of the proceedings. The text is mostly in Latin, though occasionally the scribe recorded direct quotations in the vernacular. When the leaves were stitched together into their current form, they were assembled out of order, and with several folios concerning an unrelated matter inserted in the middle. Sorting through the details of the bishop's investigation therefore requires careful reading to set matters in the correct sequence.

The evidence cannot tell us whether Constancia and Felip's story was one of coercion, seduction, simple temptation, or even love. The fate of their child, surrendered to a local hospital, is equally ambiguous. However, the case provides a window into understanding the place of this Benedictine nunnery among its neighbors in the town of Girona and the nearby countryside in the fourteenth century. The nineteen individuals questioned by the bishop included nuns, priests, and assorted lay people. They spoke with varying degrees of frankness, many of them naming other people who had told them details of Constancia's situation, others referring vaguely to others they could not remember. Together they show how the nuns cultivated certain social ties and inadvertently created others. These religious women were subjects of conversation among a wide range of their neighbors, both clerical and lay, illustrating how deeply they were embedded in the surrounding society. For these nuns, community lay not solely inside the cloister walls. Through networks of social contact that linked nuns, servants, clergy, and lay commoners, they also formed part of the community of those living in the environs of Girona. Elsewhere in this volume, Miriam Shadis argues that donors and patrons must be considered part of a monastery's community; here, I seek to include humbler folk as well, including a monastery's neighbors. Such people made transactions with the nuns, saw them, and spoke of them, implicitly including them within their own community, even as the nuns dwelled apart.

Much research in recent decades has shown the ways in which the often-expressed ideal of strict enclosure for religious women became difficult or impossible in practice. Cloisters remained permeable to visitors, particularly family members, members of the clergy, and men and women employed by the nuns.[3] In this study, we see that knowledge of the nuns and their activities also spread beyond the cloister walls, and that even people with no obvious personal connection to the nuns might know a great deal about them. Though this sort of talk might seem to be precisely the sort of scandal that many medieval clergy feared would damage religious women's reputations, it is unclear that such damage actually occurred. Rather, much of their talk suggests a widespread awareness of the nuns as objects of interest, and a tacit acceptance of the nuns' social interactions as ordinary aspects of social life in this community.

In 1367, the monastery of Sant Daniel was already a venerable institution. Founded in the early eleventh century by the dowager Countess Ermessenda of Barcelona (ca. 975–1058), widow of Count Ramon Borrell (r. 992–1017), Sant Daniel had once been situated on the outskirts of the city of Girona, a core part of the comital domains. By the late fourteenth century, the city had expanded toward the site of the monastery, with a bustling suburb of artisans now surrounding the northern road that extended toward Sant Daniel.[4] The nuns still occupied a liminal location, on the edge of the settled urban/suburban space. Beyond the nunnery extended the valley of Sant Daniel, scattered with peasant farms. To this day, the monastery of Sant Daniel sits at a transition between the town of Girona and the nearby countryside.

The monastery's population ranged from twenty to twenty-seven during the fourteenth century. The women came from the ranks of the petty noble families of Catalonia's counties, particularly those of Girona and Empúries, though some of them came from wealthy urban families. Once one of a very few nunneries in the entire region of Catalonia, by 1367 Sant Daniel existed in a crowded religious landscape. Girona alone housed its cathedral, two collegiate churches, a community of Benedictine monks, Franciscan and Dominican convents, and a Clarissan convent. In spite of the popularity of mendicant houses in the late Middle Ages, Sant Daniel continued to attract nuns taking vows; though its size and endowment were relatively modest, its nuns had a long and honorable history, if not always a tranquil one. In the earlier 1300s, an assortment of quarrels and financial difficulties had driven the bishop at that time to appoint a male procurator to handle the nuns' temporal affairs, as well as to outline a stricter standard of enclosure.[5] By 1367, however, all that was years in the past.

On April 26, 1367, Bishop Ennec de Vallterra went to the monastery of Sant Daniel to begin a routine visitation. As Vallterra had been made bishop only ca. 1361/1362, this may have been the first time he had conducted such a visitation at Sant Daniel. Though bishops were supposed to visit monasteries under their jurisdiction regularly, few visitation records regarding women's houses in the diocese of Girona have survived. The unusual nature of this case likely led to its preservation.

The visitation began with ordinary questions: the bishop asked whether the monastery buildings were in good repair, whether the chaplain performed his duties adequately, how many nuns there were, whether the nuns attended mass and the offices regularly, ate and slept in common, and so forth. He interviewed, in turn, the abbess, Ermessenda de Trilla; the prioress, Sibilia de Vilamarí; and the steward, Elisenda Aliona (or d'Alió). The women's replies reveal only ordinary kinds of problems—the nuns did not sleep in a common dormitory, for example, as the roof leaked in that part of the building.[6] The scribe included marginal notes with instructions for monastic officials: the procurator should be directed to have the roof repaired by All Saints, for one thing.[7] In the course of these routine queries, the bishop asked Elisenda Aliona how many nuns were present. She mentioned that Constancia de Palol had been absent from the monastery during Lent, possibly without license from the abbess, and Elisenda did not know where she was. Elisenda here may have been offering the bishop a pointed hint, and breaking the silence which both the abbess and the prioress upheld.

The following day, the bishop returned to interview the infirmarian, Agnès de Mata. Though the scribe recorded her name and the date, no statement follows.[8] Either the interview did not occur, or Agnès spoke to the bishop in confidence, perhaps under the seal of the confessional. As infirmarian, she had reason to know about Constancia's pregnancy. If

Agnès did not speak to the bishop, perhaps Elisenda's hint set him on a new path of inquiry. Either way, when the bishop resumed his interviews on May 6, he was on the trail of Constancia's transgression.

On that date, Bishop Ennec questioned three priests beneficed at Sant Daniel. Two of these, Bonanat Hospital and Pere Bernat de Perles, the nuns' chaplain, spoke briefly, generally on matters concerning the monastic routine: communal sleeping and eating and celebration of the Divine Office.[9]

The third priest, Jaume de Soler, told a longer story. According to him, three local priests, Felip de Palau, Domènec Cardona, and Ramon Scuder, had visited the monastery. Felip and Domènec had also entered Constancia's dwelling within the cloister to visit her. When asked whether the nuns lived chastely, Jaume said yes, but added a somewhat convoluted anecdote: he said that the steward, Elisenda d'Alió, had brought a priest from Girona and a Jewish surgeon into the monastery to see one Constancia, the servant of Constancia de Palol. Hearing complaints that someone was defamed, Jaume had spoken to another woman, Lunarda, who said that Constancia had requested license to be absent from the monastery during Lent due to her pregnancy, and had been staying in the household of En Romaguers in the parish of Llambilles, some eight kilometers to the east of Girona.[10] Why this place was chosen is not clear from the sources; though the monastery of Sant Daniel owned scattered parcels of land throughout the region, the monastery's documents do not indicate a prior connection to Llambilles or the Romaguers family.

From here, Ennec de Vallterra's questions focused on the issue of Constancia's chastity. On May 12, he questioned Pere Berenguer de Casesnoves, a canon of the cathedral chapter who was also the nuns' procurator, handling their temporal affairs. Pere Berenguer said that Constancia was widely reputed as unchaste. He identified the father of Constancia's child as Felip de Palau, and said that one Berenguer Gironés had told him that the abbess had ordered Constancia to stay at the Romaguers household during her pregnancy. According to Pere Berenguer, Berenguer Gironés had served as a messenger between the monastery and the Romaguers household, ultimately escorting Constancia back to the monastery just before Palm Sunday. The canon Pere Berenguer also named other individuals who had visited the monastery, and frequently stated that he knew things because he "had heard it said" by assorted unnamed individuals.[11] He thus passed on information to the bishop without, in general, claiming to be an eyewitness, and contributes to the impression that Constancia's situation was much talked about.

Felip de Palau must have been well known to Ennec de Vallterra. Felip was, like Pere Berenguer, a cathedral canon, and had also served Ennec de Vallterra as an emissary and procurator in the past.[12] Felip had been close to the previous bishop, Berenguer de Cruïlles, and had been an executor of Berenguer's testament when that bishop died in 1362.[13] In 1367, Felip was rector of the hospital maintained by the cathedral chapter; the hospital was located outside Girona's walls, not far from Sant Daniel. His post therefore placed him in proximity to the nunnery.

The bishop next questioned a Girona priest, Pere Nironi, who said that he had heard from many people that Constancia had given birth to a child in the parish of Llambilles, and that that child had been fathered by Felip de Palau. According to Pere Nironi, however, it was Pere Berenguer de Casesnoves who had sent a servant to accompany Constancia back to Sant Daniel, suggesting that the procurator was more complicit in concealing the situation than he had admitted. Pere Nironi, too, relied on reporting other people's words, though he had himself seen Felip de Palau talking to the nuns many times, apparently outside the monastery. He had seen Felip visit the abbess and other nuns as well, accompanied by Domènec Cardona, and he had heard it said that Felip gave gifts to Constancia, though he could not recall who told him this. He was precise about what he had witnessed; when asked if he had seen Constancia enter Felip's home, he said no, but he had seen her come out.[14]

Pere Nironi's testimony, like that of Pere Berenguer de Casesnoves, suggests that Constancia's situation was well known in the town of Girona. Visits to the nuns, gifts to them, and other activities were noticed and remarked upon, by so many people that neither man could recall or name their informants. Remarks like these are common, illustrating both the reach of information about the nuns, and the way the speakers situated themselves in social networks.[15] The nuns were known by name and reputation to many, and were a visible part of Girona's social activity.

The bishop next approached people associated with the "new" hospital of Girona. Founded in the thirteenth century and maintained by the municipal council, the hospital was no longer precisely new, but it retained that name to contrast it with the "old" hospital associated with the cathedral, the one of which Felip de Palau was rector.[16]

Constancia's child had been entrusted to the new hospital. Margarida "Spitaleria" testified that a newborn had been abandoned at the hospital in the month of April, and that she did not know the child's parentage. The baby had been accompanied by a small sum of money, and a note naming him *Johan*, and so he was baptized. Asked whether she knew anything about a nun's pregnancy, Margarida said that she did not know herself, but that Anabona of Aiguaviva, the infant's wet nurse, had told her the baby must be the nun's.[17] Francesc de Savarrés, the head of the new hospital, similarly testified that the infant had been given to the hospital on April 1, and entrusted to Nicolau Vinyes of Aiguaviva for a monthly fee of fourteen *solidi* and an allotment of bread. Like Margarida, Francesc said he did not know the identity of the baby's parents, but Nicolau Vinyes had told him that it must be the child of the "venerable and religious lady Constancia de Palol, nun of the monastery of Sant Daniel de Girona, and Felip de Palau, priest and rector of the hospital of the cathedral of Girona."[18] Francesc did not know how Nicolau Vinyes had come by that information. The hospital's rector, Guillem de Condamina, claimed to know nothing of the child's parentage or any nun's ill fame.[19]

Margarida and Francesc's testimony illustrates both the extent of knowledge about the case and the care that witnesses took to distinguish between what they "knew" and what they had been told.[20] In making such distinctions, those questioned not only indicate what they themselves had witnessed, they offer testimony to the extent of knowledge among the wider community. For Francesc and Margarida, though they were based in Girona and in contact with the abandoned infant, their information came from the villagers of Aiguaviva rather than from the Girona townsfolk. Like earlier witnesses, they distinguished between what they knew and what they had "heard said;" in this case, Nicolau Vinyes and Anabona were their sole informants.

In contrast to the limited connections of the people working at the new hospital, the next witness, a priest of Girona named Francesc de Soler, was thoroughly plugged into networks of conversation. He said that the nun Elisenda d'Alió's servant Lunarda had told him that Constancia de Palol was pregnant and staying in the parish of Llambilles; that a Dominican friar, Berenguer Camites, told him that Sant Daniel's abbess had given license for Constancia's absence (contradicting Elisenda's original claim to the bishop); that a man named Joan had said that Constancia was "*grossa*"; and that the nuns' infirmarian, Agnès de Mata, had told him that the prioress begged the abbess to show mercy to Constancia.[21] Nuns, their servants, and other members of both clergy and laity spoke freely to Francesc, who in turn passed on these colorful details to the bishop. When asked who had impregnated Constancia, Francesc said that both rumor and Lunarda had told him it was Felip de Palau.[22]

The bishop seems not to have sought out Lunarda, nor several of the other witnesses mentioned. He did, however, question Nicolau Vinyes of Aiguaviva, the infant's caretaker. Nicolau said that his sister Anabona or Bona, the child's nurse, had told him the baby was the child of a nun, born at the Romaguers household.[23] Anabona's informant was a neighbor of theirs in Aiguaviva, a widow called Correguera, who had learned it while visiting her married daughter in Llambilles. Knowledge of the nuns, therefore, traveled from village to village through family members and neighbors, linking the nuns into the wider lay community of the region. For some reason, Nicolau told the bishop that he could not name the nun involved, knowing only that she was a nun of Sant Daniel (even though, according to Francesc de Savarrés, he had named her before). Like others, Nicolau had heard that Felip de Palau was the father. And yet, when asked if he had heard any defamation of the nuns, he replied no.[24]

Several other individuals were then briefly questioned on May 15. Bonanata, wife of Guillem Manet of Girona, said that she had heard about Constancia's pregnancy from some women at the new hospital. Jacoba of Aiguaviva, formerly living at Sant Daniel, had heard about Constancia and Felip from a friend called Bonanata Marquesa.[25] Berenguer Martí, identified as the nuns' *nuntius*, was the man who had been dispatched by the abbess to escort Constancia back from Llambilles, but he had been told that Constancia suffered from a fever and a cough. It was a man called Lomde from the parish of Quart, whom Berenguer Martí met along the way, who had told him that Constancia had given birth.[26] Margarida, a widow from Llambilles, had met Constancia there. She had heard that Constancia had given birth, though she could not recall who had told her so. She did not know who had impregnated Constancia, though she listed several people who had frequented the house where Constancia stayed, and could state when Constancia had arrived in Llambilles, as well as when and how she departed (the Saturday before Palm Sunday, riding a mule).[27] These details illustrate the visibility of Constancia's stay, as well as the awkwardness of the timing: one suspects that Constancia returned before Palm Sunday so that no absence from Holy Week celebrations could raise questions.

The bishop's inquiry then languished for a month. On June 15 he resumed questioning, and at that time interrogated Berenguer Domènec de Cardona. This appears to be the same Domènec de Cardona who, according to the clerics Jaume de Soler and Pere Nironi, had accompanied Felip de Palau when he visited Constancia at the monastery of Sant Daniel. Berenguer Domènec, asked whether he or anyone else had special familiarity with the nuns, talked extensively of Felip de Palau's connection to Constancia de Palol.[28] He admitted that Felip had given Constancia gifts, that Felip had celebrated mass at Constancia's request, and that he and Felip had eaten at the monastery of Sant Daniel together. According to him, the monastery's prioress, Sibilia de Vilamarí, had told him that Constancia visited Felip's home. In spite of Cardona's own social connections to both individuals, he said that it was Bernat Oliva, a priest of the cathedral chapter, who told him of Constancia's pregnancy. He had heard about the birth, and the infant's arrival at the new hospital, but could not recall who had told him of these matters.[29]

Berenguer Domènec de Cardona's testimony appears self-serving, distancing himself from any association with Constancia and Felip's illicit relationship. However, he maintained distinctions that show us contemporary attitudes toward the idea of defamation. To him, it seems, Constancia's visiting Felip's home was not itself evidence of defamation; only the report that others considered the pair to be defamed carried that status. What mattered was public opinion. Cardona admitted to visiting the nuns of Sant Daniel, suggesting that such social visits were not unusual, and did not pass beyond the bounds that local people considered appropriate. Such acceptance itself indicates that these nuns maintained social ties that went beyond the convent walls, integrating them into a community of neighbors, friends, and acquaintances. Paying social calls seems to have been viewed as ordinary, in spite of decades-earlier orders regarding enclosure.

In Constancia's case, her social connections also included a lover. While visiting people in Girona, in and of itself, does not seem to have affected her reputation, there may have been something about Constancia and Felip's interactions that led others to believe their connection was more intimate, and thus worthy of defamation. One recalls the case of Giovanni and Lusanna, in fifteenth-century Florence, where witnesses to a lawsuit cited details of the couple's conduct that led them to believe the two were married.[30] In the case of Constancia and Felip, no witnesses describe their behavior together, so whatever actions or expressions might have contributed to their public defamation are unknown. It is possible that their relationship had initially been discreet, growing out of a genuine friendship, and had only attracted critical attention once Constancia's pregnancy became publicly known. There is no real way of knowing.

Finally, in late June, the bishop interviewed Constancia de Palol herself. By this time, he must have been well aware of the facts of the situation. Constancia, however, gave away little: to the first questions, she replied that all the nuns lived chastely, and none had had a child. Did she know of the bishop's queries? Perhaps not; he seems not to have questioned any of the nuns of Sant Daniel or their servants after his initial visitation in late April. Constancia did admit that she had stayed at the Romaguers household, but said she had been ill with a fever. When asked about Felip de Palau's visits to Sant Daniel, she said she had seen him talking with the abbess, minimizing her own connection to him. She said that she and the prioress, Sibilia de Vilamarí, had visited his house together, just as they visited other people in Girona.[31]

With Constancia's statements, the scribe's notes end. If the bishop accused her once she was done, or imposed any kind of penance or punishment on her, it went unrecorded. The testimony of the witnesses, partial though it is, provides a window into the social networks surrounding the monastery of Sant Daniel. It is clear that the nuns maintained numerous connections. In addition to the clergy holding benefices at the nuns' church, they received visitors from other members of the clergy, and perhaps also from lay neighbors. The nuns also conducted social visits themselves, leaving the monastery to do so. They employed both male and female servants, including a nuntius, Berenguer Gironès (or Martí), who carried messages and did errands for the nuns, including escorting Constancia back to the monastery. When it was decided to house Constancia outside the monastery as her pregnancy came to term, during one of the most important seasons of the liturgical year, the nuns found a friendly contact who hosted Constancia at some distance from the monastery. They evidently also successfully persuaded En Romaguers and his family to keep Constancia's situation relatively discreet; at least, the family did not take the matter to the bishop themselves. All these connections are testimony to the breadth of the nuns' community.

At the same time, if Constancia, the abbess, and the prioress hoped to keep Constancia's circumstances entirely secret, their strategy failed miserably. Relocating Constancia to the Romaguers household in Llambilles made more people aware of Constancia's pregnancy, rather than concealing it. People saw her in Llambilles and remarked on her presence there. The cover story that Constancia suffered from a fever was widely disbelieved, perhaps because she was visibly pregnant. The preparations for childbirth and the presence of a newborn in the Romaguers household must have been obvious to curious neighbors, as the widow Margarida's testimony suggests. Na Correguera's visit to Llambilles also took news of Constancia's presence there back to the village of Aiguaviva, where she spoke to Anabona and Nicolau Vinyes, who in turn told Francesc de Savarrés of the new hospital that the foundling placed in his custody must be the child of Constancia de Palol and Felip de Palau.

These incidents show that the nuns were talked about, even by those with no direct contact with the nuns. To be sure, the monastery of Sant Daniel had extensive land holdings in the region; many lay people in the area must have been the nuns' tenants, or have held adjoining properties, or have taken their grain to be ground in mills owned by Sant Daniel. The nuns' church, with its lavishly decorated shrine to St. Daniel, also attracted local worshippers. Even beyond such ties of economics or devotion, the religious ladies of Sant Daniel were objects of interest and subjects of conversation among clergy and laity in Girona, Llambilles, Aiguaviva, and other nearby villages. Constancia's pregnancy was, no doubt, an especially juicy piece of gossip for many of these neighbors, but the extent of their interest, and their knowledge, shows how deeply the monastery was embedded in the local social environment. The monastery of Sant Daniel was an institution with far-reaching connections to its neighbors.

Though medieval stereotypes held women as gossips, in this situation, priests played crucial roles in passing on rumors.[32] While several of the witnesses questioned said they had heard certain things from many people, many of the priests had talked to numerous specific individuals, enabling them to combine information from different sources. Francesc de Soler, for example, had details from Sant Daniel's infirmarian, from the servant of a different nun, from a Dominican friar, and from an otherwise unknown layman. Jaume de Soler's informants likewise included monastic servants; Pere Berenguer de Casesnoves named several individuals who frequented the monastery. Other priests, such as Pere Nironi, relayed their own eyewitness testimonies, as well as the words of anonymous others. All of these men observed social connections and, through their talk with others, helped form them.

Even though Constancia's pregnancy and her affair with Felip were widely known, no surviving records indicate that either had been disciplined for sexual transgressions prior to this point. Many of the witnesses, in fact, temporized; even when asked directly whether the nuns of Sant Daniel were chaste, people like Jaume de Soler and Nicolau Vinyes responded "yes" or "I don't know" immediately before repeating rumors about Constancia's pregnancy that they had heard from others. As noted previously, those questioned, or the scribe, maintained a distinction between things they "knew," "saw," or "had heard." They were, perhaps, reluctant to give too much credence to hearsay, or simply had a desire to be precise in the face of an official episcopal inquiry.

It is also possible that, prior to this point, Constancia and Felip's relationship had been treated as acceptable, within the realm of tolerated conduct, with anything transgressive merely a matter for speculation and gossip. Yet gossip itself could be a serious matter in the late Middle Ages; public talk formed reputations, and could create scandal.[33] Witnesses' words allowed them to participate in creating and enforcing social norms.[34] In this case, the witnesses chose what information to reveal and what to conceal. Constancia herself, even while concealing her pregnancy, admitted that she had visited Felip de Palau's home and eaten there. She had done so accompanied by the prioress, she said, suggesting that such visits could be construed as acceptable so long as she was not alone. Berenguer Domènec de Cardona also reported Constancia's visits to Felip, without apparently considering that evidence of "defamation." The witnesses thus seem to treat visits between a nun and a priest as ordinary rather than shocking, in spite of the fact that previous bishops of Girona had limited such contact earlier in the century.[35] Late medieval nuns frequently did not live according to the strictest ideals of enclosure found in spiritual literature, but witness statements like the ones found here suggest that laity were not disturbed by their social interactions, as long as vows of chastity were not obviously violated.

Not only did the witnesses hesitate to assert that the nuns were unchaste or defamed, only Constancia was mentioned as possibly infamous, even though other nuns of Sant Daniel also visited outside the monastery and spoke with male visitors inside it. While ecclesiastical superiors seem to have feared that any hint of transgression would taint the entire community, Sant Daniel's neighbors distinguished between Constancia's behavior and that of the other nuns.

The text of the source simply ends, with no indication of resolution or further inquiries. If Ennec de Vallterra chose to discipline either Constancia de Palol or Felip de Palau, that discipline does not survive in episcopal records. Perhaps the matter was handled privately, with one or both subjected to penance or temporary disciplines. In addition, no new exhortations regarding enclosure of the nuns appeared until September 1368. At that time, Girona's clergy were forbidden from entering the monastery of Sant

Daniel, but the date, over a year after the inquiry, seems late to be directly motivated by Constancia's circumstances.[36]

Whatever may have happened in the short term, Constancia de Palol remained both nun and subprioress until sometime after 1392, her last appearance in the monastery's documents.[37] By that time, she had been a nun for over forty years and served as subprioress, managing the altar of St. Benedict, for over thirty. Felip de Palau, for his part, was still rector of the cathedral hospital in 1390.[38] With their child given up, their old affair had little outward effect on their lives. We do not know how often, if at all, they saw each other again. Of their son, we know even less; he disappears from the historical record after his birth.

NOTES

1. Identified as subprioress in Arxiu de Sant Daniel #878 (June 13, 1360); first mentioned in ASD #833, dated 1351.

2. Arxiu Diocesà de Girona (ADG), Processos Medievals 303.

3. As discussed in Lehfeldt, *Religious Women*; Makowski, *English Nuns*, 16–21, gives a brief overview of the difficulties around enforcing enclosure in the later Middle Ages. The full dimensions of the ideal and reality of enclosure go beyond the scope of this essay, but valuable interpretations can be found in Schulenberg, "Strict Active Enclosure"; Uffman, "Inside and Outside"; and Gill, "*Scandala*."

4. For the history of Girona, see Guilleré, *Girona al segle XIV*; for a general history of the Crown of Aragon, see Bisson, *Medieval Crown of Aragon*.

5. As discussed previously in Herder, "Substitute or Subordinate?"; the appointment of a procurator can be found in ADG, Cartoral de Capmany, fols. 5–6 verso; for an order of stricter enclosure, see ADG Notularum G-6, fols. 94 verso–95.

6. ADG, Processos Medievals 303. As noted above, the leaves are also out of order. Abbess Ermessenda's testimony is on fols. 11–12; Sibilia de Vilamarí's, fols. 12–13; and Elisenda d'Alió's, fols. 17–18.

7. ADG, Processos Medievals 303, fol. 12.

8. The heading can be found on fol. 13 verso.

9. ADG Processos Medievals 303, fols. 18 verso–21; Jaume de Soler's statement is on fols. 19 verso–21.

10. ADG Processos Medievals 303, fols. 20 verso–21.

11. ADG Processos Medievals 303, fols. 21 verso–23.

12. Such as in 1365: ADG Litterarum U-50, fol. 156.

13. ADG Notularum G-42, fols. 163 verso–164.

14. ADG Processos Medievals 303, fol. 24 verso. Pere Nironi's testimony can be found on fols. 23 verso–25.

15. See McDonough, *Witnesses, Neighbors, and Community*, especially 46–48, for more on the construction of witness testimony.

16. Brodman, *Charity and Welfare*, 38.

17. ADG Processos Medievals 303, fols. 25–26.

18. ADG Processos Medievals 303, fol. 26 verso.

19. ADG Processos Medievals 303, fol. 27.

20. The same distinction is observable in other legal testimony; see Wickham, "Gossip and Resistance," 4.

21. ADG Processos Medievals 303, fol. 28.

22. ADG Processos Medievals 303, fol. 28 verso.

23. ADG Processos Medievals 303, fol. 29; Bona is called Nicolau's *fratra* rather than *soror*.

24. ADG Processos Medievals 303, fol. 30.

25. ADG Processos Medievals 303, fol. 30v.

26. ADG Processos Medievals 303, fols. 31–32.

27. ADG Processos Medievals 303, fol. 34.

28. ADG Processos Medievals 303, fols. 13 verso–14; Cardona's testimony occurs on fols. 13 verso–16 verso.

29. ADG Processos Medievals 303, fol. 16.

30. Brucker, *Giovanni and Lusanna*, 15–25.

31. ADG Processos Medievals 303, fol. 2 verso; Constancia's statement can be found on fols. 1–3.

32. See the introduction to Bardsley, *Venomous Tongues*, and Lochrie, *Covert Operations*, especially 135–36, for a discussion of the gendered nature of speech stereotypes.

33. Further discussion in Fenster and Smail, *Fama*, especially 1–8.

34. See McDonough, *Witnesses, Neighbors, and Community*, 46–48, and Wickham, "Gossip and Resistance," 6–9.

35. ADG Notularum G-6, fols. 94 verso–95.

36. ADG Litterarum U-57, fol. 300.

37. ASD #1010.

38. ADG Litterarum U-79, fol. 32 verso.

BIBLIOGRAPHY

Primary sources

ADG. Arxiu Diocesà de Girona
    Litterarum series.
    Notularum series.
    Processos Medievals 303.

ASD. Arxiu de Sant Daniel de Girona
    Parchments
Secondary Sources
Bardsley, Sandy. *Venomous Tongues: Speech and Gender in Late Medieval England.* Philadelphia: University of Pennsylvania Press, 2006.

Bisson, Thomas. *The Medieval Crown of Aragon: A Short History.* Oxford: Clarendon Press, 1986.

Brodman, James William. *Charity and Welfare: Hospitals and the Poor in Medieval Catalonia.* Philadelphia: University of Pennsylvania Press, 1998.

Brucker, Gene. *Giovanni and Lusanna.* Berkeley: University of California Press, 1986.

Fenster, Thelma, and Daniel Lord Smail, eds. *Fama: The Politics of Talk and Reputation in Medieval Europe.* Ithaca NY: Cornell University Press, 2003.

Gill, Katherine. "*Scandala*: Controversies Concerning Clausura and Women's Religious Communities in Late Medieval Italy." In *Christendom and Its Discontents: Exclusion, Persecution, and Rebellion, 1000–1500*, edited by Scott L. Waugh and Peter D. Diehl. Cambridge: Cambridge University Press, 1996.

Guilleré, Christian. *Girona al segle XIV.* 2 vols. Girona: Ajuntamant de Girona, 1993.

Herder, Michelle. "Substitute or Subordinate? The Role of a Male Administrator at a Benedictine Women's Monastery," *Journal of Medieval History* 31, no. 3 (September 2005): 231–42.

Lehfeldt, Elizabeth A. *Religious Women in Golden Age Spain: The Permeable Cloister.* Farnham UK: Ashgate, 2005.

Lochrie, Karma. *Covert Operations: The Medieval Uses of Secrecy.* Philadelphia: University of Pennsylvania Press, 1999.

Makowski, Elizabeth. *English Nuns and the Law in the Middle Ages: Cloistered Nuns and Their Lawyers, 1298–1540.* Woodbridge, Suffolk: Boydell, 2011.

McDonough, Susan Alice. *Witnesses, Neighbors, and Community in Late Medieval Marseille.* New York: Palgrave MacMillan, 2013.

Schulenberg, Jane. "Strict Active Enclosure and Its Effects on the Female Monastic Experience, 500–1100." In *Medieval Religious Women: Distant Echoes*, edited by John A. Nichols and Lillian Thomas Shank. Oxford: Cistercian, 1984.

Uffmann, Heike. "Inside and Outside the Convent Walls: The Norm and Practice of Enclosure in the Reformed Nunneries of Late Medieval Germany." *The Medieval History Journal* 4, no. 1 (2001): 83–108.

Wickham, Chris. "Gossip and Resistance among the Medieval Peasantry." *Past and Present* 160 (August 1998): 3–24.

11

Minerva of Her Time

Luisa Sigea and Humanist Networking

RACHEL F. STAPLETON

When Spanish-Portuguese humanist Luisa Sigea (b. ca. 1522) died in 1560, neither her fame nor name died with her.[1] In the decades after her death, she continued to be the subject of elegies by humanists, poets, and literati across Europe; poet Pedro Laínez penned a lengthy epicedium in Castilian to "*Aloysiae Sygeae Toletanae*," which culminates with the lines: "Here lies the most famous Sigea, in rare perfection, esteemed without equal in a world girded by the sea and surrounded by the sun, stolen by Death before her time."[2] Juan Merulo, a noble Toledan, wrote: "Here, beneath the icy marble, lies the learned Sigea; mournful Hesperia moans 'Alas!' on account of her death. And rightly so! For from this girl, expert in Hebrew, Greek, and Latin, and no less in the tongue of her fatherland, cruel Death has seized so many languages, which were to be admired in a tender maid who was adorned by them all. Luisa Sigea of Toledo, the Minerva of her time!"[3] This description of Sigea as "Minerva of her time" followed her for decades after her death, and speaks volumes to the level of her renown.

Her literary career garnered Sigea international recognition, as she participated in the intellectual conversations of her era and in the social activities of the royal households to which she was attached. The youngest daughter of Franco-Spanish humanist Diego Sigeo, she studied and worked her adult life in humanist circles.[4] In the 1540s, when she first begins to make a name for herself, Sigea was in her early twenties and firmly ensconced at the court of the Infanta María of Portugal—an influential patron of both religion and culture, and one of the few courts that valued the expression of women's knowledge.[5] There she was employed as a Latin tutor to the princess and participated in the social activities of María's court circle, which also included Sigea's sister, Ángela, Paula de Vicente, and Joana Vas.[6] During this time, Sigea received a salary of 16,000 reis, significantly more than other *moças de câmara* (chamber ladies).[7] Sigea's earliest surviving writings are from this period, and show that she was already corresponding with humanists throughout Iberia and across Europe, on her own and her patroness's behalf.

As with many humanists, the frivolity of courtly life was a frequent topic of criticism in Sigea's letters and in the *Dialogue of two virgins on the public or the private life* (*Duarum virginum colloquium de vita aulica et privata*), in which her interlocutors, Blesilla and Flaminia, find in favor of the private life.[8] In addition to the *Colloquium*, Sigea's Latin poem *Syntra*—which recounts a meeting with a nymph in the woods of Sintra on the outskirts of Lisbon, which is supposed to prophesize the Infanta's future marriage— and some shorter poems in Castilian have also survived. Important for understanding Sigea's professional career is that her profit from the *Colloquium* and *Syntra* was in renown rather than cash.[9] And while only some twenty-two of Sigea's letters are extant, they are suggestive of a much larger correspondence.[10] Living at the western edge of continental Europe and the Holy Roman Empire, Sigea's correspondence allowed her to travel not only to distant geographies but also, with the help of a network of humanists and patrons, to social and political environments that were otherwise out of her reach. This network, however, was largely—if not uniquely—comprised of male humanists, although Sigea's patrons were more frequently women (the Infanta María of Portugal and the Empress María of Hungary, sister of Charles V).

I argue that Sigea's letters allow us to gain understanding of one woman's entrance into the humanist networks and communities of her time, particularly the ways in which she actively seeks out recognition from individuals who can further her career and celebrity. This essay examines letters from Luisa Sigea to three different correspondents, written at different points in her career, and for different purposes, letters which, respectively, establish, preserve, and rely on her reputation and fame. The first letter, addressed to Pope Paul III, brings herself to his notice for her scholarship; with Paul's reply, an exchange is created that grants Sigea recognition on an international scale.[11] The second letter demonstrates Sigea's concern for her reputation and how to preserve it; it is one of two extant letters addressed to Álvar Gómez de Castro, a fellow humanist and long-time friend, with whom she shared the epithet "*toledano.*"[12] The last is a single letter in which Sigea offers advice to an aspiring young female scholar, Magdalena de Padilla, on the best manner of being a humanist and resisting the temptations of courtly life, gleaned from Sigea's own experience. And while so few letters have survived, these three letters by Sigea (and the reply from Paul III) that I include here allow us to understand her entrée into, and depth of her participation in, the intellectual communities of sixteenth-century Iberia and Europe.

Prior to the invention of modern technologies of communication, letters were the primary means of building and maintaining community and relationships across distance. They functioned at least in part as Seneca imagined in his *Moral Epistles*: as pictures of absent friends.[13] This classical metaphor appears repeatedly throughout humanist and early modern discussions of letter writing; in his 1522 *De conscribendis epistolis*, Erasmus attempts to define what makes a letter, and comes to the conclusion, "I think that I cannot define it more concisely than by saying that the wording of a letter should resemble a conversation between friends. For a letter, as the comic poet Turpilius skillfully put it, is a mutual conversation between absent friends, which should be neither unpolished, rough, or artificial, nor confined to a single topic, nor tediously long."[14] The conceit of face-to-face conversation in the light of physical absence reappears over and over again: in a 1534 letter writing treatise (also titled *De conscribendis epistolis*), Spanish humanist Juan Luis Vives writes: "A letter is a conversation by means of the written word between persons separated from each other. [...] 'The purpose of the letter,' said Saint Ambrose to Sabinus, 'is that though physically separated we may be united in spirit. In a letter the image of the living presence emits its glow between persons distant from each other, and conversation committed to writing unites those who are separated. In it we also share our feelings with a friend and communicate our thoughts to him.'"[15] The sharing of thoughts and feelings is inseparable from the medium of the letter, as even the most stilted epistolary tone can help elucidate the nature of the writers' relationship. And while Luisa Sigea's letters vary in formality as she adapts her tone according to her addressee, her style is fluid and natural and illuminates her relationships with her correspondents.

The letters of Luisa Sigea are important not only as documents of historical record, but as testimonials of individual lived experience. Letters can be read as documents of self as well as of history, enabling us to better unpack the complex ways in which historical letters, often formulaic in structure, participate in and challenge contemporary discourses. Roxana Pagés-Rangel notes the ways in which letters have traditionally been studied as secondary sources or historical and biographical "keys" to cast light on the primary "literary" works of an author, rather than as literary texts in their own right.[16] That letters function both as sources of historical interest and as creative and literary texts makes them particularly productive, as evidenced by a growing number of studies in the past decade. These studies highlight not only the materiality of letters, but their function as active texts that are full of auto/biographical potential, as Jacques Presser and Rudolf Dekker suggest with the term "egodocument."[17]

The importance of the "ego" is particularly central in reading letters by women. Because women are so often erased from or marginalized by the historical record, letters allow us entrance into women's first-person points of view.[18] In the historical and literary records, letters are one of the richest sources of documents by women; Pagés-Rangel argues that writing letters is one of the areas in which women most regularly employed both their literacy and literary skills, and she notes further the particular importance of epistolary exchange for women, who were "traditionally displaced from public spaces and spaces of power, authority, and the rhetoric of print culture."[19] The frequent exclusion of women from public discourses means that letters are doubly important in studying women: they are a liminal genre, often permeating physical or social borders and boundaries that the writer might not otherwise be able to traverse, simultaneously private and public documents that create conversation while remaining silent.

The other surviving letters in Luisa Sigea's corpus are as much to do with business and advancement as they are with friendship, but in all instances they build on the presumption of a relationship forged in pen and ink. While some of Sigea's correspondents are far above her in social hierarchy (she writes to monarchs as well as popes), even in these cases Sigea's literacy and literariness function to allow her to assume a relationship of, if not social equality, then of literary parity with her social superiors. With those she views as her equals, Sigea is assertive and confident in her position as a woman "without equal."

LETTERS TO A POPE: RECOGNITION AND FAME

In 1546, in a masterful display of humanistic learning, Sigea wrote a letter to Paul III for which she would garner international recognition and fame. The letter was written in Latin, but she included copies which she herself had translated into Greek, Hebrew, Arabic, and Syriac.[20] Enclosed with these translations was a gift Sigea wished to present to the pope: her poem, *Syntra*. Paul III, a well-known patron of the arts and lover of pomp and circumstance, was an obvious recipient of Sigea's skill as a letter writer and a poet.[21] Sigea's letter was carried to Rome on her behalf by Italian humanist Girolamo Britonio, and through Britonio's own networks, Sigea's letter reached the papal court, where it seems to have been received with wonder and amazement by the Pope and his secretaries.[22] Some months later, Paul replied to Sigea, explicitly recognizing her talent and effectively granting a papal seal of approval to her studies.

In her letter, Sigea attempts to gain favor from Paul through modesty and subtle flattery, while simultaneously mobilizing her exceptional learning and mastery of languages as a rationale for recognition and potential patronage. Elsewhere in her letters, Sigea creates an autobiographical accounting of her life and accomplishments to support her claims, but that account almost invariably relies on the recognition she eventually receives from Paul. In addressing him in this letter, Sigea emphasizes her membership in humanist networks through her connection with Girolamo Britonio, who "some six years ago, arranged for my immature scribblings—which I sent with the audacity of youth—to reach your Holiness";[23] no copy of this earlier letter, presumably written around 1540, when Sigea was still in her teens, survives, nor is there a record of it having been received in Rome.

Sigea addresses herself to the pontiff in the hope of gaining notice, writing modestly of her previous efforts that "It has been some time now since I presented to Your Holiness a few flower buds of my humble talent, in the manner of the faithful farmer who garlands the altars of the gods with the tender shoots newly blossomed, so that, under their protection, they [the plants] may grow to their full maturation, and produce more abundant fruits."[24] Her rhetorical humility continues through the metaphors of inspiration and abundance; here, the divine protection of the gods demands Paul's in turn, that Sigea's "fruits" may ripen under the papal aegis. Dismissing her earlier offerings as the unripe products of an immature mind, she builds on the pastoral metaphor of flowers growing into fruits, but where only patronage and recognition can act as the warming sun necessary for the ripening and "full maturation" of her work. Without such nurturing warmth, Sigea's efforts, both in this letter and the earlier one that has not survived, will be deemed those of a precocious schoolgirl showing off, instead of a scholar producing serious work.

Not counting the four translations which accompanied it, Sigea's 1546 letter is one of her shorter surviving letters, showing off her brevity along with her wit, both desirable traits in humanist letter writing. Vives advises: "If you omit what is necessary, all letters are too brief; if you cram them with superfluities, they are all too long."[25] Well familiar with edicts of this kind, Sigea makes good use of her words. Towards the end of the letter she writes that she desires "not to tire the ears of your Holiness with a too-long letter," and Sigea quickly moves on to present her poem, *Syntra*, as a gift to Paul—although it is the letter itself, rather than her poem, which most contributes to her subsequent renown.[26]

In the final rhetorical move of her letter, Sigea suggests to Paul precisely how he might nourish her: "But if, during the flourishing of your Most Holy Pontificate, Your Holiness should begin to favor my sex, my talent, and my learning, this immortal benefit, joining countless others, will be celebrated by all posterity."[27] The "immortal benefit" is deliberately vague, and the relationship between it and papal favor suggests that Paul's foresight in recognizing Sigea will reflect her brilliance back on him. But in the end, it is his recognition of Sigea's sex, as much as her talent, and learning, that is the center of the fame that Sigea mobilizes throughout her career, both in forging relationships with other humanists, in speaking from a position of authority, and later, in seeking employment for herself and her husband after they have left Portugal. That she calls on Paul's recognition as authoritative throughout her later life suggests that she perhaps had some idea in advance as to how valuable it would be to her to have an ultimate authority recognize and approve of the combination of her learning and talent with her female gender, and in the end, Sigea, if not Paul, is remembered by posterity for this letter.

The superlativeness of Sigea's display of talent—especially her linguistic brilliance—clearly captured Paul's attention; Paul's reply to Sigea, dated January 6, 1547, was accompanied by translations of the Latin into Syriac and Arabic by papal secretary Guillaume Postel. Paul's letter comments on Sigea's learning and accomplishments with great admiration, and he expresses his pleasure in receiving the multilingual letter, but "at the same time as we have marveled before the fruits of the genius of a woman who, according to what we have heard, possesses honest and pious customs. For all this, we give thanks to Almighty God who has bestowed this precious gift of the knowledge of many languages, a talent that is rare among men, but rarer still among women."[28] In a few short lines, Paul acknowledges his pleasure in receiving the letter, undoing the possibility of presumption on her part in writing to him in the first place. The condescension of the move opens a space for a relationship or exchange, although Paul's use of the royal "we" negates any possibility of equality.

While praising Sigea's talents, Paul places just as much emphasis on the pious customs that have allowed her dedication to intellectual pursuits without running afoul of religious censure. Sigea has emphasized that in the court of her "Most Serene Princess," she speaks, works, and teaches among women, not men. Yet in praising Sigea, both for her pious customs as well as for her talent and her gifts, Paul compares Sigea not only to the literate and educated among her own sex, but to the majority of male humanists: she is "rare among men, but *rarer still* among women" (emphasis added). Sigea clearly stands out among her contemporaries for the rare combination of her sex and her talent. Paul continues: "Therefore you also should give continual thanks to God and you should adorn—as you do—this talent with honor, piety, and other virtues."[29] This talent is also a gift, and Sigea's honest and pious customs mean that this gift is not only from God, but also to be used in the service of God—Sigea's work is neither religiously nor politically radical, but rather wholly humanistic, and deserving of fame.

A draft of a second letter from Sigea to Paul later in 1547 survives, although records do not indicate whether it was ever sent, received, or responded to. There is no record of any further correspondence from Rome. Yet despite silence from Sigea's potential patron, the acknowledgement she received in the pope's letter of January 1547 provides Sigea with enough social capital to solidify her position within the intellectual networks of the Portuguese, Spanish, and Hapsburg courts and circles. The fame of recognition from an arbiter of taste and morality such as Paul III provides a seal of approval for Sigea's ongoing intellectual activities. She is no longer simply bound to teaching Latin at the court of María of Portugal, but has received sanction to circulate her original work, the "mature and abundant fruits" of her God-given talents, among like-minded humanists.

While by 1546 Sigea already had a secure post with the Infanta, and some recognition from her contemporaries, the multilingual letter she wrote to the Pope catapulted her to a whole new level of fame. Precisely how news of Sigea's linguistic talents spread is unknown, although Guillaume Postel is a likely culprit, given his later praise of Sigea (discussed below); Britonio is also likely, as his role in bringing Sigea to Paul's notice was vital to her success. Yet while the precise trajectory of Sigea's rise to fame is hidden from us, its basis on her letter to Paul is clear: throughout her later correspondence she refers to her unique status, "a woman ordained for an uncommon destiny" as she writes to her brother-in-law, Alonso de Cuevas.[30]

Sigea's other surviving letters engage mostly with humanist colleagues or with potential patrons, providing evidence of her epistolary network. Like her contemporaries, Sigea wrote vividly of the issues of her time; Prieto Corbalán emphasizes Sigea's fluency, describing hers as a "living Latin" that felt natural and easy, the Latin of one who spoke as well as wrote it.[31] For Sigea and many of her humanist correspondents, Latin was alive and thriving in the sixteenth century. Yet Sigea's Latin letters to potential patrons, whether to the Pope or to María of Hungary and Philip II of Spain, effectively functioned also as her portfolio, a way to demonstrate her skills and training. Seeking employment as a Latin tutor or secretary, the command of the language displayed in her letters was always her first and perhaps most important opportunity to showcase her talents. Latin-fluency also served as an important in-group marker for the humanist community. Prieto Corbalán emphasizes the awareness among humanists of the ways in which this cultural and intellectual community was largely supported by letters. We can think not only the number of epistolary treatises produced, but also by the sheer volume of letters that have survived from this period (although relatively few of those have been written by or to women). For Sigea, letters enabled her to participate fully in her intellectual community, demonstrating her erudition, along with her more personal feelings and experiences.[32] Her letters, and in particular two surviving letters from 1558 addressed to Spanish humanist Álvar Gómez de Castro, function as a microcosm of these humanist communities and friendships.[33]

A common frustration for scholars of letters is that one half of a correspondence is often missing; scholars are forced to infer the recipient's responses from clues in the letters before them. Fortunately, in the case of these two letters to Gómez, Sigea explicitly states the points in Gómez's letter to which she is responding. By 1558 Sigea and her husband, Francisco de Cuevas (whom she had married in Portugal, in 1552), had moved to his hometown of Burgos, and the year before, Sigea had given birth to their only child, a daughter, Juanita. Both Sigea and Cuevas had also been employed in the service of María of Hungary, until her death in October 1558.

From the first of the two letters to Gómez, we can surmise that Sigea had previously sent him a letter, perhaps written in careless haste. Gómez corrected Sigea's Latin in that letter and returned it to her so that she might learn from her errors. Such attention and diligence act as a display of friendship, demonstrating the care with which Gómez engages with Sigea's letters and the regard in which he holds her: he does not wish her to be embarrassed, it seems, by making similar errors in a letter to someone who might judge her more harshly than her friend. This creates a fascinating moment in the construction of an epistolary conversation, as the friendship of the correspondents comes into conflict over a letter. The comfort and naturalness with which Sigea made her Latin her own also meant that letters written in haste to friends rather than to patrons could be riddled with language that might be deemed infelicitous to a stickler of Latin grammar. Such is the case, it seems, in the missing letter at issue here.

In her surviving reply to Gómez, Sigea declines to return the corrected letter to him, which he seems to have requested. Sigea presents her refusal in the humblest of terms, giving her thanks for his correcting of her errors, but she argues that he cannot possibly wish to have such a flawed token of their friendship, just as she would not willingly allow her flaws to be so exposed—and nor should he want her flaws to be, either. His demand thus transforms him from a gentle corrector to a "cruel judge," which Sigea cannot imagine to be his real intent, and his request must therefore be ignored.[34] It seems that Sigea is taking the opportunity to flout Horace's warning that *nescit vox missa reverti*, a word sent forth cannot be called back.[35] She *can* call back her words in this case, and with thus the errors contained in them; she can hide her shame away, or perhaps burn it.[36]

For Sigea, as for other humanists, friendship and community are inextricable from letter writing, and her friendship with Gómez requires that she deny his request, just as his friendship with her requires not only his gentle correction of her errors, but should also have prevented him from asking to keep the proof of her inadequacy in the first place.[37] Her performance of modesty makes her reluctant to have a flawed letter of hers loose in the world; what if Gómez were to show it to someone? How might her reputation be affected? Her refusal is the simplest statement in the letter, a short sentence of firm negation: *Non igitur remitto epistolam*, "Therefore I will *not* return my letter."[38] She instead focuses on the corrections Gómez has made, choosing to view them not as evidence of her faults, but as tangible reminders of Gómez's friendship and regard for her.

Gómez's request to return the corrected original to him once she has taken note of the errors and their corrections highlights the friendship he feels for Sigea, his wish to preserve the material object of her letter. But the paper which stands in for her physical presence in the classical and humanistic metaphor of the letter also preserves a flawed textual body. She asks, "Why would you want, in effect, to preserve next to you a page full of faults, when you have claimed that you corrected it so that it might not be shown to others as a reminder of the inadequacy of my learning?"[39] The memento which her faulty letter constitutes is too powerful, and it would be impossible for Gómez to be a generous judge and friend when her sins are constantly before him. Instead, Sigea encourages him to emulate God's judgment, while at the same time gently remonstrating with him, "'Though your sins are like scarlet, they shall be as white as wool, and I shall not remember them.'"[40]

At the end of this letter to Gómez we find one of the most sentimental moments in Sigea's surviving correspondence, a short postscript in Castilian, emphasizing the friendship she shared with him. This is the only intrusion of the vernacular into Sigea's surviving Latin letters, and in this note to her countryman, Sigea's tone is teasing as she offers to give to Gómez a little bird who has been distracting her and is responsible for her errors: "Sir, if your worship would like a parrot, I have one here, who will not let you do anything properly for her constant chatter! I will send her to you, for she has made me erase this page two or three times; her name is Juanita. Your worship must lay the blame at her door, not at mine!"[41] Not only does this vernacular postscript break the formality of Latin-based humanistic intellectual exchange, but in invoking her little parrot, her toddler daughter, Sigea gestures explicitly to her motherhood as an excuse for her failures as a correspondent. There is something particularly endearing about this addendum, reflecting one of the few mentions of her child in Sigea's surviving works. At the same time, its inclusion suggests a familiarity with Gómez beyond the exchange of intellectual ideas: it speaks to the personal and the feminine in a way that also suggests that Gómez would appreciate the joke. Indeed, in the second surviving letter to Gómez, although much more serious in tone and entirely in Latin, Sigea ends again with a farewell from herself and her *graeco psittaco*, her little Greek parrot.[42]

BUILDING COMMUNITY: ADVICE TO A YOUNG HUMANIST

Along with her correspondence with established humanists across Europe, Sigea also undertook the role of guiding aspiring scholars. In ca. 1556/1558, not long after leaving the court of María of Portugal, Sigea penned a letter to a young woman, Magdalena de Padilla.[43] This letter of advice covers not only instructions for participation in intellectual circles but also for the successful navigation of the corrupting temptations of life at court, a favorite topic of Sigea's since her *Duarum virginum*. The career options for secular women humanists, already few and far between, were rapidly diminishing during this part of the century.[44] Service to a patron such as the Infanta María would be one of the few professional opportunities for an educated young woman.

In the opening paragraph of her letter to Padilla, Sigea sets up an extended military metaphor to frame her giving of advice. In this metaphor, Sigea is the experienced veteran soldier and Padilla the green recruit presented to her for approval and training. The veteran, Sigea writes, "measures the recruit's courage and cleverness against the strength of his body" to ensure his ability "to endure the labors of military service."[45] But along with courage and cleverness, the veteran Sigea displays equal interest in *animi indoles*, the tendencies of Padilla's character as they are illuminated by her outward traits. Courage, cleverness, and strength cast light on these traits through a *transenna*, a lattice-work screen.[46] Transennas are a common feature of Iberian architecture, providing not only shade from the hot Mediterranean sun, but also privacy, particularly for women. Thus the recruit's external (and masculine) traits of courage, strength, and cleverness create a *transenna* that allows the discerning of interior—and potentially feminine—traits, of having "at the same time a well-proportioned body and an uncommon strength of mind/moral vigor."[47]

This metaphor is continued as Sigea describes her service in the "encampment of the Muses," but the battle joined is not just one of literary creation. Instead, the battle actually takes place at Court and "in the chambers of the Most Serene Princess" (presumably the Infanta María).[48] "Of the many kinds of style, the majestic, impetuous, fiery, and rapid," writes Erasmus, "are particularly suitable for encouragement . . . the style should be masculine and, if I may say so, robust, impressive, and vigorous."[49] The military metaphor that Sigea invokes suggests, in particular, the masculine traits that are prized within the intellectual community to which Sigea belongs, and Magdalena hopes to belong. At the same time, I would argue that there is something subversive about her extending the metaphor to such a degree when writing to another woman; Sigea never hides her gender, and her exceptionality and recognition in large part depend on it. To invoke a martial metaphor to demarcate the parameters of her advice to Padilla rather than, say, a maternal one, is to refuse to accept that women cannot participate equally in the intellectual community and with the same language as male humanists—even if perhaps only when speaking to each other.

Sigea is also skeptical as to whether Padilla is actually as green as she claims: "at times you [Padilla] denied knowledge of the Latin tongue as on your first campaign, at other times you admitted to a modicum of knowledge."[50] The false modesty that Sigea sees in Padilla is unbecoming in her, "and that with your charming wits, your gracelessness was plainly counterfeit before me";[51] these actions are simulated and inauthentic, as so much is at court, as opposed to the authenticity Sigea values so highly in private life. Instead, she says, "When you occupy yourself with the affairs of Court, speak not of the Muses, and when you occupy yourself with the Muses, put aside the cares of Court," and warns the young woman of the dangers: "take care, renowned Magdalena, for venom is always bestowed wrapped in honey, and if you wish to savor fully the fruit of the Muses and to enter into their presence to which the courts of all the princes are considered secondary, and to live in familiarity with them, reject haughtiness of mind and set aside your superciliousness."[52] Sigea's concern for Magdalena is that the latter not appear affected or artificial, and she argues that the Muses always demand honesty from their acolytes, not false modesty or a superiority. The irony, of course, is the superiority with which Sigea makes her arguments, but it is a superiority earned by her years of study, by her modesty in her relationships with other humanists, and, of course, by the recognition of her talent granted to her by Paul III.

CONCLUSION: PRAISING MINERVA

Paul III's recognition of Sigea answers her belief that it is an "immortal benefit, joining countless others, will be celebrated by all posterity,"[53] a prediction that comes true, both in the sheer volume of praise directed toward her during her life, and in the eulogies written in her honor after her death. Guillaume Postel, a contemporary of Sigea's as well as Paul III's translator, mentions her by name in his 1553 work, *Tres-merveilleuses Victoires des Femmes du Nouveau Monde* ("The Most Marvelous Victories of the Women of the New World"), where he writes of "the lady Luisa Sigea, who, in her twenty-second year, demonstrated her experience by writing most learnedly in Latin, in Greek, in Hebrew, in Syriac, and in Arabic to Pope Paul . . . how much knowledge there is in her!"[54] In Postel's words, Sigea writes most learnedly of her knowledge and learning, and that he emphasizes, as well her youth, suggesting even further the uncommonness of her accomplishments.

Even decades after her death in 1560, new poems of praise for her virtue and intellect were being circulated, and her linguistic skills were almost always mentioned. Portuguese humanist André de Resende penned a touching tribute: "Here lies Sigea: this is enough. Who knows no more is a boor and cherishes not the Liberal Arts."[55] Among the other eulogies collected by Andreas Schottus are poems by Francisco López, Álvar Gómez de Castro, and Sigea's husband, Francisco de Cuevas, who had her tomb engraved with the epitaph *foeminae incomparabili*, a woman without compare.[56]

Luisa Sigea's position in her community was thus reinforced posthumously, always invoking her fame as a learned woman of genius. For decades beyond her death, her name continued to be hailed as a paragon of the liberal arts. Despite the relatively small number of her surviving letters, it is clear that Sigea's position was one deeply immersed in the conversations of her time. She was a professional humanist, supporting herself, and later her family, through her intellectual endeavors, rather than an amateur who studied during her leisure time. Her letters are one of the principal ways she participated in her communities, and she created a place for herself with her contemporaries with her linguistic and epistolary skill.

NOTES

1. Earlier scholarship placed her date of birth nearly a decade later, in 1530, but research published in 1970 by Léon Bourdon and Odette Sauvage argues convincingly for this earlier date ("Recherches," 33–79). Prieto Corbalán concurs with Bourdon and Sauvage's conclusions but notes in particular the difficulty of narrowing down a date of birth with any firm certainty, due in large part to conflicting documentary sources (*Epistolario Latino*, 54).

2. Laínez, "Aloisiae Sigeae," 134. All translations are mine.

3. Merulo's elegy of Sigea is one of many included in Andreas Schottus, *Hispaniae bibliotheca seu de academiis ac bibliothecis*, 342.

4. Sigea was not the only woman humanist of the period; Anne Cruz notes the excellent humanist educations received by Beatriz Galindo and María Pacheco, and, in the seventeenth century, Juliana Morell and Ana Francisca Abarca de Bolea. See Anne J. Cruz, "Women's Education," 30.

5. Bergmann, "Spain's Women Humanists," 222.

6. Saen de Casas, "Juana de Austria," 31.

7. Nieves Baranda notes that as a comparison in 1550, Joana Vaz, employed as a Latin teacher, received a salary of 10,000 reis. See Baranda, "Words for Sale," 61.

8. This dialogue, while well received at the time, was used a century later by Nicolas Chorier in 1660 as evidence for attributing his erotic dialogue, *Satyra sotadica*, to Sigea. Chorier's dialogue continued to be attributed to her until 1862, when Pierre Allut conclusively disproved the claims. The title page of the 1660 edition reads, "The Sotadic Satire of Luisa Sigea of Toledo, on the secrets of love and sex; Luisa wrote the Spanish; Johannes Meursius translated it to Latin" (*Aloisiae Sigeae Toletanae satyra sotadica de arcanis Amoris et Veneris; Aloisia Hispanice scripsit; Latinitate donavit Ioannes Meursius*). Meursius's involvement with the work was also fabricated, although his character seems to have been less tarnished by the suggestion. The *Satyra sotadica* takes the form of a dialogue between two women, the elder of the two is charged with the sexual initiation of the younger. The

dialogic form is, thanks to the *Duarum virginum colloquium*, part of the evidence Chorier used to add credibility to his claim. However, the titillation of a woman being named as its author no doubt helped reinforce this attribution. See Paul Allut, *Aloysia Sygea et Nicolas Chorier*.

9. Baranda, "Words for Sale," 61.

10. Sigea's letters can be found in the Biblioteca Nacional de Madrid, the British Library, the Archivo General de Simancas, and the Archivo Histórico Nacional.

11. Pope from 1534–1539.

12. Prieto Corbalán, *Epistolario latino*, 39.

13. Seneca, *Ad Lucilius epistulae morales*, 40.1.

14. Erasmus, *De conscribendis epistolis*, 20. Charles Fantazzi describes the first part Erasmus's treatise as "giv[ing] voice to his more liberalizing and practical concepts of style," ("General Introduction," 11).

15. Erasmus, *De conscribendis epistolis*, 23.

16. Pagés-Rangel, *Del dominio público*, 4.

17. Dekker, *Egodocuments and History*, 7. On studies of the materiality of letters, see also: Antonio Castillo Gómez, "Del tratado a la práctica: la escritura epistolar en los siglos XVI y XVII"; Daybell, *Material Letter*; Martín Baños, *El arte epistolar*; Schneider, *Culture of Epistolarity*; Steen, "Reading Beyond the Words,"; Stewart and Wolfe, *Letterwriting*, among others. Also of interest is recent research into letterlocking and epistolary security by Jana Dambrogio (MIT) and Daniel Starza Smith (King's College London).

18. Volumes such as this one continue the ongoing scholarly labor of re-centering female and feminine experience in the historical and literary records.

19. Pagés-Rangel, *Del dominio público*, 19.

20. Unfortunately, only the Latin version of this letter survives. The Latin *syriace* ("caldeo" in Spanish) refers to Eastern Middle Aramaic, the classical and liturgical language of Chaldean Christianity.

21. In addition to being an active and generous patron, Hohl describes Paul III as having "a tendency to support the Renaissance in an extravagant manner" ("Paul III, Pope," 23). Among other things, Paul commissioned Michelangelo to paint the Sistine Chapel, and was instrumental in the design and construction of the Farnese Palace.

22. Girolamo Britonio (1491–ca. 1549), was a member of the circle surrounding the Italian poet Vittoria Colonna; other members included Michelangelo, Ariosto, Sannazzaro, Tasso, et al. From 1535, a large number of his works were dedicated to Paul III, and printed in Rome, suggesting at least some access to the Vatican. See Gianni Ballistreri, "Britonio, Girolamo."

23. Sigea to Paul III, 1547, 81.

24. Sigea to Paul III, 1547, 81.
25. Vives, *De conscribendis*, 127.
26. Sigea to Paul III, 1547, 81.
27. Sigea to Paul III, 1547, 81
28. Paul III to Luisa Sigea, January 6, 1547, 83.
29. Paul III to Luisa Sigea, January 6, 1547, 83.
30. Sigea to Alonso de Cuevas, 1554, 101.
31. Prieto Corbalán, *Epistolario latino*, 78, 79.
32. Prieto Corbalán, *Epistolario latino*, 78.
33. Álvar Gómez de Castro (1515–1580) was a native of Santa Olalla and Toledo. The letters are found in BN MS 18.673. Sauvage dates these letters to 1552, but Prieto Corbalán argues for a later date of 1558, which I follow here: Prieto Corbalán, *Epistolario latino*, 115, n. 78.
34. Sigea to Álvar Gómez (I), 1558, 89.
35. Horace, *Arte poetica*, 390.
36. On the burning of letters, see Arnold Hunt, "'Burn This Letter.'"
37. Prieto Corbalán, *Epistolario latino*, 80.
38. Sigea to Álvar Gómez (I), 1558, 90.
39. Sigea to Álvar Gómez (I), 1558, 89–90.
40. Sigea to Álvar Gómez (I), 1558, 90. The reference here is to Isaiah 18:1 and 43:25.
41. Sigea to Álvar Gómez (I), 1558, 90.
42. Sigea to Álvar Gómez (II), 1558, 92.
43. Odette Sauvage suggests Magdalena might be a daughter of María Pacheco and Juan de Padilla, to whose children Diego Sigeo had at one time acted as tutor; Prieto Corbalán prefers not to make any particular claim as to Magdalena's identity but argues that we can at least deduce that Magdalena was a young lady of the court, most likely in the service of Sigea's former patron, María of Portugal. Sauvage dates this letter as 1558, noting that the letter is signed from Valladolid and thus assuming that Sigea wrote it while in the employ of María of Hungary. However, Prieto Corbalán argues for an earlier date of 1556, arguing that Sigea's *nudiustertius*, "the day before yesterday," while not necessarily an accurate accounting of time, suggests a recentness to the encounter, perhaps along the lines of "when I saw you the other day." Corbalán further argues that if Sigea had been in the service of María of Hungary at this time, she would have mentioned her patron explicitly in the letter. Corbalán thus concludes that the letter being signed from Valladolid is most likely attributable to one of many transcription errors and inconsistencies made by copyists of Sigea's correspondence.
44. From the 1550s onward, it became much more difficult for a *docta puella* to exercise her talents outside of a convent (Baranda, "Words for Sale," 62).

45. Sigea to Magdalena de Padilla, 1556, 112.

46. The word "transenna" persists in modern Portuguese; the Spanish equivalent is "celosía," with the implications of not only privacy but also of jealousy.

47. Sigea to Magdalena de Padilla, 1556, 112.

48. Sigea to Magdalena de Padilla, 1556, 112.

49. Erasmus, *De conscribendis*, 90.

50. Sigea to Magdalena de Padilla, 1556, 112.

51. Sigea to Magdalena de Padilla, 1556, 112.

52. Sigea to Magdalena de Padilla, 1556, 112.

53. Sigea to Paul III, 1546, 81.

54. Quoted in Bourdon, and Sauvage, "Recherches sur Luisa Sigea," 38.

55. Schottus, *Hispaniae bibliotheca*, 342.

56. Schottus allots two pages to Sigea in his collection; as a point of comparison, Saint Teresa de Jesús, whose entry directly follows Sigea's, receives one paragraph.

BIBLIOGRAPHY

Primary Sources

Erasmus, Desiderius. *De conscribendis epistolis; conficiendarum epistolarum formula; De civilitate; De pueris Instituendis; De recta pronuntiatione*. Translated by Charles Fantazzi. Toronto: University of Toronto Press, 1985.

Horace, "De arte poetica liber." In *The Works of Horace, Translated Literally into English Prose; For the Use of Those Who are Desirous of Acquiring or Recovering a Competent Knowledge of the Latin Language*. Translated by C. Smart, 347–90. Philadelphia: Joseph Whetham, 1836. Perseus Digital Library, Gregory R. Crane, ed. Tufts University. http://data.perseus.org/texts/urn:cts:latinLit:phi0893.phi006.perseus -lat1, (accessed June 13, 2019).

Laínez, Pedro. "Aloisiae Sigeae Toletanae epicedion, Petro Lainez auctore," In *Clarorum Hispaniensium epistolae ineditae ad humaniorum litterarum historiam pertinentes*, edited by Adolfo Bonilla y San Martín, 127–34. Paris: n.p., 1901.

Paul III. To Luisa Sigea, January 6, 1547. In *Bulletin des études portugaises*, edited by Léon Bourdon and Odette Sauvage, 83. 1970.

Prieto Corbalán, María R., ed. *Epistolario latino de Luisa Sigea*. Madrid: Akal, 2007.

Schottus, Andreas (André Schott). *Hispaniae bibliotheca seu de academiis ac bibliothecis: item elogia et nomenclator clarorum hispaniae scriptorum*. Frankfurt: Marnius, 1608.

Seneca, "Seneca Lucilio suo salutem (On the proper style for a philosopher's discourse [40.1]." In *Ad Lucilium epistulae morales*, Vol. 1. Translated by Richard M. Gummere. London: William Heinemann, 1925.

Sigea, Luisa. To Alonso de Cuevas, 1554. In "Recherches sur Luisa Sigea," *Bulletin des études portugaises*, edited by Bourdon and Sauvage, 101–2. 1970.

Sigea, Luisa. To Álvar Gómez (I), 1558. In "Recherches sur Luisa Sigea," *Bulletin des études portugaises*, edited by Bourdon and Sauvage, 89–90. 1970.

Sigea, Luisa. To Álvar Gómez (II), 1558. In "Recherches sur Luisa Sigea," *Bulletin des études portugaises*, edited by Bourdon and Sauvage, 91–92. 1970.

Sigea, Luisa. To Magdalena de Padilla, 1556/1558. In "Recherches sur Luisa Sigea," *Bulletin des études portugaises*, edited by Bourdon and Sauvage, 112–15. 1970.

Sigea, Luisa. To Paul III, 1546. In "Recherches sur Luisa Sigea," *Bulletin des études portugaises*, edited by Bourdon and Sauvage, 80–81. 1970.

Vives, Juan Luis. *De conscribendis epistolis*. Translated by Charles Fantazzi. Leiden, Belgium: Brill, 1989.

Secondary Sources

Allut, Paul. *Aloysia Sygea et Nicolas Chorier*. Lyon: N. Scheuring, 1862.

Ballistreri, Gianni. "Britonio, Girolamo," In *Dizionario biografico degli Italiani*, 1972.

Baranda, Nieves. "Words for Sale: Early Modern Spanish Women's Literary Economy." In *Economic Imperatives for Women's Writing in Early Modern Europe*, edited by Carme Font Paz and Nina Geerdink, 40–72. Leiden: Brill/Rodopi, 2018.

Bergmann, Emilie L. "Spain's Women Humanists," In *The Routledge Research Companion to Early Modern Spanish Women Writers*. Edited by Nieves Baranda and Anne J. Cruz, 219–35. New York: Routledge, 2017.

Bourdon, Léon, and Odette Sauvage. "Recherches sur Luisa Sigea." *Bulletin des études portugaises* 31 (1970): 33–176.

Castillo Gómez, Antonio. "Del tratado a la práctica: la escritura epistolar en los siglos XVI y XVII." *La correspondencia en la Historia: modelos y prácticas de escritura epistolar. Actos del VI Congreso Internacional de Historia de la Cultura escrita*. Vol. 1. (2002): 79–108.

Cruz, Anne J. "Women's Education in Early Modern Spain," In *The Routledge Research Companion to Early Modern Spanish Women Writers*, edited by Nieves Baranda and Anne J. Cruz, 27–40. New York: Routledge, 2017.

Dambrogio, Jana and Daniel Starza Smith. "Letterlocking." MIT. http://letterlocking .org, (accessed June 13, 2019).

Daybell, James. *The Material Letter in Early Modern England*. Basingstoke UK: Palgrave Macmillan, 2012.

Dekker, Rudolf, ed. *Egodocuments and History: Autobiographical Writing in Its Social Context since the Middle Ages*. Hilversum, Netherlands: Verloren, 2002.

Fantazzi, Charles, ed. "General Introduction." In *De conscribendis epistolis of J. L. Vives*, 1–20. Leiden, Belgium: Brill, 1989.

Hohl, C. L. Jr. "Paul III, Pope," In *The New Catholic Encyclopedia*, 21–23. Gale, 2003.

Hunt, Arnold. "'Burn This Letter': Preservation and Destruction in the Early Modern Archive," In *Cultures of Correspondence in Early Modern Britain*, edited by James

Daybell and Andrew Gordon, 189–209. Philadelphia: University of Pennsylvania Press, 2016.

Martín Baños, Pedro. *El arte epistolar en el renacimiento europeo, 1400–1600*. Bilbao: Universidad de Deusto, 2005.

Pagés-Rangel, Roxana. *Del dominio público: Itinerarios de la carta privada*. Amsterdam: Rodopi, 1997.

Saen de Casas, Carmen. "Juana de Austria como modelo de feminidad regia en *La hija de Carlos Quinto* de Mira de Amescua." *Bulletin of the Comediantes* 68(1), no. 1 (2016): 19–38.

Schneider, Gary. *The Culture of Epistolarity: Vernacular Letters and Letter Writing in Early Modern England, 1500–1700*. Newark NJ: University of Delaware Press, 2005.

Steen, Sara Jayne. "Reading Beyond the Words: Material Letters and the Process of Interpretation." *Quidditas* 22 (2001): 55–69.

Stewart, Alan, and Heather Wolfe. *Letterwriting in Renaissance England*. Washington DC: Folger Shakespeare Library, 2004.

12

So That They Will Remember Me

Seroras and Their Testaments in the Early Modern Basque Country

AMANDA L. SCOTT

As she reached the end of her long life, Doña Ana de Alzate looked back on her many years and took stock of what had been most important. As the daughter of the lords of Alzate and Urturbia, Doña Ana had secured an equally prominent marriage and joined the noble house Samper. Yet all of this had happened in her youth. Now, in 1593, she was an old woman and a widow, and the cares of her past were increasingly distant. After years of serving her parish community in a secular capacity as patron and noblewoman, she finally found a new calling, this time in the service of the spiritual well-being of her community as *serora mayor* at the shrine of Our Lady of Muskilda in Ochagavía, Navarre. Many of the previous networks and relationships she and her husband had cultivated remained important to her, but as serora she also hoped to build new ones, especially with other pious men and women of her parish community. As she prepared to enter the *serería* and her final phase of life, Doña Ana drew up a testament that looked both forward and backward, and seamlessly joined her secular and spiritual vocations.[1]

Doña Ana is one of only a handful of seroras who composed testaments; like most early modern people, most seroras departed from their lives and vocations in states of humble poverty with few goods and little wealth.[2] Still, when compared to other women in the early modern Basque Country, seroras were proportionally much more likely to compose testaments than were their lay counterparts. These testaments preserve, in written word and legal form, the networks, obligations, friendships, debts, hopes, and fears that existed outside of formal records, and which shaped the day-to-day experiences seroras shared with their communities. Moreover, occasionally these testaments were challenged legally; when this happened, the legal documentation produced captured the tense ongoing conversations about controlling and defining seroras and their responsibilities to their communities. Doña Ana's testament was among those testaments that were litigated, and in this way, it offers a vivid glimpse into the ways in which seroras saw themselves as dual religious figures and community members, and how these definitions were challenged in the post-Tridentine years.

Neither fully lay nor fully religious, seroras existed in the blurry middle ground of the world of devout laywomen. In the post-Tridentine reform period, as devout laywomen, seroras were pulled in various directions, and often became catalysts for conversations about the necessity for reform and how it should respond to local needs. Seroras defined their work in mixed religious terms, seeing it as benefiting equally the institutional church and the parish community. Still, despite internal and external pressures to push the seroras into roles more akin to traditional nuns, seroras deflected such reforms, clearly asserting their identities as local religious women. Moreover, as they cared for shrines and ministered to their neighbors, seroras were centrally important in focusing and invigorating the material and spiritual piety of the laity; they helped anchor the parish community to local sites through communal devotions, charity, and above all, testamentary bequests. In many ways, Doña Ana's brief years as serora of Muskilda—and the events following her death—encapsulate the experiences of many seroras and act as a synecdoche for understanding the vocation as a whole, as well as understanding the ways in which seroras were tied to their communities.

Seroras were caretakers—spiritual, as well as material caretakers—of the devotional objects and practices that gave texture and meaning to ordinary people's religious experiences. Their caretaking duties put them into the same world as the male hermits stationed at shrines all around Europe; however, the seroras' labors were considerably more institutionalized and socially prominent. Though the seroras were undoubtedly shaped by the same impulses that led women such as the better known beguines, Italian penitents, and Castilian *beatas* to seek spiritual fulfilment outside the traditional (and cloistered) path of monasticism, the seroras and their parish communities created a form of religious life for women unmatched by manifestations of lay devotion elsewhere in Europe at the time.[3] Variations of all these forms (except the beguines) were available to women in the Basque Country; nonetheless, Basque women often chose the seroría over these other forms, underscoring the perceived benefits and flexibility of the vocation. The decision to enter the seroría placed them at the center of local religious life, all the while allowing them to remain in and among the people and spiritual geographies that gave life to their connection to the holy.[4]

The seroras were also considerably more financially autonomous than their peer devout laywomen. Seroras were licensed and examined by the diocese in processes much like those that regulated the male clergy, and they were supported by a combination of alms and stipends drawn from the parish benefice structure. Indeed, seroras shared much in common with sacristans and other lower clergy entrusted with the smooth functioning of day-to-day parish life.[5] Seroras also took no vows, meaning that unlike other women pursuing religious callings, seroras were free to leave their vocation if they chose. Once licensed, seroras were guaranteed their positions for life, and though the option to return to the fully secular life was always available, few seroras chose to leave. Permanency was preferred, and the vocation was not intended to be a temporary stop-over before or in-between marriages. For those that stayed, they were well-supported by the diocese, the parish clergy, and their parish communities. In addition to their stipends and job security, seroras received free housing, ceremonial alms connected to baptisms and funerals, and the right to take precedence in communal devotions. Working closely with rarely more than one or two others, seroras also enjoyed the not-inconsequential perk of being allowed to live and work closely with other women, outside the confines of the monastery and domestic household, and free from the burdens and dangers of child-bearing. Many seroras reported close friendships with other seroras, as well as with nieces and sisters who joined them in the serería. Others proudly described their fundamental caretaking roles for their parish churches and shrines, noting that it was their responsibility alone to make sure that repairs were completed, church furnishings accounted for and parishioners welcomed to mass.

Seroras could not be married at the time they entered the vocation (though some were widows), and following Tridentine-era synodal meetings in the later sixteenth century, the Diocese of Pamplona also insisted that they be at least forty years old "and of good life and habits."[6] Once selected by their local communities and confirmed by the bishop, seroras began their caretaking duties. These varied somewhat depending on location, but most seroras washed and set out church linens and mantels, kept inventories of church furnishings, collected wax, refilled vessels of holy water, swept aisles, and locked the church every night.[7] Many were also entrusted with ringing the bells—a duty which required no small amount of skill and strength.[8] Others operated small pilgrim hospitals, some were charged with educating young girls, and a few even were responsible for dressing the priest before mass.[9] Seroras primarily served shrines and parish churches across the Basque Country, but a handful were appointed to larger institutions, such as Cathedrals in Tudela and Bayonne. Regardless of where they served, their labor and caretaking duties were essential in keeping the parish running smoothly on a day-to-day basis.

WOMEN AND TESTAMENTARY CULTURE

Though they shared much in common with devout laywomen elsewhere in Europe, the seroras were unique to the Basque Country. No other iteration of devout female lifestyle exhibited this full complement of stipend, licensing, parish service, and job security. Moreover, the vocation responded directly to demographic pressures of the early modern Basque Country, in which men were away for months or years at a time as they worked in the Atlantic fishing and whaling fleets, shepherded flocks of sheep across the Pyrenees, or migrated to the New World to contribute their expertise in mining industries. The testaments written by seroras situate them in a decisively unique world, in which women were a demographic majority and in which social and migratory pressures made it normal and expected for women to take a leading role in various domestic, community, and religious leadership roles.[10] In addition to providing insight into the life and work of the seroras, the seroras' testaments provide an important perspective on how women positioned themselves in their communities vis-à-vis wealth, property, and social commitments that are often absent in the documentary records.

Compared to elsewhere in early modern Europe, Basque women were exceptionally well-represented in the limited testamentary record, and among these, seroras are even better represented.[11] The wealth of the Basque notarial archives makes it impossible to assess sixteenth- and seventeenth-century testaments comprehensively, but through random sampling of sub-notarial districts in Navarre and Guipuzcoa, it appears that approximately 37 to 51 percent of testators were women, though of course these numbers reflect only the small portion of the entire population that chose to write wills. More importantly, the sampling suggests that about 50 percent of *all* seroras wrote testaments either before or after entering the serroría, meaning that as women, their voices are exceptionally well preserved in the testamentary record.[12]

Such numbers are largely an effect of the Basque marriage contract. Marriage contracts reflected sexual, economic, and social unions between two families, and families often made use of this broad definition of marriage in the fullest sense. It was not uncommon for marriage contracts to handle dowries, *arras* payments, and the birth of future children in almost the same breath as they transferred property belonging to other siblings and made plans for the funerals of the bride and groom, as well as their parents, sisters, cousins, or other members of the extended Basque household. Thus, women who were part of a marriage contract—either their own, or of a close relative such as a daughter or sister—often had no need to plan for the transfer of other property following their deaths; instead, this was handled by the very documents that contracted their nuptials or those of their daughters and sisters. For example, when Margarita de Essandi and Charles Landa married in Ochagavía, in 1645, their marriage contract addressed matters pertaining to Margarita's brother, sister-in-law, and uncle, as well as Charles's parents and his brother and sister. Margarita's dowry was spelled out in numbers of sheep and hard currency, but both families also took advantage of having already contracted a notary to make plans for sending one brother to the university, as well as supporting an unmarried sister for as long as she chose to live at home (or perhaps until she entered the seroría).[13] Similarly, when Catalina Joan Beliz and Joanes Zarraluzque drew up plans to marry, they also made plans for Catalina's mother's funeral, even though Catalina's mother was still quite alive at the time of her daughter's nuptials.[14] These expansive documents neatly packaged a variety of tangential matters, precluding the need to pay a notary to handle additional business.

Because seroras had to be unmarried during their service and at the time of their appointment, most were not primary members of an active marriage contract at the time they entered the seroría. Of course, many widows entered the seroría (as well as spinster sisters of married couples), but entering the vocation provided women a moment to rewrite or discard old contracts and begin afresh.[15] Indeed, many parishes encouraged their seroras to write wills prior to entering the seroría, arguing that anything written afterward presented logistical complications in how to fairly separate a serora's property from that of the church where she served.

Many seroras followed this advice, though some also wrote testaments following years or lifetimes within the seroría. Notably, both newer and older seroras shared a similar outlook on the parameters of the vocation, and all consistently identified primarily as lay women, employed by the church, but with their strongest ties linking them to the non-religious men, women, and children within their communities. Regardless of how long seroras had served the church, in their testaments, seroras followed familiar family inheritance strategies, remembered friendships with other women, or favored young nieces, nephews, or cousins. For example, though the serora María de Azcarraga had served the parish of Andoaín for most of her life, at the time of her death, she specified only limited pious gifts, leaving most decisions in the hands of her nephew, whom she named as her universal heir.[16] Likewise, Joana de Hossa of Elorrio had been close to her cousin Juan, and in her will, she stipulated that the two should not be parted even in death, and would share a tomb together.[17] Ana de Barrenechea, property owner of Urretxu and serora in Villareal, could have been buried in her parish church with other seroras; instead, she wanted to be buried with her mother and "the bones of her father." She left small gifts to the church where she served, but most of her wealth went to paying for a series of anniversary masses for her beloved mother. She named her sister, Mari Joaniz, her universal heir and executor "because she and her husband are most familiar with my property and [what should be done with it]."[18]

Few seroras left significant portions of their wealth to the churches or shrines where they served, or to the male clergy with whom they worked. Like the parishioners they served, most seroras conformed their pious bequests to the rote offerings recommended by notaries of a few *reales* to each of the local shrines or, at most, the establishment of a small perpetual chaplaincy. The most substantial gifts and transfers of property stayed within family circles, between seroras, or between close friends. These personal testamentary bequests point to the close relationships seroras forged with other women in their communities, alongside and apart from their formal spiritual obligations to the parish.

For example, when Catalina de Luzuriaga died of plague in 1564, a number of other shrine staff and seroras reported that she had promised them gifts of bedding, sleeves, collars, and other items of clothing.[19] Similarly, María López de Zelaya, serora of Aozaratza, left a detailed list of small remembrances to the chapels within the orbit of her local spiritual geography, while the rest of her testament primarily benefited friends and family members surviving her. Included among these small gifts were a few linens and several measures of oil paid to each of the shrines in the area, as well as "two masses costing two reales each, said at the main altars of Mondragón," "a devotion to St. Francis, paid from my estate," and "nine masses said for my soul at the church of Aozaratza."[20] One unnamed person was ordered to make a small pilgrimage to the shrine where María López served and to pay for an additional six masses once she arrived there.[21] Depending on the location, such funerary gifts were obligatory and part of how benefices were structured for the clergy and the seroras, and thus say less about personal devotions and more about how the community supported the local church.

These devotions were certainly important to María López de Zelaya and the other seroras and priests with whom she lived and worked, yet they were largely standard and impersonal; similar gifts of oil and instructions for masses were a set feature in her neighbors' testaments as well. Instead, and like other seroras, evidence of María López's most important social times come to us through the next set of instructions: María López had received numerous household goods from the previous serora, gifts for which she was apparently still very grateful. These gifts were not part of the shrine fabric, but rather the personal possessions of the seroras who served there. Including a cider-pot, a chest, a copper cauldron, some dishes, and weaving implements, María López instructed her executors to make sure these goods passed on to the next serora, and that they added to it "some spoons, earthenware jars, and iron frying pans,"[22] which she had accumulated during her life. These household goods would help support the next serora, carrying on her legacy and making sure that seroras remained a central part of the local devotions in Aozaratza. They also emphasized the close relationships between seroras and how they viewed their maintenance as reciprocal and at least partially autonomous from the support of traditional parish clergy.[23]

In small villages where nearly everyone was related to one another, friendships with female family members that went above and beyond familial obligation were also common. For example, after leaving money for the lighting of the church and for the "redemption of Christian captives,"[24] the serora María de Minteguiaga made plans to have masses said over the tombs of her family members and leave specific gifts to close relatives, so that they would remember to pray for her soul. Her sister Cathalina was named as her principal heiress, but María also recognized the affections of her two young nieces. Agustina and Mariana de Galarrage received several clothes chests and other furniture. Mariana, however, also received "the bed in which I lay sick, along with its canopy and curtains."[25] Perhaps later, sleeping in the bed, Mariana would remember her late aunt, and her work as serora, and be inspired to pay for subsequent masses or make other devotions to María's beloved shrine.[26]

Finally, seroras' testaments also reveal their central roles within their communities as suppliers of liquid capital. Though most seroras lived and died in relative poverty, some managed to accrue enough wealth that their parishioners came to rely upon them for loans, or as guarantors for other economic transactions. In these cases, seroras devoted a substantial portion of their testaments to recovering old debts (and occasionally forgiving them in acts of charitable benevolence). The seroras who did list debts-owed tended to have numerous debts linking them to large swaths of their parish community. For example, when the serora Juana de Salanoba died in Maya, in 1631, among her debtors were the widow María Joan de Barrechea, who owed twelve reales; Pedro de Bordav-echerea, who had owed forty-three reales to Juana's brother, (though Juana had later bought this debt); Graciana de Lastiri, who owed one ducat worth of flax; María de Arguinona and her sister "little María," who each owed eight reales; the lords of the houses Arraztoa and Arrigada, who owed six ducats, but had "only paid back twelve reales in bacon"; "Maricuri and his wife," who owed nine reales for unstated services; Juana de Arracha, who owed twenty reales; and Domenja de Armendarrez, to whom Juana "had lent one *robo* of wheat for this year's planting, on the condition that she pay it back in double . . . and also she still owes wheat from last year."[27]

Similarly, in 1645, Ana de Yrunaga, serora of Mutriku, left instructions that 210 reales be dispersed among the shrines and other religious sites of Mutriku (ten of these went to alms, the other 200 paid for funeral masses for Ana herself). Yet, this generosity was dwarfed by 636 reales that Ana was owed by her parishioners. Most of these debts were owed by women, most were under one hundred reales, and most were held in structured interest-bearing loans (*censos*).[28] Ana probably received at least part of her own stipend and alms in hard currency; in turn, she could provide small loans to needy women in her community, possibly under terms that they would not be collected until years later. However, upon Ana's death, her two nieces and heirs, Catalina and María Fernández de Corostola, were ordered to pursue these debts, and then inherit Ana's estate in its entirety. "It is my will," wrote Ana, "that Catalina and María [collect these debts] and enjoy them . . . so that they will remember me."[29]

As devout laywomen holding crucial responsibilities for the spiritual wellbeing of their parish communities, such testamentary bequests and acts of testamentary charity carried additional weight. Planned and executed in the name of these special women, such financial transactions represented more than just gifts or loans between relatives or friends. They were statements by the seroras that their places were among the laity they served, and that they would continue to look after their parish communities in death, just as they had in life.

THE SERORA OF MUSKILDA

These testamentary patterns are well-documented in the testaments dictated by seroras across all the Basque Provinces. They also speak to broader difficulties in defining seroras as devout laywomen, neither fully lay nor fully religious, with affiliations and obligations spanning both worlds. This is particularly evident in the testament of Doña Ana de Alzate, whom we met at the beginning of the chapter. Doña Ana, and the other women that lived beside her in the serería of Our Lady of Muskilda, formed part of a particularly well-established and large community of seroras. Located on the top of a small hill overlooking the village of Ochagavía, the basilica of Muskilda supported as many as three or more seroras, a hermit, a chaplain, and several servants. Like many shrines, Muskilda represented a communal focal point for the parish, and parishioners reported taking great pride in serving as churchwardens, visiting the shrine, and overseeing its day-to-day operations. It hosted community festivities and religious processions, but unlike other communal shrines, Muskilda also drew devotees from throughout the Basque Country and sometimes even France. With such prestige, it made sense that a woman of Doña Ana's stature might be drawn to Muskilda. Doña Ana only lived for three more years after her entrance as serora, but her short tenure nonetheless left a big mark on the community.

Like many other seroras, Doña Ana planned ahead and wrote her testament some time before her death. Her preamble was standard, if perhaps a bit more florid than normal. Admitting that "nothing was more certain than death or more uncertain than the hour of death," she continued with the somewhat less usual warning that "even if during the years leading up to death, the person makes plans for the care of her soul and for the dispersal of the goods that God has given her [but only does so orally], then death can be the cause and occasion for her debtors, relatives, and other people to argue and fight over those worldly goods. Such does not serve God in the least."[30] This fear that death might lead to community discord proved all too prescient. Doña Ana's testament was indeed contested, leading to two subsequent lawsuits and numerous notarized witness statements and memorials. At stake was an ample estate, several large debts and loans, and ultimately, jurisdictional authority over the seroras between the diocese and the parish community.

As noblewoman turned serora, Doña Ana brought with her numerous debts, obligations, and social connections that were enhanced and complicated in her new role as serora. Yet, her appointment to Muskilda was opportune for all parties involved. For Doña Ana, it provided a respectable and prestigious place to end her days in service of God and community; while for the parishioners of Ochagavía, it represented the potential influx of considerable wealth into their community and its religious sites. As a devout laywoman who straddled the secular and religious, Doña Ana and her potential for charitable giving promised benefits across both overlapping worlds.

Wealthier than most seroras, Doña Ana made full use of her testament as a statement of social status as well as a mechanism for exercising charity. Amounts of funerary wax, bread, and candles were limited by Navarrese law, but Doña Ana ordered that the full legal amount be extracted from her estate and used during her funeral. A funeral *novena* was to be said, as were two sets of thirty masses, and fifteen masses on the last day of the year. Ten ducats were left to the church of San Pablo in Labiano, part of which was to be spent on buying an expensive "candelabra to put in front of the body of Saint Felicia."[31] Finally, she established a well-endowed chaplaincy paying its holder three ducats a year for performing six anniversary masses each year. Don Antonio de Góngora, Lord of Góngora and St. Adrián, was named first patron of this foundation, as well as general executor for the entire testament.

None of these plans ended up being particularly problematic, especially since in broad terms they benefited both the parish community as well as the Church. Doña Ana's other plans, however, created a rift between the Church and her executor, on one side, who argued that Doña Ana's wealth should be distributed as she saw fit, and the parishioners of Ochagavía, on the other side, who ironically argued that it could only be given to the Church. Like many female testators, much of Doña Ana's material wealth was made up of household goods and clothing—items that would be passed on among women many times over again. A number of chests, silver spoons, and skirts were doled out, and the priest of Ochagavía was remembered in particular with a special allotment of linen napkins. To Doña Mariana Ruíz de Bergara, Lady of Góngora, and her daughter Catalina, went six "fine, new linen sheets . . . so that they remember to pray my soul." Doña Ana's niece Ana de Chacón received two more; but another niece named Juana de Chacón, who currently lived with Doña Ana in the serería, received eight, as well as several curtains, blankets, and pillows. In addition to these itemized gifts, Juana was named heiress, with the understanding that she would use her inheritance as a dowry to become a serora like her late aunt. Juana's inheritance also hinged upon tracking down items that Doña Ana had loaned to various community members, including numerous sleeves, collars, and petticoats, as well as "five old napkins, currently in possession of Rodrigo de Erasso," and "one [women's] headdress, of the style worn in Álava," which was inexplicably in the possession of a man named Tristán de San Martín.[32]

Difficult as wresting these items away from their current holders might have been, Doña Ana's instructions regarding the liquidation of a censo proved even more challenging. Guaranteed by property owned by Miguel de Azpilcueta, Lord of Amunarrizque and two of his associates, the loan was currently paying Doña Ana 6 percent yearly interest. In turn, Doña Ana owed her executor, Don Antonio, 100 ducats, and she ordered that this be paid back through her censo, either immediately, or through a transfer of future interest. Several other smaller debts and pious donations likewise were to be paid from this investment.[33]

Yet with her considerable wealth at stake, upon Doña Ana's death, her definition as neither fully lay nor fully religious was open for challenge. Sensing that Doña Ana's considerable wealth was about to slip through their fingers, the parishioners of Ochagavía and the other seroras of Muskilda challenged Doña Ana's testament on the grounds that "from time immemorial, it is customary in these parts . . . that seroras cannot bequeath property to people outside their basilicas, as everything they own is owned by the basilica."[34] Moreover, they challenged, it had been inappropriate for Doña Ana to make plans for her niece Juana to follow her into the seroría; this privilege of naming seroras belonged to the parish alone.[35] In becoming serora, the Ochagavíans claimed, Doña Ana had given herself over completely to the Church, property and all, and now that she was dead, control over that property (and related decisions) had passed to the community of Muskilda automatically.

Superficially, it seemed the parishioners were arguing for a stricter definition of devout lay service, and one that more closely resembled professed nuns. In the post-Tridentine years, such questions about the exact status of religious men and women were at the forefront of diocesan reform programs, and bishops regularly moved toward stricter definitions intended to better separate the clergy from the laity. In this light (as well as from a financially pragmatic standpoint), it would have made sense that the bishop of Pamplona would have sided with Ochagavía and ordered Doña Ana's estate sequestered for the Church.

However, the bishop saw the conflict not as a property dispute, but rather as a challenge to diocesan authority coming directly from the parish community. Working closely with Don Antonio, the bishop's attorney informed the parishioners that seroras "could disperse their goods as they see fit . . . because they are not professed religious, but rather [devout laywomen]."[36] Moreover, he continued, ultimately, localities did not have the authority to define seroras' obligations to the Church, financially or otherwise, since "even though [the parish of Ochagavía] may be the patron of the said basilica, it is nonetheless one of the bishop's reforms that mayors and town councils do not have authority over seroras, but rather they [have seroras because the bishop allows this]."[37] In challenging Doña Ana's testament, the parish was usurping Church authority and interfering with Tridentine reforms that sought to definitively separate lay and female religious worlds, thus complicating how seroras were defined as lay or religious.

CONCLUSION

The conflict between Doña Ana's executor, the bishop, and the parishioners of Ochagavía speaks to an overarching problem that haunted the seroría in the post-Tridentine period. Following the Council of Trent, bishops increasingly sought to suppress or cloister semi-religious women like the seroras and faced mixed reactions from both the women and their communities. In line with Tridentine reforms, the Diocese of Pamplona debated the "problem" of having seroras. Ultimately, they decided that if seroras were licensed and supervised by the Diocese, they were not uncloistered religious women, but rather, diocesan employees.[38]

The diocese saw this as a solution to what was otherwise a violation of its own reform program; indeed, up until the reorganization of benefices under the Bourbon reforms of the eighteenth century, the bishops of Pamplona were mostly happy to let the seroras continue to serve their local shrines and churches. However, the nature of this compromise—hinging upon increased diocesan oversight into how seroras were selected, supported, and most of all, how they embodied a link between the diocese and the local community—was not always embraced by local communities. Yet, this did not mean that parishioners were misinformed about the Tridentine reform program. Diocesan court records of the period show parishioners repeatedly attempting to appropriate Tridentine rhetoric and deploy it to serve parish community interests.

Within these protracted negotiations, the seroras found a strong voice of their own in their testaments and bequests. Even if the diocese and the parish never fully decided upon a definition that was either fully lay or fully religious, the seroras nonetheless articulated a definition for themselves. They clearly understood the importance of their work in religious terms, benefiting the Church, the local spiritual geography, and above all, the parish community. However, they were also fully comfortable rejecting expectations that pushed them closer to traditional nuns, and away from their familiar town communities. Though they faced pressures to devote themselves spiritually and materially to the Church, most seroras used their bequests to emphasize their social and economic ties to the secular world and to the people of their parishes. Through gifts of property and the transfer of censos, seroras remembered their affiliations and affections to lay men and women outside the Church. The naming of nieces and nephews as heirs—and not the Church—moreover, accentuated their continued commitment to familial inheritance strategies, even under pressure to eschew these older obligations. The bulk of their wealth usually stayed within small networks of friends and families, and through these remembrances, seroras stated that they were first and foremost lay daughters, sisters, aunts, and cousins of the lay parish community.

NOTES

1. Unless to distinguish between the different Basque provinces, in this chapter I refer to the Basque Country in its comprehensive cultural sense to include both the administrative Basque Country and Navarre. Archivo Diocesano de Pamplona (ADP), C/183 n1.

2. For a full history of the seroras, see Scott, *Basque Seroras*, and especially chapter 4 for an in-depth analysis of seroras and testamentary culture, including more context for some of the anecdotes discussed in passing in this chapter.

3. For a small sampling of the rich work on devout female religious life in late medieval and early modern Europe, see Simons, *Cities of Ladies*; Gill, "Open Monasteries for Women"; Weber, *Devout Laywomen*; and Diefendorf, *From Penitence to Charity*.

4. The dense networks of shrines that spiderweb across the Basque Country created a particularly rich sense of religious connection to physical place for early modern devotees. Even the Basques who migrated to the New World seem to have maintained a sort of mental map of sites of spiritual importance and devotion, recalling, years later, special attachments to familiar shrines, hermits, priests, and seroras. This overlay of physical geography with spiritual connection was even more closely felt by those people that moved about these places on a daily

basis, and the seroras helped receive and channel material items given in honor of these holy sites.

5. The roots of the vocation are obscure, but folklorist Roslyn Frank argues for a structural (if not functional) continuity between the role of women in pre-Christian Basque religious practice and the later seroras. Frank, "A Diachronic Analysis." For the parallels between seroras and sacristans, see Garmendia Larrañaga, *Seroras y Sacristanes*, and for more information on hermits in Navarre, Goñi Gaztambide, "La vida eremítica."

6 Rojas y Sandoval, *Constituciones synodales*, fol. 93v.

7. Archivo Histórico Diocesano de San Sebastián (AHDSS), sig. 2352/008–01.

8. For example, ADP, C/690 n.16, fols. 35v and 37r and AHDSS, sig. 2352/008–01.

9. For example, Archivo Histórico Provincial de Bizkaia (AHPB), Prot. Not. Antonio Garaizabal, sig. 719, fols. 90r–v and Archivo Histórico Provincial de Álava, Esc. Martín de San Román (1564), prot. 11512, fols. 12–13v.

10. These patterns compare to Allyson Poska's findings from Galicia where there was also considerable male migration. Poska, *Women and Authority*.

11. The literature on the intersections between gender, inheritance law, and testamentary practice in medieval and early modern Europe is extensive. Among many excellent works, see French, *People of the Parish*; Coolidge, *Guardianship, Gender, and the Nobility*; and the essays in Rollo-Koster and Reyerson, "Salvation of my Soul."

12. See Scott, *Basque Seroras*, chap. 4.

13. Archivo General de Navarra (AGN), Prot. Not. Hernando Labari, Ochagavía, Caja 12273/2, no. 18.

14. AGN, Prot. Not. Hernando Labari, Ochagavía, Caja 12273/2, no. 54.

15. I have found few mentions of seroras with living children (and none with young children), suggesting that widowed mothers were less likely to enter the serería, or that they were considered less viable candidates by their communities.

16. Archivo General de Gipuzkoa (AGG), PT2094: fols. 21r–22v.

17. AHPB, Prot. Not. Pedro Ibáñez de Esteibar, sig. 680, s/n.

18. Archivo Histórico de Protocolos de Gipuzkoa (AHPG), sig. 1/4070, fols. 99r–100v.

19. Archivo Histórico Provincial de Álava, Esc. Martín de San Román (1564), prot. 11512, fols. 12–13v.

20. AGG, PT93: 148r–149r.

21. AGG, PT93: 148r–149r.

22. AGG, PT93: 148r–149r.

23. AGG, PT93: 148r–149r.

24. AGG, PT2089: 34r–35v.

25. AGG, PT2089: 34r–35v.

26. AGG, PT2089: 34r–35v.

27. AGN, Prot. Not., Iñigo de Maya, Caja 15084/4.

28. Ana did not consistently differentiate between *reales de oro* and *reales de vellón*, but it appears that most of her counts were in vellón. In the seventeenth century, one ducat was worth about 216 reales de vellón.

29. AHPG, sig. 1/2628, fols. 20r–21r.

30. ADP, C/183 n1, fol. 7r.

31. The relics of St. Felicia of Labiano were venerated at the Shrine of San Pablo in Labiano, Navarre. She should not be confused with either St. Felicitas of Rome or St. Felicitas of North Africa.

32. ADP, C/183 n1, fols. 179r–181v.

33. ADP, C/183 n1, fols. 7r–12v.

34. ADP, C/183 n1, fol. 18r.

35. ADP, C/148 n3, esp. fols. 43r and 95r–99r.

36. ADP, C/183 n1, fol. 20r and ADP, C/148 n3, fol. 56r.

37. ADP, C/183 n1, fol. 20r and ADP, C/148 n3, fol. 56r.

38. Rojas y Sandoval, *Constituciones synodales*, fol. 93v.

BIBLIOGRAPHY

Primary Sources

ADP Archivo Diocesano de Pamplona
    C/148 n3.
    C/183 n1.
    C/690 n16.

AGN. Archivo General de Navarre
    Protocolos Notariales Hernando Labari Caja 11273/72.
    Protocolos Notariales Iñigo de Maya, Caja 15084/4.

AGG. Archivo General de Gipuzkoa
    PT2094.
    PT93.
    PT2089.

AHDSS. Archivo Histórico Diocesano de San Sebastián
    Sig. 2352/008-01.

AHPB. Archivo Histórico Provincial de Bizkaia
    Protocolos Notariales Antonio Garaizabal.
    Protocolos Notariales Pedro Ibáñez de Esteibar.

AHPG. Archivo Histórico de Protocolos de Gipuzkoa
    Sig. 1/4070.
    Sig. 1/2628.

Archivo Provincial de Álava

    Esc. Martín de San Román (1564) 11512.

Rojas y Sandoval, Bernardo. *Constituciones synodales*. Pamplona, 1591

Secondary Sources

Aguirre Sorondo, Antxon. "La mujer en la religiosidad popular: Las seroras." In *Sukil, Cuadernos de Cultura Tradicional*, Vol. 1. Pamplona: Ortzadar Euskal Folklore Taldea, 1995.

Aguirre Sorondo, Antxon and Koldo Lizarralde Elberdin. *Ermitas de Gipuzkoa*. Ataun, Gipuzkoa: Fundación José Miguel de Barandiarán Fundazioa, 2000.

Álvarez Pérez-Sostoa, Denis and Iñali Garrido Yerobi. *In Dei Nomine: La Hondarribia del Siglo XVI através de sus Testamentos*. Hondarribia: Hondarribiko Udala, 2014.

Arregi Azpeitia, Gurutzi. *Ermitas de Bizkaia*. Bilbao: Diputación Foral de Bizkaia, Instituto Labayru, 1987.

Azpiazu, José Antonio. "Las seroras en Gipuzkoa (1550–1630)." *Cuadernos de Sección: Antropología-Etnografía* 13 (1995): 41–66.

Brunêt, Serge. *Les prêtres des montagnes: la vie, la mort, la foi dans les Pyrénées centrales sous l'Ancien Régime (Val d'Aran et diocèse de Comminges)*. Aspet, France: Pyré-Graph, 2001.

Caro Baroja, Julio. *De la vida rural vasca*. 3rd ed. Donostia: Editorial Txertoa, 1986.

Coolidge, Grace. *Guardianship, Gender, and the Nobility in Early Modern Spain*. Burlington VT: Ashgate, 2010.

Diefendorf, Barbara. *From Penitence to Charity: Pious Women and the Catholic Reformation in Paris*. Oxford: Oxford University Press, 2004.

Frank, Roslyn M. "A Diachronic Analysis of the Religious Role of the Woman in Basque Culture: The Seroras and Her Helpers." Published originally as "Euskal Herriko Eginkizun Erligiosoaren Inguruko Azterketa Diakronikoa: Serora eta bere aguntzaileak." In *La mujer en Euskal Herria: Hacia un feminismo propio*, edited by Miguel Angel Barcenilla, Roslyn M. Frank, Anne-Marie Lagarde, Isaure Gratacos, Xabier Amuriza, Nejane Jurado, Marta Agirrezabala, Alizia Stürtze, and Arantxa Erasun, 65–103. Donostia: Basandere Argitaletxea, 2001.

French, Katherine. *The People of the Parish: Community Life in a Late Medieval English Diocese*. Philadelphia: University of Pennsylvania Press, 2000.

Garmendia Larrañaga, Juan. *Seroras y Sacristanes: Etnografía e Historia*. Donostia: Eusko Ikaskutza, 2009.

Gill, Katherine. "Open Monasteries for Women in Late Medieval and Early Modern Italy: Two Roman Examples." In *The Crannied Wall: Women, Religion, and the Arts in Early Modern Europe*, edited by Craig A. Monson, 15–47. Ann Arbor: University of Michigan Press, 1992.

Goñi Gaztambide, José. "La vida eremítica en el reino de Navarra." *Príncipe de Viana* 98–99 (1965): 77–92.

Poska, Allyson. "Gender, Property, and Retirement Strategies in Early Modern Northwestern Spain." *Journal of Family History* 25, no. 3 (2000): 313–25.

———. *Women and Authority in Early Modern Spain: The Peasants of Galicia*. Oxford: Oxford University Press, 2006.

Rollo-Koster, Joëlle, and Kathryn L. Reyerson, eds. *"For the Salvation of my Soul": Women and Wills in Medieval and Early Modern France*. St. Andrews, UK: University of St. Andrews, 2012.

Scott, Amanda L. *The Basque Seroras: Local Religion, Gender, and Power in Northern Iberia, 1550–1800*. Ithaca NY: Cornell University Press, 2020.

Simons, Walter. *Cities of Ladies: Beguine Communities in the Medieval Low Countries, 1200–1565*. Philadelphia: University of Pennsylvania Press, 2001.

Weber, Alison, ed. *Devout Laywomen of the Early Modern World*. New York: Routledge, 2016.

Conclusion

Iberian Women and Communities across Time

ALLYSON M. POSKA

During the Middle Ages and early modern period, an individual's survival was regularly threatened by disease, poverty, war and other forms of violence. Unable to rely on state structures that were often diffuse and unstable, people looked to locally-constituted communities to provide a variety of protections, including affective ties, economic support, connections to the divine, and behavioral regulation. Although many scholars have examined the formation and dynamics of these different communities, Katherine Lynch's *Individuals, Families, and Communities in Europe, 1200–1800: The Urban Foundations of Western Society* proved to be profoundly influential for a generation of scholars who, in the intervening decades, have explored the ramifications of her work in a variety of European contexts.[1] Indeed, this collection of essays follows up on Lynch's work, focusing on what was likely the most complicated collection of communities in Western Europe, the Iberian peninsula. In addition to the majority Christian population, the kingdoms of Portugal, Castile, and Aragon were home to significant populations of Jews and Muslims, as well as conversos and Moriscos, whose conversions to Christianity spanned the spectrum from coerced to voluntary. The authors examine nearly 500 years, during which a complex set of relationships and associations evolved within each of these communities. At the same time, each community faced constantly shifting dynamics in terms of its interactions with the other communities, which were framed by spatial boundaries and prohibitions on economic and physical interactions, on the one hand, and the realities of interpersonal relationships, on the other hand.

Within each of the faith communities, women created and relied upon a variety of relationships beyond the family. When Sarah Ifft Dekker's Goig began lending money, she created the opportunity for other women in Vic's Jewish community to do the same, expanding Jewish women's social interactions as well as their economic prospects. Grace Coolidge shows how Castilian women used testamentary bequests to create and reinforce bonds with other women, some of whom were relatives, and some of whom were not. In fact, women who might otherwise be marginalized by their social or economic circumstances often looked to women in their communities to help them through difficult times. In Comas-Via's contribution, the widow Margarida made a formal agreement to take care of the widow Romia, creating an association that would help ensure the survival of both women. Although it is not surprising that the single mother Na Oliva and her mother Guillema lived together, Armstrong-Partida's reading of their case reveals how they relied on neighbor women for support and comfort after being attacked by the parish priest. As Michelle Herder demonstrates, when the nun Constancia became pregnant, her sisters in religion at the convent of Sant Daniel de Girona rallied around her, finding a place for her to give birth and attempting to hide her pregnancy from episcopal inquiry. These essays reveal that unlike the stereotypes promoted in Iberian literature, neither widows, nor single mothers, nor pregnant nuns found themselves isolated by their lack of traditional family ties. Nor were these women exceptional. In the Middle Ages and early modern period, a significant number of women never married, and, over the course of a lifetime, spousal death meant that even those who did marry were often single for longer than they were married. Unable or unwilling to rely on men, it was critical that women fostered mutually productive relationships with other women in their communities that provided them comfort, care, and support in their times of need.

In premodern Iberia's complicated socio-religious context, women often acted as links between different faith communities. For instance, as conversion tore at marital bonds, some Jewish women used their property to maintain their connections with their New Christian relatives. Guerson and Wessell Lightfoot show that when the husbands converted but the wives remained Jewish, those women became key social and economic connectors between the two religious communities, and even willfully transgressed community boundaries ostensibly created by conversion. They tell the story of the widow Gracia in Girona who did not deny her converted son Joan his inheritance; rather she gave him her dowry and marital property long before she was required to do so, presumably so he could marry. Although conversion often fractured familial ties, driven by maternal duty and affection, women like Gracia placed themselves squarely on the line between the Jewish and converso communities. In fact, community ties were particularly critical for female converts, whose place in the Christian community was never secure. As Stephanie Cavanaugh shows, when Christian authorities in Valladolid attempted to break up the enclave in which they lived, Morisca widows actively participated in the negotiations for an Edict of Grace and the establishment of the *situado*, a protection tax, to which they also contributed. It was not enough for women to maneuver successfully within their own communities; their survival depended on their ability to defend their communities from Christian intervention.

At times, even Christian women facilitated connections, not between their own communities and those of Spain's religious minorities but between Christian religious and lay culture. For nuns, their vows and the cloister ostensibly created well-defined boundaries between themselves and the world beyond; yet, those women did not cease to exist as members of their secular communities. Although the permeability of the medieval cloister has been well documented, these essays remind us of the vibrant relationship that existed between convents, the nuns that they housed, and their local communities. Miriam Shadis moves us beyond the confines of the cloister to explore the connections between the convent of Santa Maria de Celas in Coimbra, and the donors, patrons, and business partners who gave or sold property to the community. Through these transactions, the local lay community maintained social, economic, and political ties to women inside the convent's walls that connected many more women (and some men) to the convent in its early years. Michelle Herder has uncovered an array of less formal connections between the convent of Sant Daniel de Girona and the nearby community. The inquiry into the nun Constancia's pregnancy revealed that not only did Constancia's paramour have enough access to her to get her pregnant, but both the nuns and members of the local community knew exactly what was going on. In fact, these studies of Iberian convents and communities present an interesting parallel with the *juderías* and *morerías* that were supposed to separate Jewish and Muslim women from the Christian community. In all of these cases, the physical barriers established to separate women of one community from another community did little to hinder the affective and economic connections that women nurtured beyond the man-made walls.

While the emphasis on lending and property transactions in these chapters is clearly a consequence of the authors' extensive employment of notarial records, this documentation does provide us with an important perspective on how women from varied social and economic statuses and faiths took advantage of their property rights to create community. Grace Coolidge shows that single women and widows were not alone in their employment of property to form and reinforce their connections to other women (as well as to men other than husbands). Married women also knew that relationships beyond their immediate families were valuable emotionally and could be key to success, and even survival. According to Sarah Ifft Dekker, Reina and the other female Jewish moneylenders in Vic extended nearly 40 percent of loans made to the Christian community. Thus, their access to economic resources and their ability to strategically employ those resources were critical to both the financial stability of their own community and, interestingly enough, the development and expansion of the Christian community. This was also true in the case of Natalie Oeltjen's study of Mallorcan Jewish women and conversas, whose dowries made them the focus of attention from their exiled families and from the

Crown of Aragon. In Amanda Scott's study of Basque seroras' testaments, we see these women, whose place in the religious hierarchy was somewhat unclear, using property to create and maintain connections that supported their devout but lay status. Their bequests were vivid reminders that despite their piety, they were, as Scott argues, "first and foremost lay daughters, sisters, aunts, and cousins of the lay parish community." In all of these cases, Iberian women used property to define themselves and their communities beyond those articulated by religion, family, or the law.

Finally, a number of the authors examine the power of insults, gossip, and violence to enforce community norms. Sometimes a community used words (or the lack thereof) to marginalize problematic women. When the men of Girona refused to testify against the bullying priest Joan, Armstrong-Partida shows how they reinforced Guillema's reputation as a scold who deserved the cleric's violence. Similarly, in Valencia, Mark Meyerson found that when community conflict erupted, male attackers shouted insults at women in an attempt to damage their reputations, just as they injured their bodies. Despite attempts by her sister nuns to cover up the scandal, local gossip eventually exposed the pregnant Constancia in Michelle Herder's article. In the case of Luisa Sigea, Rachel Stapleton demonstrates how the humanist used words to create community. Although marginalized from broader intellectual circles by her gender, she assertively used her writing skills to seek recognition and participation in the community of letters. Community identities were tied to particular expectations about women's behavior, and words were powerful weapons in their regulatory arsenal.

When words failed, men's violence against women delineated clear boundaries between the perpetrators' ideal community and that of the victims. For instance, through his violence, Armstrong-Partida's cleric, Joan, reasserted his role as enforcer of community authority, as did the house attackers in Mark Meyerson's piece. As Meyerson notes, "Yet, paradoxical as it may seem, violent contests for honor, in which household assaults were a central element, contributed to a sense of community in Valencia's neighborhoods precisely because all of the neighbors participated in them, whether as assailants, victims, or all-too-interested bystanders."[2] The violence that men perpetrated against women prioritized their own idea of community at the expense of women and their families whom they deemed noncompliant with those community norms.

Even as some of this research underscores the dangerous repercussions of community for medieval and early modern women, overall, the emphasis in this collection is on women's agency—and it is fascinating to see how a focus on communities actually amplifies women's independent actions.[3] First, the emphasis on communities moves us firmly beyond any narrative of the exceptional woman who found ways to engage in independent political, social, or economic activity within otherwise constraining legal and social norms. Women, both as individuals and in groups, had the knowledge and skills to successfully interact with a variety of communities, and even create new ones when necessary. Those communities also reveal the degree to which communities were structured around women's agency. Whether Jewish, converso, Morisco, or Christian, communities expected women, (again, as individuals and in groups), to act on their own and on their community's behalf. By moving beyond the binary of inclusion/exclusion, these authors acknowledge the ability of patriarchal norms to constrain women's activity *and* at the same time, for women to take action on behalf of themselves and their families.[4] Finally, these essays reinforce the utility of intersectional analysis in considering how some women might facilitate or constrain the agency of other women and how religious difference and marital status informed or mitigated that agency.

This collection not only presents a complex view of Iberian women and their communities, but over the centuries we see significant changes in the meaning of community for women and the intensity of enforcement of community boundaries by and against women. Although women's gendered experience of community during the multireligious Middle Ages was marked prescriptively by strict separation, we also find it marked by surprising moments of integration and interaction. Certainly between 1391 and 1492, violence and the pressures of assimilation for converts and potential converts from Judaism and Islam accentuated women's ability to adapt to ever changing and often dangerous circumstances and to maneuver through the complicated expectations of multiple communities.

Then, after 1492, conversas and Moriscas found themselves betwixt and between, connected by birth to a prohibited faith community on the one hand, but rejected by the Christian community on the other hand. Although Christian women did not face the same radical transformations that Jewish, Muslim, converso, and Morisco women experienced, they nevertheless had to constantly negotiate and renegotiate their place in their own communities vis a vis men, as well as other women, both religious and lay.

During the Middle Ages and early modern period, Iberian women of all faiths grappled with the complicated and often contradictory expectations of their own communities, as well as the social and legal constraints that attempted to define their interactions with other communities. Indeed, the communities that provided women with care, comfort, protection, and resources also employed social and legal coercion and violence to force women to comply with community expectations. One day a woman could be a part of a community, and the next day she could be harassed, threatened, or rejected by that same community. Yet, across medieval and early modern Iberia, women's bodies, women's words, women's relationships, and women's decisions defined, shaped and reshaped, protected and transgressed the communities that framed their lives.

NOTES

1. Lynch, *Individuals, Families, and Communities*, 1–2.
2. Meyerson, chapter 5 this volume.
3. Certainly, premodern women's agency has been hotly debated by women's historians. Judith Bennett has emphasized the power of patriarchy to constrain women's activity in chapter 4 of *History Matters*. African historian, Lynn Thomas has cautioned against the dangers of agency becoming "safety argument" in "Historicizing Agency," 329. Margaret Hunt has asserted that the argument for women's agency is beset by other issues, including the fact that archival materials may disproportionately represent agentic acts over those that acquiesce to patriarchal expectations, and that feminist scholars tend to prioritize female solidarity over exploitation. See Hunt, *Women in Eighteenth-Century Europe*, 5–7. For some interesting perspectives on the role of patriarchy and agency, see Muravyeva and Toivo, *Gender*.
4. Cohen, "Women on the Margins," 316.

Bennett, Judith M. *History Matters: Patriarchy and the Challenge of Feminism.* Philadelphia: University of Pennsylvania Press, 2006.

Cohen, Elizabeth S. "Women on the Margins." In *The Ashgate Research Companion to Women and Gender in Early Modern Europe,* edited by Allyson M. Poska, Jane Couchman, and Katherine A. McIver. Farnham, UK: Ashgate, 2013.

Hunt, Margaret R. *Women in Eighteenth-Century Europe.* Harlow, UK: Longman, 2010.

Lynch, Katherine A. *Individuals, Families, and Communities in Europe, 1200–1800: The Urban Foundations of Western Society.* Cambridge: Cambridge University Press, 2003.

Muravyeva, Marianna G., and Raisa Maria Toivo, eds. *Gender in Late Medieval and Early Modern Europe.* New York: Routledge, 2013.

Thomas, Lynn M. "Historicizing Agency." *Gender & History* 28, no. 2 (August 2016): 324–39.

CONTRIBUTORS

MICHELLE ARMSTRONG-PARTIDA is an associate professor of history at Emory University, whose research focuses on gender and sexuality. She is the author of *Defiant Priests: Domestic Unions, Violence, and Clerical Masculinity* (Cornell, 2017). Her current project is a comparative study of concubinage in the late medieval Mediterranean.

STEPHANIE M. CAVANAUGH is a historian of early modern Spain who writes about Moriscos, conversion, and identity-making in the sixteenth century. She is the Sir John Elliott Junior Research Fellow in Spanish History (1400–1900) at the University of Oxford's Exeter College (2019–2021).

MIREIA COMAS-VIA is an adjunct professor of medieval history at the University of Barcelona. She has published works on widowhood and women's writing in the Middle Ages. She is the author of *Entre la solitud i la llibertat: Vídues barcelonines a finals de l'Edat Mitjana*, with a forthcoming English version.

GRACE E. COOLIDGE is professor of history at Grand Valley State University in Michigan. She is the author of *Women, Guardianship, and the Nobility in Early Modern Spain* (Ashgate, 2011) and the editor of a collection of essays titled *The Formation of the Child in Early Modern Spain* (Ashgate, 2014). She is currently working on a book about illegitimacy and the noble family in early modern Spain.

ALEXANDRA GUERSON is a lecturer at New College (University of Toronto) where she teaches world history at the International Foundation Program and coordinates New One: Learning without Borders. Her current work is a collaborative project with Dana Wessell Lightfoot, funded by an SSHRC Insight Grant, on Jewish women and *conversas* in Girona after the anti-Jewish violence of 1391.

MICHELLE HERDER is associate professor of history at Cornell College. Her research focuses on disorder and enclosure in late medieval women's religious communities.

SARAH IFFT DECKER is a social and economic historian of the medieval Mediterranean, focusing in particular on gender and religious difference. She is currently a postdoctoral fellow in the Borns Jewish Studies Program at Indiana University, and received her PhD from Yale University in 2017.

MARK MEYERSON is professor of history and medieval studies at the University of Toronto. Among his publications are *The Muslims of Valencia in the Age of Fernando and Isabel: Between Coexistence and Crusade* and *A Jewish Renaissance in Fifteenth-Century Spain*. He is currently completing *Of Bloodshed and Baptism: Violence, Religion, and the Transformation of Spain, 1300–1614* and, with Thomas Burman and Brian Catlos, *The Sea in the Middle: The Mediterranean, 650–1650*.

NATALIE OELTJEN has published on the *conversos* of Mallorca at the turn of the fifteenth century in *Jewish History* and *Sefarad*. After a postdoctoral fellowship at the Hebrew University of Jerusalem, she settled at the Centre for Reformation and Renaissance Studies at the University of Toronto.

ALLYSON M. POSKA is professor of history at the University of Mary Washington in Fredericksburg, Virginia, and the author of four books, including *Gendered Crossings: Women and Migration in the Spanish Empire* (New Mexico, 2016) and *Women and Authority in Early Modern Spain: The Peasants of Galicia* (Oxford, 2005).

AMANDA L. SCOTT is assistant professor of early modern European history at The Pennsylvania State University. She is the author of *The Basque Seroras: Local Religion, Gender, and Power in Northern Iberia, 1550–1800* Ithaca NY: Cornell University Press, 2020.

MIRIAM SHADIS is an associate professor of history at Ohio University. She is the author of *Berenguela of Castile (1180–1246) and Political Women in the High Middle Ages* (Palgrave, 2009) and a number of essays on elite women in France and Iberia. Her current project focuses on the royal women of early Portugal (1100–1250).

RACHEL F. STAPLETON is based at the Centre for Comparative Literature at the University of Toronto. Her research focuses on the rhetorical uses of life experience in early modern women's letter writing from the British Isles and the Iberian Peninsula. Her work has been published in *Medieval Feminist Forum*, *Lives & Letters*, and *L'histoire comparée de littératures de langues européennes*. She is coeditor, with Antonio Viselli, of *Iconoclasm: The Breaking and Making of Images* (McGill-Queens University Press, 2019).

DANA WESSELL LIGHTFOOT is an associate professor of history at the University of Northern British Columbia, Prince George BC, Canada. Her monograph, *Women, Dowries, and Agency: Marriage in 15th c. Valencia,* was published by Manchester University Press in 2013. Her current work is a collaborative project with Alexandra Guerson on Jewish women and *conversas* in late medieval Catalonia. This project is funded by the Social Sciences and Humanities Research Council of Canada.

INDEX

All premodern names are alphabetized by first name.

Bellaire (wife of Guillem Bernat Desmaestre), 139, 141

Bennett, Judith, 63, 275n3

Bensch, Stephen, 29

Berenguer Domènec de Cardona, 222, 226

Bernard Gui, 138

Bernat Sanç, 116

Bernat Vidal. *See* Caravida Vidal

Black Death, 21

Blanca (Astruga, wife of Samuel Faquim), 49

Blanca (wife of Bernat Falcó), 140–41

Blanca (wife of Miguel de Sent Pere), 55n9

Bonafilla (wife of Caravida Vidal), 142–45

Bonafilla (wife of Mosse Bellshom Falcó), 139–40

Bonastruch Desmaestre (rabbi), 139

Brodman, James, 184

Burgos, 169n54, 238

Burns, Robert I., 24

Camarasa, Jordina, 186, 191n24

Cara de la Paz, 65

Caravida Vidal (Bernat Vidal), 142–45, 183

Castelló d'Empúries, 21

Castile, 3, 6, 61, 133, 156, 160, 163, 165n1, 269

Catalina de Luzuriaga, 256

Catalina de Ortiz, 69–70

Catalina de Vargas, 60–61

Catalina Joan Beliz, 255

Catalina López, 59–60, 71

Catalonia, 30; charitable institutions in, 185, 190n20; economy of, 91; role of women in, 34; violence in, 107, 120n10, 127n62. *See* religious institutions

Caterina (wife of Johan Buixó), 117

Caterina (wife of Johan Gil), 115

Caterina (wife of Miquel Manyiques), 114

Caterina (wife of Miquel Torres), 113

Caterina la Romana, 115

Catlos, Brian, 156

Cebriana Ruiz, 59, 65

census, 159–61, 164

charity and charitable institutions, 9, 178, 191n24, 192n42, 252–53, 258–59; Bací de Pobres, 182–83, 186–87; children surrendered to, 215, 220, 222, 224; and guilds, 190n14; Hospital de la Misericordia, 71; Hospital de la Santa Creu, 184–85, 188; Hospital de Santiago, 64; Hospital of Ortabello, 184; Hospital of Girona, 220; Hospital of São Nicolás, 202; Hospital of the Haudriettes, 184; hospitals, 184–86; informal, 180–81, 186–88, 192n42; and Pia Almoina of Barcelona, 181; registers, 3, 184–85; testamentary bequests for, 53, 64–65, 68, 74n29

Charles V, King of Spain, 158

charters, 3, 198, 200–204, 207–9; ecclesiastical, 3, 9, 199, 203; sale/purchase of, 196

chastity, 107, 116, 118, 126n55, 218, 226

Chojnacka, Monica, 88

Christian-Jewish relations, 18–19, 23, 30–33, 41–42, 44–45, 132–33, 137–41, 143–44, 145–46

Cistercian Order, 196, 198, 201–2, 207

Clara (widow of Guillem Comes), 180

Clara (widow of Humbert de Vilafranca), 183–84

Cohen, Elizabeth, 164, 167n35

Coimbra, 9, 195–97, 202

community: converso, 43, 53; definition of, 4–5, 18, 84–85, 88, 98n5, 196, 207, 215; and family, 145; and gender, 4, 274–75; historiography and, 2–3; intellectual, 235, 238; and neighbors, 87–88, 109–10; religious, 163, 196–97; violence as constitutive of, 96–97, 106–7; women as links in, 5, 34, 271; women's role and status in, 84, 87. *See also* marriage

Moriscos, 11; definition of, 152–53; expulsion of, 151, 165n1, 168n41; relocation attempts by, 154–55, 157–58, 161, 163, 168n40. *See also* crypto-Islam

Morujão, Maria do Rosário Barbosa, 199, 204

Mossé Bellshom Falcó, 139–40

motherhood, 51, 65–66, 70–71, 89, 132, 145–46, 153, 200, 238–39, 240, 265n15

Nader, Helen, 62, 169n50, 170n59

Navarre, 260

networks. *See* community

North Africa, 46, 49, 51–52, 55n11

notarial records, 5–6, 10, 19, 44, 53–54, 59–60, 69, 133, 139–40, 141, 144, 145, 155, 254, 272. *See also* Libri Iudeorum

Ochagavía, Navarre, 259–60

Ogilvie, Sheilagh, 19

Oliva of Lledó, 83, 86–90, 94, 98n1, 270

Pagés-Rangel, Roxana, 233

Pamplona, 253

parishes, 4, 7, 10, 83–85, 90–91, 93, 96, 181, 182–83, 188, 190n20, 250–251, 252–53, 256, 258, 262, 263–66; Santa Maria del Pi, 183, 186, 187, 189n3, 191n21; Sant Quirze de Muntanyola, 17

Pasqualla (wife of Johan de Sison), 110

Pasqualla (wife of Martí Roiç), 118, 122n25

patriarchy, 2, 11, 86, 157, 274, 275n3

patronage: intellectual, 231, 234, 235, 238–39, 241, 245n21; religious, 66–67, 75n39, 199, 201–3, 207, 215, 250, 261, 263

Paul (saint), 136–37

Paul III (pope), 232, 234–38, 243, 245n21

Pedro (Bishop of Coimbra), 200–201

Pedro Laínez, 230

Peratallada, 142

Periculoso of Urban VI, 197

Perpignan, 21, 56n12

Perry, Mary Elizabeth, 153–54, 165n3

Philip II, King of Spain, 163, 238

Prieto Corbalán, Maria R., 238, 246n43

polygamy. *See* marriage, bigamy

Portugal, 9, 195–96, 202, 207, 231, 236, 238

poverty, 4, 10, 53, 88–89, 91, 122n25, 177–88, 190n15, 191n38, 250–51; and the "deserving poor," 178, 181, 182, 183, 186, 189n3, 190n20

priests, 83–84, 86–87, 89–91, 92–93, 96, 226, 253; and sexuality, 85. *See also* violence

procurator (legal agent), 28, 135, 139, 217, 218–19, 227n5; women as, 55n9

Puigcerdà, 22, 99n18

Ramon Mercader (Caravida Mercadell), 145–46

rape, 84, 117–18, 126n55, 127n62, 180

Regina (wife of Pere Joan Falcó), 132–33, 134, 141–42

Regina (Elionor) (wife of Caravida Vidal), 143–44, 145

Reina (widow of Bonjueu Canviador), 24

Reina (wife of Jucef Darahi, Astrug Caravida), 17–18, 26, 28, 32–33, 35n1

Reina Cabrita, 18, 22

religious institutions: and women, 195–209, 214–27; in Catalonia, 216; Celas além da Ponte 202, 207; Celas de Alenquer, 201, 202; confraternity of, 67; and cloistering of women, 63, 191n32, 197, 216, 226, 263, 271–72; confraternity of San Miguel, 53; and convents, 9, 196, 201, 215, 216, 271–72; foundation charters of, 9, 196, 197–98, 203; Monastery of Poblet, 181; Our Lady of Muskilda, 250, 259–60, 262;

widows, 59–61, 68–72, 112, 114, 140, 141, 154, 156–50, 177–88, 208, 253, 255, 270–71, 272; charitable assistance for, 178, 181–86, 190n14; and economic hardship, 10; as guardians, 69–70; legal autonomy of, 68, 160, 163–64

wills, 6, 10, 53, 61–62, 140, 205, 209, 251; challenges to, 125n51, 262–63; pious and charitable bequests in, 53, 68, 74n29, 189, 182–83, 191n21, 256–57, 258; women as testators, 24, 59–73, 140–41, 204, 206–7, 250–51, 250–64, 270, 273

Winer, Rebecca, 28, 56n12

women: as executors, 60, 66, 69–70, 256; as heads of household, 7–8, 51, 60, 68, 86, 93, 154–55, 159–61, 163, 169n54; low status of and violence against, 89; and property rights, 49, 59–61, 65, 68–69, 156–57, 159, 200, 201, 203, 208, 273. *See also* wills

women, Jewish: and conversion 41–54, 132–33, 141–42, 145–46, 147n18, 153; as widows, 21–22, 26–27, 33, 55n9, 56n14. *See also* moneylending

women, Muslim, 153, 156, 272

Yom Tov Ishbili (rabbi), 47

In the Women and Gender in the Early Modern World series:

Women and Community in Medieval and Early Modern Iberia
Edited and with an introduction by Michelle Armstrong-
Partida, Alexandra Guerson, and Dana Wessell Lightfoot

Pathologies of Love: Medicine and the Woman Question in Early Modern France
By Judy Kem

The Politics of Female Alliance in Early Modern England
Edited by Christina Luckyj and Niamh J. O'Leary

Women's Life Writing and Early Modern Ireland
Edited by Julie A. Eckerle and Naomi McAreavey

To order or obtain more information on these or other University
of Nebraska Press titles, visit nebraskapress.unl.edu.

CPSIA information can be obtained
at www.ICGtesting.com
Printed in the USA
BVHW042139250822
645571BV00002B/13

9 781496 205117